Peiping ◉

Tientsin ◉

Hwang Ho R.

Shanghai ◉

I N A

Chungking ⊛

Yangtze Kiang

Kunming

B U R M A   *R O A D*

Si Kiang

BURMA

Canton ◉

Lashio ◉

◉Maymyo

FORMOSA

Mandalay

Hong Kong

Irrawaddy

◉Toungoo

HAINAN

◉ **Rangoon**

F R E N C H   I N D O - C H I N A

Mekong R.

SOUTH

THAILAND

CHINA

BRITISH
MALAYA

THE LADY AND THE TIGERS

The author.

The *LADY* and
THE TIGERS

By

OLGA S. GREENLAW

*Illustrated with Photographs
and an Endpaper Map*

1943
NEW YORK
E. P. DUTTON & CO., INC.

PRINTED IN THE UNITED STATES OF AMERICA
BY THE WILLIAM BYRD PRESS, INC.
RICHMOND, VIRGINIA

TO MY FATHER

EDWARD B. SOWERS

ACKNOWLEDGMENT

I want here to acknowledge my indebtedness to Mr. Bogert Rogers for his assistance in editing the material in this book.

O. S. G.

ILLUSTRATIONS

THE LADY AND THE TIGERS

Chapter I

ON the night of July 17, 1941, in the Peninsula Hotel, Hong Kong, I had a hell of a row with a certain Mr. Harvey K. Greenlaw. Mr. Greenlaw was then and still is my husband, but we do not always see eye to eye. This particular little marital misunderstanding was no more acrimonious than others we have enjoyed from time to time but it was a great deal more important. I had reached a crisis in my own personal career and was trying to run away from the most exciting experience of my life—without realizing it, of course.

The scene of the fracas was the Peninsula's gay and colorful grill room with its windows facing from Kowloon across the wavering lights of the harbor to Victoria's steep hills on the Crown Colony side. In those days the grill was a charming and convivial cross-roads of the Orient. I shudder to think how, now, it must be crawling with splay-toothed little Japanese, hissing and bowing around the premises and trying to act as if they belong in such a nice hotel.

I was as mad as a hornet that evening—justifiably, of course. The only reason I refrained from throwing things, which I frequently do, was that I had been brought up to regard it as extremely unmannerly for a lady to heave objects at her husband in public. So with what I thought was commendable restraint, I said:

"Okay, Harvey, okay. You run right along to Burma with your sour-faced little pal, Colonel Chennault. Run right along and don't even give me a thought because I will be somewhere else!"

The gentleman who is my husband said:

"Louder, Olga—some people over there in the corner can't hear you."

That irritated me. "Look, Harvey," I hissed at him, "let's get this straight. You, for some stupid reason, want to go to Burma. I do not. As you very well know, I simply lo-o-oathe Burma, and as for Rangoon—" I recall holding my nose in a lady-like gesture—"the place stinks."

I meant that literally. If there is a dirtier, smellier town than Rangoon west of the Date Line it has not assaulted my nostrils—and up and down China and Malaya I have sniffed some pretty gamey municipalities. While I was running such a nice vindictive temperature I went on to make it clear that I hated airplanes and everything about them, including men who flew them, and I particularly disliked a gent in the Chinese Air Force named Claire L. Chennault and wished he would either go somewhere or back to Water Proof, Louisiana, from whence he came—and quit selling my husband screwball ideas like going to Burma.

Perhaps the weather had something to do with the way I felt. South China mid-summer heat combines the worst thermal features of Kansas City, Washington, D. C. and a Turkish bath. The shocking social truth of the matter is that all women in Hong Kong, including the wives of high British diplomats and officials, do not merely perspire freely—they sweat profusely and it puts them in a bad humor. But the heat was only aggravating what to me had become a gnawing obsession, which was a desire to stand at the rail of a clean white ship and blow bushels of farewell kisses at the odors and noises, the discomforts and inconveniences and the mounting unrest, suspicions and fears of the Far East as I sailed out of Hong Kong harbor on my way back to America.

For a long time I had been telling myself, "T'hell with the Orient." During the better part of eight years—virtually all of our married life—I had gotten a full dose of it. I had first gone out to China in 1933, a few months after we were married, to join Harvey who had resigned an Army Air Corps commission to become a member of the aviation mission to the Chinese

Government headed by American Colonel John H. Jouett. We remained until late 1936. After a long year home, we went back again in 1938, this time with Harvey representing North American Aviation Co., originally to superintend the assembling and testing of planes sold by that company to the Chinese and thereafter in various capacities. We had lived and traveled pretty much everywhere from Shanghai to the deep interior and there wasn't much of China that we didn't know something about. It was shortly after my 1933 arrival that I first met Madame Chiang Kai Shek, and of course we knew Colonel Chennault almost from the day he first stepped off the boat.

So anyway, there I was, the wife of an aviation expert, fed up with China—which I like ordinarily—and determined to go home. Specifically, to sail on August 4th, on the *President Coolidge*—now resting on the bottom of the ocean. Nothing would stop us this time—nothing could stop us. My husband had the tickets in his pocket—if he hadn't lost them—and there was no further reason for us to stay in China. Harvey could go right on selling airplanes to Oriental governments if he cared to—but the American State Department wouldn't permit them to be delivered. It had finally opened its eyes to what everyone in the Far East had known for a long time— that war in the Pacific was inevitable.

The trouble really started with a phone call. I was in the middle of packing—my life for the past three years, so it seemed, had been a constant merry-go-round of packing and unpacking. I was surrounded by tin trunks, bags, camphor chests—there was not a spot in the room that was not piled with evidence of our Oriental experiences: Cambodian silver, Borneo war drums, Hanoi bronzes and innumerable knives, pipes and other oddments. Harvey was asleep in the bedroom. He is the type who is invariably 'exhausted' when packing has to be done. The telephone rang. I answered, then shouted:

"Harvey—it's Mac on the telephone."

Without opening his eyes: "Which Mac?"

"Little Mac, the C.N.A.C. pilot," I screamed.

Mr. Greenlaw is a man who occasionally must be screamed at and "C.N.A.C." is China National Airways Company, that tough and tenuous aerial lifeline which, against fantastic odds, had done such a magnificent job of maintaining swift and reliable Chinese communications.

With his eyes still closed, Harvey stumbled to the telephone. I went on with my packing, paying little attention until I heard "Chennault"—which buzzed me like an electric current. I eavesdropped as usual. The Old Man is back, I thought, although only a few days before someone had said he was still in California. Harvey was saying, "Sure, that's fine, Mac—I'll see him at five, at your flat."

An almost imperceptible eagerness in his voice should have warned me. He was grinning complacently when he entered my room. Funny how he was no longer tired nor sleepy—but his eyes were evasive. I had a hunch right then that something was about to go wrong.

"Listen, you—if this has anything to do with our not going home—if you are even thinking of such a thing—" I felt I was on the verge of becoming a bit hysterical.

"Now, babe," he said, still grinning, "just keep your shirt on. I haven't the least idea what the Old Man wants to see me about—Mac wouldn't tell me. Might be almost anything—something trivial, probably."

He dressed and went out.

I puttered along with my packing, but my efforts seemed futile and unimportant. I ordered iced tea and sat down to think the situation over. The last time I had seen the "Old Man," as the boys called Colonel Chennault, he was standing by my bed in his blue pajamas looking like a little boy who had been caught being naughty. It was a night when I had returned to Hengyang from Canton on a troop train, arriving coincidentally with a flock of Jap bombers. Harvey had remained in Hong Kong. I had to rush from the train to hide in a pit with Colonel Mah Ting Wei, the Chinese chief test pilot, and his wife, Helen, who was born in Boston. Then we tried to cross the river in pitch darkness and the guards shot at us. Finally home, I knocked on the outer gate for twenty minutes before a servant came to open it. The boy said:

"Missy, all room full. Plenty people. No have got bed for you. Colonel Chen-Chao-ult, he sleep your bed."

All the way up the stairs I swore—audibly, I fear—at this Chinese Colonel who had usurped my bed. I didn't know who he was, or care. I'd whisk him out of there in a hurry. I was getting tired of coming home after trips and always finding someone in my bed. I threw open the door, still muttering profanity. A figure in blue leaning against the bed-post said, in a low and intriguing Louisiana drawl:

"Only an American girl could swear so picturesquely, Olga. Makes me homesick."

The Colonel had stopped over on his way from somewhere to somewhere else and knew he was always welcome. So was everyone else. It was like that wherever we were—house full, beds full, extra people for meals, Chinese officers, American officers, the C.N.A.C. boys and almost anyone who happened to be in town. The time was to come, in other houses we were to occupy, when I couldn't turn around without stepping on a "Flying Tiger." Anyway, that was us—Hotel Greenlaw—comfortable beds and good meals at all hours.

We had spent a lot of time at Hengyang in 1938. From San Francisco we sailed to Hong Kong and from there flew up country in an Eurasia Airlines tri-motored Junkers plane, flown by an excellent German pilot! Our destination was Changsha and from there to Hengyang in Hunan Province, about half way between Canton and Hankow. There was nothing fancy about Hengyang, or Hunan Province, either—no Repulse Bay Hotel or Shanghai Clubs or Happy Valley Race Courses. Hunan is rough and mountainous, its people primitive, hard-working peasants. Except for the missionaries, there were few white men or women in Hengyang. Even the Japs hadn't gotten around to violating it then, which was why this far-interior field had been chosen for assembly and testing of planes, which were shipped in from the United States through Hong Kong.

I was never what you might call whole heartedly daffy about Hengyang. Living arrangements were bad, sanitary facilities worse. And the smells were super-odoriferous, particularly when it rained which it did a fair share of the time.

We found temporary quarters in the Presbyterian mission, in the middle of town—nothing modern but at least clean and relatively fragrant—and then started looking for something permanent. No could do. Someone suggested we rent a floor in the best Chinese hotel and furnish it to suit our taste. That sounded sensible so we piled into dirty rickshaws—no rubber tires—and went down for a "look-see." The first thing we "look-saw" as we entered the courtyard were four large pots of human excrement! Harvey looked at me and I said: "*Meiolla*." Meaning in Chinese, "nothing doing."

We even tried to buy a large and beautiful junk to which a venerable Chinese artisan—a shipwright, I suppose—was putting finishing touches, painting it with a small sponge-like brush which he dipped in some sort of lacquer. He estimated it would take him another month to finish the job. We estimated he was an optimist and finally settled down in the mission. A Miss Gernhardt, who had one of the larger houses in the compound and who constantly spoke to me of Pearl Buck, kindly condescended to let us occupy two rooms at a Park Avenue rental. There, at night, we could fall asleep to the hymnal music of evening prayer meetings.

We were not regarded as particularly desirable guests by the missionaries. Primarily, we were war-minded—for obvious reasons. The good people who were our hosts, or landlords, clung trustingly to the quaint delusion that if they didn't think or talk about war the Japanese wouldn't either. They truly believed that a large American flag stretched across the mission courtyard would protect their lives and property from Japanese aggression. Later, this same American flag proved to be a perfect target for marauding Japanese pilots.

Harvey did not at all times manage to conform to the mission code of conduct. For one thing, he persisted in sneaking into the church and playing honky-tonk music on the melodeon. He plays quite badly but appears to enjoy it. And then one evening he gave a dinner for all the Chinese officers at the field, in the town's largest restaurant. Mr. Greenlaw is strictly a one-bottle-of-beer man. Beyond that his behavior is unpredictable. It is the Chinese custom that the dinner host must, individually, drink with all of his guests. There were forty guests. Harvey said the trouble was the beer was warm. The missionaries said the trouble was Harvey. He also acquired a bad habit of shooting firecrackers at the compound entrance to announce his arrival for dinner. China is a paradise for a man with a penchant for fire-crackers—and a demolition expert to boot, which Harvey is.

After three or four months we got tired of being lulled to sleep by the hymns—nobody seemed to be writing any new ones—so we rented a house on the outskirts of town built on the bank of the wide Siang river opposite the flying field. This belonged to the missionaries, too—including the furniture which we bought from them at certainly no less than they had paid for it originally twenty years before. After we reroofed and repainted the house and furnished it with such things as we could pick up, including some Petty girls clipped from old copies of *Esquire* and framed in carved black wood, it was really quite livable. Its four bedrooms were more than we needed at the time but not nearly enough later.

We were told that the missionary who designed and built

the place was a southerner and, indeed, it more closely resembled a corner of old Virginia than of older China.

During the few months we lived there, the war steadily closed in on Hengyang. And during that time I began to learn about China. I made friends with the Chinese officers' wives. They were intelligent and friendly and several of the younger ones were strikingly beautiful. I liked to visit their houses because they were so distinctly Chinese and they liked to visit mine because it was, in so far as possible, so distinctly American. We drank buckets of tea and played mah-jongg by the hour and I picked up my first smatterings of the Mandarin language, which is not as difficult as it sounds.

When we first arrived at Hengyang, except for the activity of the airfield across the river, where Harvey was testing his planes and Chinese pilots were flying them away, there was little feel of the gigantic struggle going on in the provinces beyond Hunan. The airdrome was a beehive—hundreds of coolies, male and female, cutting down a hill to lengthen the runways and doing it almost entirely by hand. Changsha, only ninety miles to the north of Hengyang, and Nanchang, equi-distant northwest had felt the spearhead of the Japanese land attack and were being bombed constantly. The Chinese knew the war would come to Hengyang before long and even though they would not have an adequate air force they intended to have an adequate flying field.

But the countryside was peaceful, peasants plowed their fields and threshed their rice in the slow ancient manner. To them, the flight of an airplane in the sky was still an exciting curiosity. Soon they would know it as a hideous messenger of misery and destruction.

Only the wealthier Chinese and missionaries owned radios and war news was strictly a subject of hushed conversation in the missions and homes of the landowners. Rice crops were being commandeered by the Government—but the war lords had been doing that as far back as the peasants and their cherished ancestors could remember. Then, one day a long train stopped at the village station. It was crowded with wounded soldiers headed for sanctuary deep in the interior. From far and near peasants, their wives and children flocked to the station to witness, for the first time, this living evidence of the cruelty and death that was marching across the land to their homes.

I joined a number of the Chinese women in hastily preparing food and rounding up such medical supplies as were available to relieve the seriously wounded. It was filthy work as many wounds were badly infected and there was a lack of opiates to allay suffering. It was surprising how quickly and effectively the Chinese women, old and young, joined in the work and were devotedly following the lead of that grand First Lady of China, Madame Chiang Kai Shek, helping to fill that vast reservoir of human loyalties which no mechanical juggernaut can ever permanently destroy.

One tragic incident occurred. A soldier, half-crazed with pain, got off the train, stomped up and down the platform moaning. Then with a sudden gesture he drew a hand grenade from his pocket, pulled the pin and hurled it at a group of his wounded comrades. Twelve were killed, including himself. It was quite messy.

Eventually the locomotive whistle tooted and the train began to roll. A shout broke the silence of the waiting crowd and grew into a deafening roar as the train faded into the horizon.

Thereafter, the life-pace of our neighbors began to quicken. The men seemed younger, more alert. Their plows furrowed faster. The officials' wives organized a Red Cross unit to meet other such trains which they knew would, in ever growing numbers, follow the first. Young men came to Harvey for information about volunteering for air service.

One day late in 1938, Captain Clifford Louie—"Long-legged Louie"—dropped down from the skies. Louie was a

Cantonese who had been born and for many years lived in Seattle. He had taken his first flight training under Tex Rankin. When Louie came to Hangchow in 1934, as one of Harvey's students, he was having a terrible time adjusting himself to China. He was addicted to coffee and American cigarettes, couldn't endure Chinese food and spoke very bad Cantonese. The next time we saw him, in Hengyang, he had mastered the language and liked the food, but still had to have his American coffee and cigarettes. Two years later Harvey saw him again. He was smoking Chinese cigarettes, had forgotten most of his English but still drank American coffee.

Louie had come down from Hankow where his outfit, the Gipsy Squadron, a group of Cantonese flyers flying Gloucester Gladiators, had been badly mauled attempting to keep Jap bombers away from the city. There had been one of the most spectacular air battles of the war, with seven of the Gipsies—all that were left of the original squadron—and thirty-five Russian E-15's and 16's against a hundred Japanese. Of the Gipsies, Louie alone had escaped unscathed. The squadron had been temporarily disbanded for lack of equipment as the fifty Gladiators with which they started had been used up and no replacements were available. Since then the Japs unopposed, had rained bombs on Hankow in raid after raid. Louie predicted the city would fall soon.

On station at the Hengyang field were two squadrons of Russian bombers. While they were flying for China, they were manned by regular Russian pilots and mechanics. With Russia officially at peace with Japan I never did figure how that had been worked out. The Russians were unique and amusing. The pilots, particularly, had a passion for wrist watches and wore three or four on one wrist at a time. They were paid, by Russian standards, big money by the Chinese Government and obviously spent most of it, saying it wouldn't be any good to them in Russia. Their doctor asked me confidentially to give him all the low-down I possibly could on

Mary Pickford. They were all Hollywood-mad and sent us bottles of vodka in return for our copies of dog-eared motion picture fan magazines.

Rumors of Japanese atrocities, the killing of thousands of women and children, the wanton bombing of defenseless towns began to seep in. Harvey was worried because regular and safe delivery of his airplanes was being threatened by Japanese advances towards Canton. Sooner or later, like a malignant white spot of leprosy, the Nipponese scourge would creep up to and finally engulf Hengyang. Harvey camouflaged his planes, with the help of the Chinese, and set up dummies which he hoped would fool the Jap bombers. We looked around for good deep holes near the house to dig ourselves in.

A special train passed through bearing Nazi military experts who had been relieved of their duties and were en route to Germany—an ominous sign.

Colonel Mah thought it was about time for me to be getting out. However, Harvey wasn't ready to leave and I certainly didn't intend to go wandering off to some other part of China alone.

Hankow fell—then Canton. Chinese officials retreated to Hengyang. Our house became, in effect, a hotel. Always there were half a dozen or more guests, some permanent, some passing through.

Despite the fact they had for months been constantly teetering backwards, the Chinese Army men were uniformly optimistic and patient. Captain Yuan, who commanded a group of flyers, told us:

"In China, every day eighteen to twenty thousand men come of age; Japan will have quite a time annihilating them. We have the man power—what we really need is more bombers, more fighting planes, more anti-aircraft guns, more supplies of every kind. If only America could be made to understand that the China Chinese, which they consider a backward people, are really fighting the battle for democracy."

After the fall of Hankow there had been many false air raid alarms—and then one morning it came—the real thing.

GINBAO!

That is the dread warning of approaching Jap bombers given by siren, gongs and church bells—all sorts of noises. Harvey was ill in bed with dengue, or bone-breaking fever. I ran up to the roof. People were scampering in all directions. I returned to tell Harvey. He wriggled into a bath-robe and ordered me to get into the pit—so I grabbed my camera, ordered him back into bed and rushed up to the roof. Nine Jap bombers in perfect formation glistened in the sunlight directly overhead, circling toward the field.

"They're at ten thousand feet and coming down fast," said Harvey, suddenly beside me. The anti-aircraft clattered, then successive "boom-booms" rumbled down the breeze. Great blasts of red dust geysered from the airdrome across the river, followed by belches of black smoke from a fire. In no time at all the sirens and gongs signalled "all clear." The raid had lasted only seven minutes.

Harvey ignored his fever and hurried to the field to appraise the damage. The Japs had concentrated their aim on a row of pursuit planes at the end of the runway—Harvey's dummies, made of bamboo and paper! However, bomb fragments had badly damaged five of his real airplanes which were ready to be delivered, and killed half a dozen men and women, who, poor things, thought the Japanese planes were Chinese and stood watching them from the edge of the field.

When it was all over I was surprised how little frightened I was. Later, when I had time to think it over, I couldn't understand why, for I certainly have sense enough not to enjoy being bombed—Or have I?

Our landlords, the missionaries, were still wishfully thinking that somehow sweetness and kind thoughts would prevail and that if we war-mongers would not provoke the Japs by continuing to live in Hengyang—specially in their house—perhaps there would be no more bombings. They feared the presence of high Chinese officers in the house might make it a favored target and requested we do something, *i.e.*, serve notice on our guests or leave. They were much more concerned about the safety of their property than the safety of its occupants. But maybe they were right.

The last three weeks we spent in Hengyang were a nightmare of diving into and crawling out of dugouts and pits, waking up and retreating to the outskirts of the village at all hours of the night, throwing ourselves flat on the ground as death whistled down from the heavens. The Chinese anti-aircraft resisted valiantly. One crack battery, equipped with Russian guns, accounted for eleven Japanese planes in three nights, proving they know how to use proper equipment. I remember most vividly one brilliant moonlight raid—twenty-seven Japanese bombers looking like silver toys and in perfect formation until furious anti-aircraft fire scattered them and brought four tumbling to earth in streaks of red flame. They dropped their bombs haphazardly and as no one place seemed safer than another we all thought we would be killed.

One afternoon they came over while Harvey was aloft, testing. A huge red cross placed on the field warned him they were coming. I was on the roof, watching. The plane dove and landed. A figure leaped from the ship and ran for the nearest hole just as a direct hit smashed the plane to powder!

Early in 1939 Harvey's work at Hengyang came to a standstill. The Japs were between us and the sea and there was no longer any way to get the crated, disassembled planes through to Hengyang. We decided to leave.

We had inherited an automobile—a 1928 DeSoto coupe and a noble vehicle. Harvey managed to get it running and we rattled off one morning by road, via Kwangsi, for Indo-China —with no spare tires. It wasn't an easy trip but extremely interesting. Through Hanoi and across to Haiphong and thence, by pig boat, to Hong Kong. For a time we zigzaged erratically

—up to Chungking and Kunming where Harvey had company business, back to Hong Kong, down to Haiphong again, there to stay for a time in a beautiful villa at Doson, then down to Siam and Singapore and across north to Rangoon. There we had to endure for four awful months while Harvey wrestled with hide-bound—to put it mildly!—British customs officials trying to clear fifty North Americans which had been sold to and were desperately needed by the Chinese. If you think he succeeded you are ignorant of the intricacies of British red tape as it existed in Burma at that time. All the lawyers in Philadelphia couldn't have whipped that problem.

Harvey finally said "T'hell with it," and flew over to Java by Imperial and Qantas Airways—Qantas, I believe, being the only word in or out of the dictionary where "q" is not followed by "u." Don't ask me why. He left me in Rangoon to inhale the rare fragrance of decaying jack fruit, returned briefly, went back to Java again, settled down in Bandoeng—and sent for me. My amah, Ah Yee, and my dog, "Lucy," went with me.

We liked Java and the climate high up in the mountains wasn't bad. We lived in Bandoeng, headquarters of the military. We stayed there for a full year, but in June, 1941, we boarded a ship for Manila and the next thing we knew we were back in Hong Kong again.

It was a little cooler now and getting dark, and one by one the lights on the hills across the harbor twinkled into being. Harvey had not returned. I started to dress for dinner. The door flew open and in he strode. For some reason he looked taller, straighter. He wasn't smiling. That look in his eyes—I knew it only too well.

"Never mind any more packing, Olga," he said. "Well, yes, you might as well, and send everything home. Leave out your summer clothes. You won't need any fur coats where we're going."

I said: "Cut out the double-talk, Harvey."

He said: "I'll tell you all about it at dinner"—which he did.

"For the past three months the old Man has had scouts back in the States rounding up pilots, mechanics, technicians to come out here to form a fighting unit under his command. The pilots are kids from Navy, Army and Marine corps—a picked group to protect the Burma Road. The other ranks are also service men. The Old Man wants me to join up with him as Chief of Staff and Executive Officer. We'll train and outfit in Burma, just above Rangoon. . . ."

That is where I blew up.

But even as I was squawking against Rangoon I knew it wasn't going to be any use. It wasn't the little frown of seriousness on Harvey's face, or his sincerity and enthusiasm that stirred something within me—it was just plain curiosity. I am one of those silly, curious women who is scared to death of missing something. It kills me if something that sounds exciting is about to happen and I'm not in on it. But I was still determined to go back to America—and yet . . .

"You mean this picked group of Americans are going to help the Chinese fight the Japs?" I was looking for a graceful excuse to change my mind.

Harvey responded enthusiastically. "Chennault calls it the American Volunteer Group—the A.V.G. It's important, Olga. We are going out there to fight."

I insisted I was going home.

Harvey smiled. "Then it's settled. You go home on the *Coolidge* and I'll go with the Old Man."

I said: "NO—you're going home with me."

Mr. Greenlaw can be a very persuasive man when he wants to. He did it with a look and a hand across the table, placed gently on mine.

"It may be tremendously exciting, Olga—and, I had a hell of a time getting the Old Man's permission for you to go along as a member of the group. He's death against women when there's work to be done. But of course if you don't want to come. . . ."

I knew he had me, the dog! But I wasn't going to surrender too easily.

"What will I do all the time you're gadding around with the Colonel?"

"Plenty of things," said Harvey, "plenty of things." He grinned. "The Old Man went up to Chungking tonight. I promised I'd send him a message tomorrow after I had talked things over with you. What'll it be—yes or no?"

"You've already made up our minds, haven't you?"

"That's fine, Olga," he chuckled. "As a matter of fact, I already told the Old Man it would be all right." He patted my hand victoriously.

Just to teach this Mr. Greenlaw not to be so darn smug, I said:

"Harvey, darling, you run along any place you want with your little pal Chennault, but Olga is going home!"

Chapter II

A N unique and disheartening feature of China National Airways' operations from Hong Kong to the interior was that, to insure maximum safety, the planes departed at night and, preferably, in bad weather. The first part of the flight was over Japanese-held territory and the goggle-eyed invaders had no qualms about improving their marksmanship on defenseless transports. Several C.N.A.C. airplanes had been attacked and passengers injured and killed. Foxy Kent, one of the best-liked pilots in the Orient, had been fatally wounded by an explosive bullet when he was chased to a landing and then cold-bloodedly machine-gunned by Jap fighters. So C.N.A.C. had two choices—fly by daylight and get shot at or fly at night and chance the weather. They preferred the latter.

We took off from Kai Tak airdrome, outside Kowloon, at two-thirty on the morning of August 25th. It was inky black, with rain pouring from low-scudding clouds—as unhappy a night for flying as you could imagine. But the pilot, Royal Leonard, a personal favorite of Generalissimo Chiang Kai Shek's and an old student of Harvey's at Brooks Field, Texas, was delighted with conditions.

"They'll never find us in this stuff," he beamed cheerfully.

I thought maybe we'd never find Chungking, our first stop on the way to Rangoon, in this stuff, either. Which I asked Harvey. His comforting answer was: "Oh, they don't crack up often." My only consolation was that the plane, a DC-3, like those on American air lines, was numbered "47" and all numbers ending in "7" are lucky for me. We circled over blotted-out Hong Kong, skirted Canton to avoid anti-aircraft fire, and climbed blind to 13,000 feet to clear the mountains.

27

It was sickeningly bumpy all the way to Chungking—for me, five and a half hours of torture.

We had waited for five uncertain weeks in Hong Kong while the British passport office debated whether I should be given a visa for Burma, difficult for anyone to get, especially women. Then Colonel Chennault wired that it had been arranged through the American and British Consuls at Kunming. Finally official confirmation reached Hong Kong. The *President Coolidge* sailed without me, of course. I knew it would that night in the Peninsula Grill although for several days thereafter I continued to play "hard-to-get," just as a matter of sound marital strategy. While Harvey was winding up his business affairs his dutiful wife packed the community property and with a sigh of relief shipped it all back to the States except one trunk, forwarded to Rangoon by boat, and the thirty pounds of luggage we each were permitted on the plane.

Harvey said it was a relief to be traveling light again and I said yes, it must be a great load off his mind not to have to worry about packing and unpacking for a change. But I knew we would start accumulating knick-knacks again as soon as we could find places to buy them and new trunks to put them in. Confirmed junk collectors are not easily discouraged.

In addition to things, we also collected creatures—including monkeys, Siamese cats, birds of all kinds and dogs. The only permanent member of our menagerie was Lucy, an Australian terrier bitch I had gotten in Rangoon in 1940 and had subsequently taken everywhere with us. Lucy was part of a Spitfire Fund. The veterinarian I bought her from had contributed the proceeds from the sale of the litter to the Fund. Her pedigree name was "Havoc," after a famous British destroyer, but Lucy seemed more in keeping with her personal habits as a puppy. She was small enough to take anywhere and faintly resembled an old mop.

At Chungking, we landed in a small field in the middle of the Yangtze. Approaching, we could see the city plainly—a

Harvey K. Greenlaw.

Colonel Chennault and Pilot Sawyer at a camouflaged repair shop, Kunming.

mass of ruins and destruction. Although the Japs were bombing it continuously and without mercy, the new capital of China carried on stoically. Then another four hours to Kunming, 6,000 feet up in a mountain valley in Yunnan Province. A lovely city, I thought, not knowing I would spend a great deal of time there later.

If I had had a crystal ball when we landed at Lashio, that ancient Burmese village of native wooden shacks which had almost overnight become the teeming southern terminus of the Burma Road, I might have foreseen myself, eight months later, scrambling madly to escape the Japanese onrush, barely slipping clear of the enveloping claws in a tender which "Little Olsen," an A.V.G. boy, salvaged from the R.A.F. at Magwe—without, I fear, wasting time to inform them that he was salvaging it. In that crisis there was no time to stop and explain.

Perhaps I could also have foreseen our good friend and luncheon host at the C.N.A.C. Hostel, Major General Denys, British military attaché to China who had boarded the plane at Chungking, hurtling to a sudden, firey death. But all I saw through the hostel windows that afternoon was an ever-rolling column of trucks bulging with tons of American lend-lease materials of war—but not nearly enough tons—with shouting, cursing Indian, Chinese and Burmese drivers crowding them relentlessly along the Burma Road toward embattled China.

It was at Lashio that we first met Joseph Alsop, who was on his way to join the A.V.G. as staff secretary. Joe had come down the Burma Road with a party which included an old Standard Oil friend of ours named Palmer. Joe was an extremely intelligent young man with an established reputation as a Washington columnist. At first, his Groton-Harvard accent and unfamiliarity with military operations placed him at some disadvantage. But having brains and a prodigious capacity for work he adapted himself quickly and was of great assistance to the Colonel. Unfortunately, he was sent on a special mission to Singapore and Manila, and finally Hong

Kong where he arrived precisely in time to be snatched up and interned by the victorious Japanese. We landed at Rangoon as the last rays of the setting sun were fading from the great golden dome of the Shwe Dagon Pagoda, a breathless sight— beautiful enough, almost, to make me forget that the ground approaches to this magnificent temple were a welter of rotting banana skins, cheroot butts and assorted garbage and filth— with odors to match. Rangoon is most beautiful when viewed from a safe distance.

We went directly to the Strand Hotel, first class in Burma, third class by American standards. But with first class tariffs. The Strand, which faced the docks along the Rangoon River, formerly had been quiet and orderly and the service good. But no longer. The lobby was a maelstrom of heterogeneous humanity, jabbering in all the languages of Eastern Asia. We had to fight our way to the reception desk. The Swiss manager, Mr. Vogel, promised us rooms the next day and sent us over to the Minto Mansions, Rangoon's second-best. As we entered the lobby the first thing to catch my eye was a carrot-colored head surmounting a red face powdered with freckles—above a khaki shirt, shorts and high-heeled Texas boots! He was with three or four other scarcely less colorful young men, all wide-eyed and having themselves a time. Texans no longer surprise me. You stumble on them everywhere in the world—full of Texas and ready to sing *The Eyes of Texas* at the drop of a tuning fork. On the way to our room I asked Harvey:

"Did you see what I saw?"

He grinned. "They're part of our gang."

"Those little boys? Why they're just children." They looked healthy and spirited—but very young.

"It's a young man's war," Harvey said.

"But not their war," I protested.

"Before it's over it'll be everybody's war."

I said at least these lads seemed to be having a lot of fun.

"Sure," said Harvey. "They think they're on a picnic. They

always do at first—but wait till the hard work and the boredom and homesickness set in."

It is worth recalling, I think, that at that time—August 1941—millions of Americans were still hoping and really believing their country would never be forced to take up arms, that by some miracle the United States might avoid the holocaust which was consuming the globe. "Defense" was the watchword. The Great Democracy would prepare to defend itself, supply arms to the fighting nations and emerge victorious, somehow, without spilling American blood. To us in the Far East this attitude was fantastic and absurd. We could not predict that the conflict in the Pacific would start at Pearl Harbor, on December 7th—although a few well-informed Americans in the Orient came very close to calling that shot! —but we knew that start—somehow and somewhere in the near future—it inexorably must.

China was at war. Rangoon, its docks heaped with weapons, was at war—unofficially, of course. These youngsters who had come half way around the world to join the American Volunteer Group were at war although, as Harvey said, they didn't yet realize it. We had seen enough of the smug complacency, lethargy and ostrich-like head-in-the-sand attitude of the French in Indo-China, the Siamese, the Dutch, and the British in Hong Kong, Singapore and Burma to be convinced that they, tragically too late, would discover they also were at war. It was frightening and depressing. These people simply would not believe anything could or would happen.

Don't ask me to explain the international political and diplomatic hocus-pocus which was going on at that time because I can't. Russia was at peace with Japan, but we had seen Russian military planes leaving Hengyang to bomb the Japanese. Britain was at peace with Japan, but the A.V.G., an arm of the Chinese Air Force, was training in British Burma to fight against the Japs. I guess the boys all knew what was coming and, in the final analysis, the end justified the means.

Colonel Chennault arrived the next morning in the Beech-craft, a bi-motored plane, to fly Harvey back to Toungoo, 175 miles north of Rangoon on the main line to Mandalay where the A.V.G. was assembling to start training at Kyedaw, the R.A.F. airdrome. They left before noon and I went out to stay a day or two with Edna and Stanley Robins. Stanley was a Major in the Indian Army Service Corps. I did some shopping—bought up all the Elizabeth Arden cleansing cream I could find—and several lipsticks, figuring that as I was marching off to war I had better be adequately equipped. Elizabeth Arden was my stand-by in the Orient. In Indo-China the creams were Paris-made—in the British possessions, British-made. There were very few American cosmetics out there except in Manila, although at times a Maxfactor "pancake" would manage to slip through the tariff barriers. Among the interesting people I met was a young British captain named Jelf, who had been a gunner at Dunkirk.

After a couple of days Harvey wired me to come along to Toungoo on the Mandalay "Up Mail."

I can brush Toungoo aside with a few well-chosen expletives. There was a main street, rumbling day and night with trucks bound for Lashio and the Road; a bazaar with shops on one side and open market stalls on the other; perhaps forty Europeans all told—and all the bugs God created to fly through the air or crawl on the ground, floors, walls, ceilings, into your food, down your back, up your legs and in your hair—beetles, lice, spiders, flies and fleas, moths, mosquitos, centipedes, bedbugs, ticks and a lot more you never heard of. The place was an entomologist's paradise. It was also dusty when dry, a morass when it rained, and *how* it could rain! and hot and humid always. All the elephants in Burma yoked together can not drag me back to Toungoo—which I won't have to worry about at the moment, thanks to the Japanese.

Harvey met me at the station. Some of the boys were with him—he had gotten acquainted with them quickly as he has a way of doing and they were, I was sure, curious to see his wife. What he had led them to expect I could pretty well guess. That first meeting is still vivid in my memory—the hot, muggy night—dimly-lit station platform—the sound of the "Up Mail" huffing away into the darkness—the shrill English locomotive whistle—the sudden cry of some wild beast in the jungle—a momentary surge of lonesomeness—and my first introduction to those youngsters whose deeds of valor were to make them known the length and breadth of America—and of China—as the terrible Flying Tigers. The boys didn't find out they were Flying Tigers until, months after the fighting started, they read about themselves in the headlines of stale American newspapers. To ourselves we were simply the A.V.G. and not very romantic. We were too busy to be romantic.

Harvey was advancing—"Olga, this is Jack Newkirk—" a tall boy, hawk-faced, sharp-eyed. "—and Bob Sandell—you call him 'Sandy' and he'll call you 'Olga'—and John Armstrong—" a slender black-haired lad. "Pete Atkinson, and this one's Bob Little—" his eyes were large and dreamy. "Ole Olson, the terrible Swede from Chicago—and Red Probst—" the Texas-booted red-head I had seen in Rangoon.

They were all grinning and giving me the once-over, drawing their snap conclusions about the Chief of Staff's wife. I wished I had tidied up a bit more before leaving the train—and was my lipstick on straight? I was looking them over, too—knowing instinctively I was going to like them.

The thing which impressed me most was they were so young and apparently inoffensive and so very much alive—which was cruelly ironical, for most of them are dead now, most of those youngsters I met that first night on the funny little station platform beside the railroad line to Mandalay.

But mark this: they died for a very much greater purpose than merely helping to destroy 600 Japanese planes and sending a thousand or two war-like little brown men to join their equally belligerent ancestors—or, when the showdown came and defeat was inevitable, keeping the Burma Road open so that the red corpuscles of war might flow into China's veins for a few extra days or weeks. They died to bring hope to 400,000,000 beleaguered human beings and give them spiritual strength and encouragement to carry on. They died that 135,-000,000 sleepy-headed Americans might finally wake up to the fact that China was fighting fiercely and stubbornly in the common cause and was worthy of all possible assistance which could be given. It wasn't what the American Volunteer Group did to a few hundred Japanese bodies which earned it a paragraph in history, but, rather, the bright and warming light of hope and promise it brought to the battered war-weary Chinese. The value of the A.V.G. was psychological far more than it was material—and I will always believe that that sagacious lady, Madame Chiang Kai Shek, shrewdly foresaw the result when she first proposed that the group be formed.

The boys started kidding. "Hm-m-m, not bad!" "You're going to like it here, babe." "Harvey, you lied to us—she isn't bowlegged"—"or cross-eyed." "The boss said you were short and fat." That was Jack Newkirk, who always called Harvey "The Boss." Red Probst said: "So you're the new little mama." Another one said: "Whadda you mean—little?"

We trooped across the tracks to the station restaurant for a drink and something to eat. Every station restaurant in Burma is The Savoy. The tiny room was crowded—all Americans and all mixed up—mechanics, radio men, clerks, pilots. They came there for dinner and such entertainment as they could stir up for themselves. There was no other place in Toungoo for them to go.

We finally wound up in the room Harvey had engaged for me up-stairs above the restaurant, because there were no accommodations for women in the newly-built barracks at the airdrome, which was eight miles north of the town. When they had all gone I was a little flustered and breathless—that 'gee!

—the boys-like-me' sub-deb feeling. I glanced in the mirror and decided that for a tall gal who had been around somewhat I wasn't such a bad-looker. I was still glowing a little from so much attention.

But as the days rolled along I began to see in a truer light. It was not necessarily that Olga Greenlaw was personally so popular or, by normal standards, any ravishing knockout. I still can look fairly snappy when I make an effort, and I get along swimmingly with men I like. But out there in Toungoo, miles from nowhere at the edge of the jungle, I was one of three American women among three hundred American men. The other two were nurses and, of necessity, tied down to their duties most of the time. I wasn't so much Olga Greenlaw, an individual, as I was a mirror in which these boys saw reflected the specific woman, or type of woman, uppermost in their minds at the moment of reflection. I was, I suppose you might say, a dummy they could clothe and endow with any of a thousand feminine virtues, vices and unique peculiarities. They saw me as wife, sweetheart, mother—perhaps even grandma or dear old Aunt Beulah. Sometimes, no doubt, I represented things which you won't mind if I skip, although under the circumstances they were perfectly understandable and require no apologies. These were normal young men with blood in their bodies and occasional ideas in their heads. So while I finally came to know all of them casually and many of them intimately I never kidded myself into believing it was unadulterated Olga Greenlaw they were enthusiastic about.

Harvey popped in the next morning to take me to see the house he had found for us.

"The Old Man bet me six to five I wouldn't be able to find a place," he said. "He thought maybe we'd have to build a shack for us near the airdrome."

I said I'd like that, but Harvey insisted he wouldn't.

"After being with the boys all day I want a little privacy at night—and a little rest."

I am afraid I raised my eyebrows. Privacy? Rest? Why, Mr. Greenlaw, how you talk! As it turned out, after the first alarms came, even though they were false, he spent most of his nights at the field—in the operations room on a cot. He knew all hell would suddenly break loose some day or night and wanted to be Johnny-at-the-rat-hole when it did.

"You'll like this place," he babbled. "Got it from an Indian fellow who is moving out now—very reasonable, too. Only two hundred rupees a month, which can't be more than four times the normal rental. It needs a little cleaning but you've got a knack of making a place look homelike, Olga."

A Burmese rupee was then worth thirty-three American cents.

We drove three blocks up the main road, dodging the rolling column of trucks, and turned into a bare and dirty courtyard which, at one time, had probably been a garden. Behind two frowsy banyan trees was a two-storey house. The downstairs wasn't much, but the upstairs would do. There was enough furniture, such as it was, a large living room and two bedrooms, one with a large bed, the other, which would be the guest room, with twin beds. Off the living room was a spacious veranda. Electric fans, of course, and no screens. There are practically no screens in the Orient, the theory being that they keep the air out. My weak-minded theory was that screens might also keep the bugs out, but I never had a chance to prove it.

Our bathing would be by the familiar vat-and-dipper system, with a *pani wallah*, or water boy, to attend to the filling and emptying. The sanitary facilities were what you might call the 'indoors-but-old-fashioned' type for which I managed to pick up some pretty snappy pink-enameled equipment in the bazaar.

"How do you like it?" Harvey asked cautiously.

I thought it would do—it would have to do!—but "needs a little cleaning up" was an understatement. It took me and ten

coolies ten days to muck the dirt out, but after I had unpacked
a few things, rearranged furniture, added odds and ends from
the bazaar and put my toilet articles out on the dressing table
it began to look the least bit homelike.

One hundred twenty-four Steel Road, Toungoo, Burma
—the new Greenlaw mansion—or more accurately the New
Greenlaw Hotel, which it promptly became.

That afternoon I drove out to the airdrome. Flying fields are
no novelty to me. I have dug the dust of dozens of them out of
my eyes—from Glendale to Delhi. But my first view of Kyedaw was a distinct thrill. I sensed it as the beginning of a new
and exciting adventure. Other airdromes belonged to governments or cities or corporations but Kyedaw was ours—the
A.V.G.'s!

It wasn't much to look at—a large field hacked out of the
jungle, two runways forming an "X" in the center, one hangar
and a few scattered shacks, some still under construction. The
main barracks were scattered along the road—well dispersed
against bombing raids. There were two mess halls, one for the
men and one for the pilots, made of split bamboo with thatched
palm rooves. The mess kitchens were clean and the Indian
servants and Burmese cooks dressed in spotless white. All the
large trees around the field had been felled and the stubby
teak which remained furnished little shade. I went back to
Harvey and said I'd seen everything, but where were the men
and planes?

His reply was a formal report.

"It's like this: as of today, the A.V.G. consists of 174 pilots
and men and twenty Curtiss P-40 planes or Tomahawks as
the British call them. Ten more planes are expected to arrive
tomorrow from Rangoon where they are being assembled by
C.A.M.C.O., which is Central Aircraft Manufacturing Company, Ed Pawley's outfit. We have some guns but no ammunition as yet, and one Beechcraft we wangled from the Chinese
for our own transportation. We expect another 150 men

shortly and a maximum of 100 airplanes. That hangar over there contains all kinds of tools and equipment for repairing planes."

"Aren't they new planes?" I asked.

Harvey gave me a look. "Right out of their cellophane wrappers—but they won't be so new after these young squirts get through learning to fly them."

I struggled to absorb it. Just so I'd know everything, I asked:

"How much are these boys paid?"

"I'll tell you for the last time. The A.V.G. is made up of American Army, Navy and Marine corps personnel—all volunteers. There is no military rank in the outfit. The pilots are divided into wingmen, flight and element leaders, and squadron and deputy squadron leaders. The base pay of a wingman is 600 United States dollars a month. Flight Leaders get $675 and squadron leaders $750. A bonus of $500 will be paid for every enemy plane shot down—and confirmed.

"The men grade from a few line chiefs, getting $400 a month, down to the administration clerks who have to struggle along on $150. In between are armourers, radio experts, mechanics and the rest. We have a complete medical staff of four doctors and a dentist, two female nurses and last but not least, the Chaplain. These all average about $500 a month. The nurses get $200. And oh, yes—we have a part-time embalmer."

That hit me right in the face and the face showed it. "You mean a man who—ah—" Harvey suddenly became very serious. "Look Olga, I'm going to warn you about something. I don't want you to become too attached to any of these kids. It won't be easy because they're a nice lot of youngsters. I am already pretty attached to some of them myself. But they're out here to fight a war—and—you can't fight a war without somebody getting killed."

I mumbled something about it didn't seem possible—

Harvey said: "It's more than possible—it's a cinch. And

another cinch that a few of these boys will smash up before we ever get into action. A lot of them have only a couple of hundred flying hours. We've got to make tough, resourceful fighter pilots out of them—and the airplanes are hot and hard to handle. I just want you to realize some very unpleasant things are likely to happen."

I have always found it extremely difficult to visualize death. I know for sure that some day I will die, yet I can't for the life of me visualize the time, place, circumstances or cause of my own demise—not that I try very often. By the same token it was impossible for me to visualize any of these gay, eager, vibrant youngsters cold and still in death. My imagination stopped short of that point. Maybe, I tried to tell myself, it wouldn't happen. Maybe, we'd be lucky and they would all come through unscathed. Or which one of them would get it first? It was suddenly very confusing and a little frightening. I began to wonder if perhaps the British Passport Office hadn't been right in wanting to refuse me a visa to Burma. Maybe this wasn't the place for a woman—with squadrons of men who were soon to soar into the heavens to kill and be killed.

A dusty, narrow track led to the hospital, a new building of teak beams with thatched roof and woven bamboo matting walls. I drove over there.

A very tall girl with frank blue eyes, red hair and millions of freckles greeted me.

"Hello. I'll bet you're Olga Greenlaw. I'm Red Foster."

To this day I don't know her first name. Everybody called her "Red." As the whole outfit knew, she was completely in love with one of the pilots, John Petach—nicknamed "Pete," of course. For a long time they wouldn't get married because the Colonel frowned on the idea, but finally they did—and Pete was killed in a mid-air explosion on the last day of the two extra weeks he volunteered to stay on to fight the Japs after the group had disbanded and before American replacements had arrived. Maybe Colonel Chennault was right—or maybe, things being what they were, he wasn't. That, I think, is for Red Petach to decide.

Red said they were still unpacking hospital equipment but could take care of an emergency. She walked to the end of the veranda and shouted: "Joe! Come out and meet Mrs. Greenlaw."

A gray-haired woman emerged, much older than Red. She was Mrs. Stewart, the other female nurse. They said the medical staff wasn't very busy. The boys were healthy and didn't need much attention. There were three American and one Chinese doctors: Dr. T. C. Gentry, Chief Flight Surgeon; Sam Prevo, L. J. Richards and Dr. Lee, his assistants. Later, Prevo and Richards proved their ability and courage during the terrible days in Rangoon, Magwe and Paoshan.

Red Probst volunteered to drive me home and picked up little 'Army Armstrong'. They wanted to do some shopping in the bazaar. Red drove so fast and recklessly it was a wonder we didn't kill a dozen or so natives and at least a hundred dogs. It was a miracle around Toungoo when you didn't run over dogs. Burma literally teems with thousands of the rattiest, mangiest, hungriest, crossbred, inbred, completely low-bred mongrels that ever a flea or tick called home sweet home.

As we careened along missing things by split inches, I couldn't get Harvey's remarks out of my mind. Some of these youngsters were going to be killed. I wondered who. These two boys I was with? I hoped not. Red Probst was wacky but I liked him. Little Armstrong was the kind of a boy you'd like to have your own son grow up to be, a kid from Kansas, via the Navy—willing and eager and itching to get at the Japs. It would be tragic if anything happened to him.

They stopped at the house for coffee. I explained that inasmuch as we made it a habit of running an hotel they had better start patronizing us without further invitation. Armstrong promptly fell in love with Lucy. "Where's my sweetheart?" he always asked when he dropped in—and most of the time he was there, she was on his lap or in his arms.

Red Probst stayed to help move furniture. When Harvey came home the three of us went to the station restaurant for dinner. Like the night before, it was packed to the doors. When we got back to the house Harvey asked:

"Well, how do you like it?"

I said all right so far—but without something useful to do I'd sooner or later be bored to the eyeballs.

It didn't take me long to get into the routine of housekeeping. I assembled a staff of servants—a "Nanny," or personal maid, a *pani wallah*, a bearer, which is the equivalent of a Chinese Number One Boy, and two sweepers. They sound impressive, but I'd have traded the five of them for one good old-fashioned American hired girl. Having no kitchen we ate all our meals out. However, on the back veranda was a small native brick stove on a cement base and here, with charcoal, the bearer made fires to boil water for coffee. I am the type of delicate creature who can eat anything and lots of it, but without good American coffee I am a flat tire. As soon as the rumor spread that we served free coffee at all hours the bicycles began to collect in the yard about four o'clock every afternoon. Thereafter, when anyone went to Rangoon he would generally bring back a few cans of some popular American brand.

Bicycling became the rage. In less than a week Toungoo was sold out of bikes and every train brought a new batch from Rangoon. Reckless buying turned the sleepy Burmese hamlet into a boom town. Prices zoomed sky high on everything. Bootmakers ran out of leather and merchants out of khaki and the old British settlers fumed at these extravagant Americans. One day the District Commissioner, a Burman, told me with unhappy grimaces and expressive gestures:

"No wonder prices have gone up. The people here all think you're crazy. Why the other day one of your men went into the bazaar, picked up a cheroot, handed the merchant a rupee and walked out. The fellow ran after him to give him his change—but instead of taking it your man pulled out another rupee and gave it to the merchant. Mrs. Greenlaw, here in Toungoo for one rupee you can buy *a hundred* cheroots!"

It wasn't strange that the kids tossed their money around. On off hours there was nothing to occupy their minds. At first they were allowed to go to Rangoon week ends, but not all at once. They usually skittered a bit and raised as much hell as there was to raise. They took in the races which, in turn, took them in and what money they had left they spent at the Silver Grill, the city's only night club. The Silver Grill sounds glamorous. In reality it was just another second-rate cabaret. Acts which appeared in these clubs in the Orient seemed to be deliberately following you around. You would catch one in Hong Kong one month—and the same people, singing the same songs and doing the same dances in the same costumes would pop up a month later in Singapore or Calcutta or Batavia.

During the long weeks before hell bubbled over, many of the boys were lonely and some, for a time, desperately homesick. A few simply couldn't take it, so they were sent back to the States at their own expense. Only one, as I recall, really had need to return.

On the 6th of September we had our first accident. Bob Little came to drive me up to the field. As we neared the runway a plane came in to a perfect landing but suddenly swerved into another ship parked by the runway. The pilot, Sandy Sandell, scrambled out looking most dejected. He wasn't hurt, but one of the wings of his plane was smashed and the propeller bent and twisted.

Two days later, while the Colonel was away in Chungking and Harvey in command of the Group, I was at the field watching the boys returning from routine flights. Most of the flying was done in early morning and all ships were supposed to be in before eleven-thirty. By that hour all had landed but two. Pilots Armstrong and Bright were missing. Nobody knew what had happened to them.

Armstrong!

A nasty little chill ran along my spine. Harvey said: "Just keep yourself together, babe ... they'll show up." But I knew he was worried, too. Against such emergencies as this, he had —through the police and head men of the villages—offered a standing reward to induce the natives to immediately report crashes or forced landings.

We were in the mess hall having lunch, with the atmosphere noticeably tense, when the telephone rang. The station master at a village north of Toungoo said two airplanes had collided over the jungle and gone down. He gave the location—near the Mandalay road. Harvey immediately sent three planes out to locate the wreckage and organized a crash party consisting of doctors, the engineering officer, Dick Peret, a radio man, an armourer and others. One of the pilots presently signalled back to the field that he had sighted the wrecks. The crash party whizzed off in cars. On his way to the scene Harvey met Gil Bright, scratched and bruised but otherwise all right, riding a bicycle he had borrowed from a native. He said he and Armstrong had collided during a practice dog-fight. He had bailed out but was sure Armstrong had gone down with his ship.

Finally the two planes were found, the motors drilled ten feet into the mud. Armstrong was in one. He had been unable to bail out. Poor little boy! Everyone liked him and everyone grieved for him. I recalled how I had decided in my own mind he'd be safe because he was too nice a youngster to be killed.

Gil Bright was shaken and remorseful and felt, as the boys always did when things like that happened, he was responsible —which he wasn't. I recalled Harvey's words: "You can't fight a war without somebody getting killed."

There were no caskets in Toungoo. Harvey phoned Ed Pawley, head of C.A.M.C.O. in Rangoon, and he sent up one and heaps of flowers by special truck which arrived at our house at dawn the next morning. I told the driver to put it in the large front room downstairs. The wives of the British officers in Toungoo all sent flowers and two came over to help me make wreaths. At four o'clock in the afternoon a military service was held in the mess room at the field, our own chaplain, Paul Frillman, reading the service. Armstrong was buried in a concrete vault in the Christian cemetery. The casket was covered with an American flag. All members of the group attended and all British officers in the district.

I had seen military funerals before. They were always impressive—but this one ripped large holes out of my emotions. It seemed so very personal, and there was something about being there on the outskirts of nowhere that made it doubly poignant.

After the ceremony the Chaplain folded the flag which was later sent to Johnny Armstrong's mother. Amongst the cards received, and also sent to his mother, was one from the Burma Defense Division and one from the R.A.F.

So he rests there now beside the brilliant green jungle, John D. Armstrong, of Hutchinson, Kansas, first of the American Volunteer Group to give his life in the cause of freedom.

It was dark when we left the cemetery, with an oppressive black overcast deepening our gloom. The incident had definitely sobered the boys. It was too late to go to the field for dinner so we went over to the Savoy with Jack Newkirk, Skipper Adair and Tye Lett. Adair was an old China hand who had been an instructor at Yunnanyi with several of the Americans who had subsequently joined C.N.A.C. Then he had gone to the United States to help recruit the A.V.G. and returned to become Transportation Officer. Tye Lett was the Allison Motors man, our P-40's being Allison powered. We waited around after dinner to put Tye on the train for Rangoon. Harvey left for the field and Jack, Skipper and I went back to the house, settled down on the veranda and they tried to keep cool with whisky-sodas. Jack was a hard drinking fellow but seldom, if ever, showed his liquor and he behaved himself better than most of the men in the outfit.

Sandy Sandell joined us later—dressed in the uniform the A.V.G. had adopted, which was simply shorts, khaki shirt and sun helmet. Being, then, in a neutral country, distinguishing marks or insignia were not thought advisable. Sandy said Harvey was staying the night at the field. He was in a talkative mood and among a great many other things explained how he happened to join the A.V.G.

"I was a second lieutenant in the United States Air Corps, stationed in Texas," he said, "when one of the scouts dropped in and explained the setup. It sounded good and I went for it. Why? Well for one thing there was a lot of fighting going on in the world for causes I believed were right and just—and I wanted to be in on it. I had been trained to fight but it didn't look then as if the United States would ever get into the war— and it still doesn't unless somebody pushes them in.

"I finally received a telegram to report in San Francisco to Eugene Pawley on July 5th. In the meantime I had made arrangements to resign from the Air Corps, which was pretending not to know where I was going. I drove to the coast from Dallas—to see the country. We came from San Francisco originally and I hadn't been back there since."

Sandy closed his eyes dreamily.

"That beautiful country around the Bay—that's where I'm going to buy me a ranch, settle down and raise cows and alfalfa—and children." He sighed ecstatically.

"Don't get ahead of yourself, Sandy," Jack Newkirk cut in. "How do you know we're going back?" He grinned sardonically.

"You're damn tootin' we're going back," Sandy said, "at least I am. They aren't going to bury me in this God-forsaken country."

Skipper Adair said nothing. I wished they'd change the subject.

Newkirk said: "By the way, Sandy, how come that crackup of yours the other day?"

"That? Well, you know, these little old P-40's have a knack

of getting away from you. This one slipped right out of my hand. They're pretty good crates at that."

Newkirk said: "We'll have plenty of chance to find out. ."

I poured another drink. Sandy rambled on about how he had gotten out to Burma—his few days in San Francisco where he couldn't get over the fact that where Union Square had been, right in front of the St. Francis, there was now an enormous hole, in which they were going to build an underground garage and then put the Square—monument, trees, flowers and green grass—right back again. And those glorious bridges! The thought had occurred to him as they slipped under the Golden Gate Bridge that it didn't make sense that men with brains and creative genius could spend years building something so useful and beautiful—and some little Japanese baboon could come along and utterly destroy it in ten seconds.

I asked if anybody in San Francisco knew about the A.V.G. or that the boys were headed for China to fight the Japs.

Sandy shook his head and grinned. "It was a deep, dark secret. Why, I heard a cigarette girl tell an elevator operator 'Yes, they're all going to China to keep the Burma Road open —they're sailing Monday on the *Jagersfontein!*'"

Jack Newkirk wanted the low-down on Al Probst. Sandy, who had known him in the States, said Red was one of those boys who was born with a hex on him—some people were like that.

"First thing he did when he came to Barksdale was wreck his car—" which I could easily believe! "—and spend three months in hospital. Then he tangled with some sudden weather and lost a couple of ships. Coming over, they weren't going to let us off the boat at Honolulu so we all got a little oiled, just for spite, and Red made a tour of the rigging. After they'd put a stop to that he went down to his cabin, walked in on a lurking intruder and took a terrific swing at him. The intruder happened to be Red's own image in a plate glass mirror. Red shattered the mirror—and didn't even get as much as a scratch. I guess maybe he came out to China to change his luck.

"You know, Jack, most of us are here for some reason or other—some to forget something they'd like to forget, others for financial reasons because, with a little luck, you've got a chance in this outfit to lay up a few dimes and quarters, some for adventure or because they wanted to see the world or wanted to fight—all kinds of reasons—you can't just tell what."

It went on like that. Adair finally left. Jack Newkirk and Sandy stayed until they had killed the bottle—and departed reluctantly. Eventually I learned to understand this reluctance to leave after a day of rough going or bad luck. It was better to be with someone and talk than it was to be alone and think.

Harvey came from the airdrome for breakfast. He was moaning because they hadn't been able to salvage either the radio equipment or guns on the two wrecked planes.

"Smashed all to pieces—couldn't save a thing," he groaned.

Armstrong was not mentioned again. Later I came to the sardonic realization that when a fighting unit is on its own in Burma or China or wherever, and it has no replacements or spare parts and doesn't know when it is going to get any, an extra machine-gun or radio outfit or even some silly little iron gadget may be fully as important as a man's life.

Chapter III

IF you are beginning to expect it is about time—somewhere along in the next few pages—to suddenly hear the rattle of the Flying Tigers' deadly machine guns and see their flaming victims go crashing down into the green Burmese jungle you might as well skip this chapter and most of the next.

For a period of more than three months after Pearl Harbor the American Volunteer Group was the pet and darling of the United States and the United Nations. It's amazing victories over the rampant Japanese air forces hogged headlines and feature pages. The Flying Tigers, as captivated war correspondents insisted on calling them, were the hottest of hot stuff and held the center of the martial stage longer and more completely than any single fighting unit has ever held it in this or any other war.

The reason is easy to understand. For numerous gloomy months prior to early 1942 the noble and righteous institution of Democracy had blocked repeated knockout punches with its nose, which by then resembled a ripe tomato and was twice as tender as a boil. Oh, sure—everybody knew the Japs couldn't do that to *us*—and just wait'll we get in stride—and naturally we'd win in the long run—but the fact remained that the detested dictators had our side battered and groggy and hanging onto the ropes for dear life. And to add insult to injury, the runty little brown men of Nippon were making our handsome white soldiers look ridiculous, stupid and futile. It was hard to laugh off the evidence which was piling up to prove the Japs were better trained and tougher, smarter fighting men. Millions of Americans began to wonder if there wasn't someone somewhere who could win just one single round—or even land one solid punch—against the sons of the Son of Heaven.

The situation looked gloomy indeed when all of a sudden out of nowhere came a blazing flash of light. A handful of unknown American youngsters in airplanes which had been much maligned by the British and Americans, completely on their own and constantly heckled by a hundred official, political and international stupidities, slashed through the blue Burmese skies and not only kicked the daylights out of all the Japs in sight but proved, mathematically, that one good American is a match for any twenty Japanese—and thereby saved the white man's ego from a total breakdown.

Which is perhaps what inspired one military expert to refer to the American Volunteer Group as "the most brilliant air combat unit the world has ever seen."

Maybe they were, or maybe not—but the point is that they didn't achieve perfection overnight. They grew from nothing into a superlative air fighting unit during what were perhaps four of the dullest, most unexciting and generally aggravating months any one group of people ever spent together—in Toungoo, of course.

After the first novelty of this disgusting little Burmese whistle-stop wore off, which didn't take very long, there was nothing to do. I am a fairly durable woman who will patiently stay put if any excitement is in prospect, but my diary shows that on five distinct occasions I was ready to quit cold, leave my husband, and go back to my mother where, in those depressed moments, I was firmly convinced I belonged. Had I been a man I would have gone out and gotten what the British call "blotto"—which some of our boys did on occasion and couldn't be blamed for.

Without realizing it, I was getting toughened up for the ordeals to come—as the boys in the Group were and as any good soldier must. Actually, our four months at Toungoo was our training siege before the championship battle. Colonel

Chennault and Harvey patiently and persistently converted a bunch of inexperienced youngsters into a deadly efficient fighting force and did a first-class job of it as the records prove.

Naturally, I very soon began to develop friendships. I couldn't become intimately acquainted with all 300 of the A.V.G. pilots and men, but before long I knew every one of them by face and name. I got to know perhaps fifty of them extremely well and for a dozen or more of these I acquired a deep and lasting affection.

The men in the A.V.G. were no different from those in any other American flying force—in Australia, Africa, Alaska or wherever. Most of them were swell kids—smart, courageous, loyal, enthusiastic and healthy. We had the usual handful of duds we wished we'd never seen and hoped to get rid of—the blow-hards, short-sports, bad drinkers, leadswingers and malignerers and a few who were plain rabbit-hearted and couldn't take the hard knocks. But the vast majority were the kind of American men and boys you are proud to know and glad to be with.

There was one vital difference between the A.V.G. and a regular service unit; our boys were volunteers and free to resign whenever they wished—which can't be done in the Army, Navy or Marines. To their credit—after the initial shakedown of quitters and malcontents—only one or two of them even thought of resignation, even after they had endured weeks of hell and hardship and their nerves were raw and jangling—and when day after day they had to face overwhelming odds with no prospect of relief or reinforcement. Probably there wasn't a single one of them who wouldn't have been glad to be out of there—with the possible exception of fireballs like Jack Newkirk and Tex Hill who fought for the sheer joy of fighting—but they all stuck it out—voluntarily, remember!—because they were the kind of kids who stick things out. Most American boys are.

I had better explain right here that this book is based on the jottings of a personal diary I kept while I was with the

A.V.G.—and of others which I kept from the first day I arrived in Chna. And, in spots, from the official *War Diary* of the Group, which it was my job to maintain as a member of the A.V.G. staff. "Jottings" isn't exactly the right word. I wrote in voluminous detail and many of the entries were made right on the scene, when such things as bomb raids were in progress. So don't mind me if from time to time hereafter, to lighten the task of writing a book, I crib a few of my own items. I find, for example, there are several which refer to the joys and comforts of life in Toungoo during those four dull months we spent getting ready to be sensational.

I am covered with bug bites. The servants say the bamboo seats of the chairs have small bugs, impossible to get rid of. However, I had them pour boiling water over the chairs. I hope it got rid of the bugs. I know it got rid of the paint.

Something has to be done about the drinking water—it is full of minute bugs and all kinds of little particles. We boil it—I must get a filter from Rangoon.

The prickly heat is unbearable. The Nanny (maid) prepared a whole mess of white of egg and plastered it on my face, neck and arms. Kept it on for an hour, then removed it with cotton soaked in rose water prepared by herself from fresh rose leaves. The spots are still red, but dried up somewhat. She may have something there!

The Indians are so dirty. I tell the bearer (number one boy) to do a thing and how to do it. He passes the buck to the next servant, and so on right down the line until it always ends up with the 'chokra' or small boy. He is about eleven but smart as a whip. His mother is still living in a small room of the servant's quarters. I can't get rid of her. The Nanny told me she was carrying on the oldest profession in back of the house. I ordered her to get out but she wouldn't budge. Finally I called the policeman—but she was back again the next day. I suspect the policeman may have succumbed to her charms!

Saw a terrible thing when I went to the post office to mail a letter to Edna Robins, in Rangoon. One of those big General Motors trucks, driven by a Burmese, ran over a child with both wheels—cut him almost in half. He died instantly. The parents were given one hundred rupees, more money than they have ever seen in their lives. They can have another child but not often can they see that vast amount of money.

All of which may convey a quick and vague idea of what went on.

The British colony at Toungoo was, if possible, a bit more British than any I had previously encountered. It numbered about forty loyal and completely conventional Britons, mostly husbands and wives. I am always amazed at the way the English can go thousands of miles from their native isle, live for years—and never do, wear or say one little thing which would not be considered completely proper in Mayfair, Chelsea or Blingham-on-the-Twing.

The focal point socially was the Gymkana Club, where everyone gathered Sunday afternoons for chitchat and cocktails. It was quite nice, with a well-kept nine-hole golf-course, two tennis courts, a billiard room, ballroom and pleasant little bar.

The social leaders were General and Mrs. Bruce Scott. The General was Commander-in-Chief of the British Frontier Force of the Burma Division—a handsome and affable officer of the old school. Mrs. Scott was a charming hostess. Amongst the civilians there was Mr. Fulton, the Connells, he being the Public Works Department engineer for the district, pleasant English gentlefolk who despite bugs, heat and a dozen other handicaps succeeded in making their home as English as Devonshire; Major and Mrs. Maurice Wright; the Wilsons, he the District superintendent of police; the two unmarried ladies of the town, Miss Fields, who was head of the Catholic Convent Hospital and Miss Burns, an Anglo-Burman who was accepted socially by the British ladies; and others.

Commercially, Mr. Fulton was the big shot of the village and district—Number One of the MacGreggor Company, the world's largest teak dealers. A bachelor, he dressed meticulously, always wore a monocle and was a perfect host. He had been in Burma for twenty-one years and besides being a teak expert was an elephant authority. It was his job to train the young men, "jungle *wallahs*," who came out from Scotland and were sent into the jungle by the MacGreggors for a year at a time—to learn the business. With malaria, dysentery and whatnot, very few of them could stick it out. Those who could remained for years, as had Mr. Fulton.

Colonel Chennault, Harvey and I were frequent guests at the Scott's home. One of the times we went there for dinner we met General McLeod, then Commander-in-Chief of the Burma forces. He was a sweet old gentleman, tall, a bit heavy, with perfectly white hair and a ruddy complexion. He seemed to be very pleased about everything, but maybe the whisky sodas had something to do with it.

The old custom of women leaving the table after dinner, still prevailed in Toungoo. Later, the men joined the women in the drawing room for coffee and liquors and the final *chota peg*, a small whisky and soda.

That night, I didn't want to join the women. I excused myself and remained with the men because they were discussing the Burmese Army. General Scott said the Karen was the best soldier. The Burma Rifle Corps was composed of Karens, and they were passionately loyal to the British. The Chins, inhabitants of the hills along the west bank of the Chindwin River, were the most fierce in combat. Those Chins wore blankets with their tribal designs. The Kachins, too, made good soldiers as they were the descendants of a war-like tribe that inhabited northern Burma.

When he spoke of the Karen people who occupy the eastern part of Burma between the Shan States and Siam, and also live in the Irrawaddy delta, I was much interested. The Karens make the famous Karenni drums. I was the proud owner of one of those drums which later caused me a lot of grief flying it from Burma into China, from China into India, and when I tried to get it out of there to take back to the States, the British said that it was war material as it could be used for shrapnel—an antique—160 years old! After pointing out that if it hadn't been for me, the Japs would have it, they let me take it.

During all this discussion one alarming fact became crystal

clear to me. Generals Scott and McLeod were two as charming gentlemen as you'd wish to meet—mannerly, interesting when they wanted to be, honorable to the nth degree. But I was afraid that they hadn't the faintest idea of what was going on right under their noses—or of what the terrible future held in store for them. They honestly anticipated no trouble from the Japanese. Subsequent events proved their forces were woefully inadequate, that the loyalty of the Burmese troops was questionable. They did not know, as was proven later, that the Burmese were sheltering dozens and scores of Japs who mingled with the natives dressed as Burmans and were making themselves generally useful to the Emperor. These two charming gentlemen knew Singapore was impregnable, that Britanaia ruled the waves and that the Japanese were much too smart to ever attempt to challenge the authority of their white masters. These things they knew for sure. No amount of argument or logic could have changed their opinions one single little jot. And these were the men who held in their hands the destiny of China's precarious life line, the Burma Road!

When we got back to the house we found Bob Little, Sandell and Jack Newkirk asleep on our beds! They were going to Rangoon but the train had been late. It had been raining for days and the countryside was inundated. The Sittang River had overflowed and at some places the railroad bridges were washed out.

One afternoon I went out to the field at tiffin time to sell the boys tickets for a show—the proceeds to go to the building of an animal hospital!

When I tried to sell the Chaplain a ticket he refused, saying he didn't believe in putting away dogs, or building dog hospitals.

Chaplain Paul Frillman, called "Padre" by all of us, was a Lutheran—an American born in Chicago. He was quite young, about thirty-three; unmarried and handsome. He arrived with the second group about the middle of August. He didn't know

whether to behave like a serious, dignified strict chaplain, or
to be a jovial, friendly one. The boys also did not know how
to take him. The Padre decided to be a jolly-good-fellow-well-
met. That did the trick. He never preached—just gave good
advice, take-or-leave-it. The boys usually "took it." He
played games with them and organized the theatre programs
and all forms of entertainment, which was part of his duty.

I didn't get far with the dog ticket. Sam Prevro, our surgeon,
said that it would be cheaper to kill dogs by running over
them, that he, himself killed at least two a day and could easily
run over more. He added: "How would you like to have Lucy
put away because she had fleas and ticks?" I challenged him to
find a single flea on Lucy. The boys roared with laughter and
that was the end of the dog hospital, as far as I was concerned.

Now if all this trivial gossip about the social life of Toungoo
is beginning to bore you you can imagine how much it bored
our young men of the A.V.G. The air training progressed
steadily, of course, despite drenching tropical rains. Schedules
were strenuous. A transition school was inaugurated to better
acquaint ex-Navy men who had been flying big planes with
the tempermentalities of the smaller and much trickier P-40.
Harvey insisted every pilot take the complete gunnery course
whether he had passed it before or not. More planes arrived—
and gradually, guns and ammunition—although we never had
enough of anything. Little by little the Group began to show
evidences of *esprit de corps*.

But because there was nothing to do in off hours the boys
got into considerable trouble. Some of it was funny and harmless; some of it was not. There were always fights and disorders
at the railroad station restaurant—including the night Harvey
had to pop one particularly obstreperous young man over the
head with a peppermint bottle. If the boys went hunting, they
seemed unable to avoid accidentally shooting an occasional
native; if they drank too much they shot up the village—Red
Gulch style. Harvey had a terrible time getting enough sleep

as he was constantly answering the phone at all hours to listen to complaints. There was one particular evening when a young man in his cups tried his hand at flying a switch engine which had carelessly been left beside the main line with steam up. He managed to delay both the "UP" and "DOWN" Mails for several hours, until he ran out of steam.

And then there was the evening when Red Probst, slightly jingled, climbed into General Scott's station wagon and ordered the surprised General, whom he mistook for the driver, to take him to the airdrome—which the General uncomplainingly did. Red's parting words to the Commander-in-Chief, after being deposited in front of the barracks, were a stern: "And don't ever let it happen again!"

I think the two most serious problems we had at Toungoo were the lack of mail and the lack of girls. Nobody ever could find out what happened to our mail. We just didn't get any— for literally months at a time. *Somebody* in the States must have written to our boys but the letters never arrived. There must be bags-full of them sitting around somewhere.

As for the girls—I may be wrong but I don't think you can successfully run an army for too great a length of time without a touch of romance. There were no girls in Toungoo and not many in Rangoon. On one occasion a number of Anglo-Indian young ladies were imported from Rangoon for a costume ball the English women held for charity. They were quite nice and well-behaved but some were a bit on the suntan side and not entirely appreciated. Later, a great deal of the fairly serious trouble we had with the men in Kunming was, in one way or another, over girls, or the lack of them. It wasn't that our group was any different from any other outfit of American fliers. It was just that the average American young man past voting age occasionally craves the companionship of an American—or at least approximately American—girl—and, I discovered, for the most part for decent girls.

It was in October that we had our first scare at Kyedaw.

Colonel Chennault thought two Japanese planes had flown over the airdrome on a reconnaissance mission. It subsequently turned out that they were two North Americans on their way to join the Burmese air force—which wasn't really an air force but a flying club with a few civilian members. The Burmese had repeatedly requested the British to give them a flying school but nothing was done about it. The Burmans concluded the British didn't want them to learn to fly.

Later the same day a Japanese observation plane did come over the airdrome at 30,000 feet and after circling the field flew off toward Thailand. This ship was too high to intercept. The Group was immediately put on regular alert—planes and pilots ready to take off at a moment's warning, ready to fight. The Colonel and Harvey knew that the Japanese usually preceded a bombing raid by aerial observation. Neither of them trusted the Japanese ideas of neutrality and both of them had a horror of being caught asleep on the ground, even though the proper dispersal of aircraft and equipment was emphasized at every opportunity.

Just about that time, three carloads of .30 and .50 caliber ammunition arrived from Lashio under the supervision of Captain Dan Wong. This ammunition had been sent from various arsenals in China. The ships of the Second Squadron mounted 7.92 guns in the wings and ammunition for these was obtained from the British Bush Warfare School at Maymyo.

We realized the possibilities of being unexpectedly raided and felt we would not be caught totally unprepared even though the British had no adequate warning system. At dawn, noon and dusk which were the periods the Japanese would probably attack, patrols were sent up to protect the field even though we did not want to run up motor time before we got into China and actual combat.

The pilots—and particularly myself—had no more than gotten over the hurt of Armstrong's death than our second tragedy occurred. Later we all learned to take anything up to and including a major disaster in stride and almost without emotion but in those first days at Toungoo we hadn't become quite hardened to it.

It sounds silly for me to even suggest that the Burmese 'Nats' might have had something to do with this misfortune and others which were to follow but after you've been around fliers for a time you get so you can believe almost anything— like gremlins, for instance.

It was my Nanny who told me about the Nats.

The Burmese, and particularly the Karens, are extremely superstitious. They believe the whole universe is filled with powerful, nasty-tempered little spirits which they call "Nats." They occupy every tree and rock and physical object above and even below the earth and in order to keep them in hand they must be bribed by regular offerings.

One night I was kept awake all night long by dogs baying at the full moon—a mournful sound at any time but particularly blood-chilling against the oppressive silence of the jungle. The next morning the Nanny said the dogs bayed because they were being disturbed by the Nats and that was a bad omen.

I always liked to listen to her prattle the village gossip in her soft voice. She was an attractive woman, pure Indian, and spoke English quite well as she had been brought up by one of the old Scotch settlers.

A day or two later one of the clerks dropped by to tell me a ship had spun in somewhere down along the Rangoon road and the pilot was seen to bail out. As the country was flooded at the time it wasn't known for sure whether the pilot was safe. He turned out to be Frank Schiel. He had been dog-fighting with Eric Shilling, got into an outside spin and had to jump. He wasn't badly hurt.

The next morning the Nanny said, ominously, that the Nats had caused Schiel's accident. They were not satisfied with Armstrong's death—they demanded more victims. I thought of the old Air Corps superstition of the "rule of three." The Nanny explained more fully:

"Before the field at Kyedaw was cleared, eight families lived there near the banyan tree that is on the left side of the road near the entrance. The British moved these families out when they started to build the field. The soil in that section is bad, and the natives living there were very poor and only raised a few chickens.

"A Nat lived in the banyan tree and every evening the people placed offerings which kept him happy and appeased. But now, there is no one there to give offering and he is angry. Of course, we do not blame the Americans because they do not know. The British cleared the field and moved out the people. Too bad your American friends have to suffer for it. . . .

"The Burmese have been worshipping at the temples all afternoon to appease this Nat who is so very angry and will eat the Americans who through no fault of their own are at Kyedaw."

Silly as it sounded, the idea disturbed me.

It wasn't until several days later that I began to take the Nats seriously. It was two o'clock in the morning and I was sitting in a car alone by the side of the road, waiting for the men to emerge from the jungle with the body of Maax Hamer, our second training casualty. He was an Illinois youngster who had only been with us a week.

Harvey had telephoned me about the crash. I went to the field about dinner time and found him and the Colonel talking about it. The plane had spun into a heavy thicket and it was suggested the search be left for early morning, but Harvey said the body should be recovered immediately—that it must for the morale of the boys.

The searching party was A.V.G. men and Burmese trackers. They all wore khaki shorts and shirts and rubber boots to keep the mosquitos and the leeches from their ankles. Most of them carried pistols, jungle knives and flashlights.

When we got to the part of the road where the small trail started off into the jungle, everybody disappeared in the darkness towards the scene of the accident. Left alone, I was quite frightened. I took several drinks of water out of a bottle and smoked many cigarettes to keep the mosquitoes off.

Finally the party returned. They had located the crash but it was impossible to get the body out until daylight. Two men were left guarding it.

Hamer's funeral was delayed—the truck bringing the tin-lined coffin from Rangoon was late. Everyone in the village knew of the accident. The phone rang continuously, British women asking if they could do anything to help. They sent flowers, the same as they did when Armstrong was killed. The same empty room downstairs was used again as the funeral parlour.

The funeral took place at three in the afternoon. I didn't attend as I wasn't feeling too well and it was pouring rain. Every time I didn't feel well, I figured I had worms—a common malady in the Orient. Every foreigner whether young or old had to take some kind of worm medicine periodically. So far, I hadn't had any—I didn't forget the possibility and would get indignant when Harvey told me I had them.

The Nanny had little to say after Hamer's crash but I knew she blamed the banyan tree Nat.

I was ill at ease for the next two or three days expecting something to happen at any moment. Then it came—Pete Atkinson this time. His ship exploded in the air at 5,000 feet. I went to the field to find out about it. The boys were badly broken up as Pete was well liked by both pilots and men. He was a devout Catholic who never missed a Sunday mass and was a favorite with the Italian priests who had been recalled from their stations and were concentrated in the Toungoo area. Pete, on a test flight, had apparently ripped off the tail surfaces in a terrific power dive.

This third fatality left me very downhearted. It was beginning to hit me every time one of these boys was killed. I had come to accept them as part of our family.

I knew, of course the Nats couldn't have been responsible

any more than they could have been months later when Frank Schiel was finally killed after he had transferred to the Army Air Forces. And yet, I wondered . . .

I arranged a Catholic burial and all the next day made wreaths—a lovely cross of white lilies from myself and Harvey and one of red roses from Colonel Chennault. The ceremony was most impressive—a high mass with the bishop and twenty priests and one hundred choir boys. A Gurkha soldier sounded taps—over the graves of three American boys buried side by side in that Christian cemetery in the shadow of the jungle. Three of them gone already—and our war hadn't even started yet.

I returned to the house. The downstairs room was cluttered with withered flowers and palm leaves—the chairs were still in place. It seemed as if everything was waiting for another coffin to take the place of the one we had just moved away . . .

I don't recall exactly when we adopted the shark-tooth paint job which gave the A.V.G. planes such a vicious and distinctive appearance but this is how it really happened:

In an English magazine Eric Shilling saw a picture of a shark-tooth painted P-40 which belonged to some R. A. F. outfit in the Middle East. He showed it to Harvey. All the boys liked the idea so it was tried on a few planes and then on all of them. Whether it had any psychological effect on the Japs I don't know—nor think anyone else does. The squadrons also adopted individual markings—an Adam and Eve for the First Pursuit, a Panda bear for the Second, and a somewhat hippy and dishabille lady for the Third.

New arrivals came along steadily for a time and among those I was to know particularly well were Tom Jones, Greg Boyington, Bob Prescott, Freddie Hodges and R. C. Moss.

Before I knew Boyington's name, I used to call him the "Bulldog." He was about five feet eight inches tall, with tremendous shoulders and narrow hips; his head held on by a strong neck. He had coarse features, large eyes, wide, flat nose, and heavy jowls. An ex-Marine Corps Captain, he was the toughest of the lot and most of them were a little afraid of him.

Bob Prescott was a tall, rangy Texas boy who never looked well-groomed, no matter how he tried.

Freddie Hodges reminded me of a bird. He too, was tall, but very thin—with a sharp, pointed face with a long nose. He was terrified of bugs—all kinds of bugs—which was why the boys called him "Fearless Freddie."

Tom A. Jones hailed from Washington State and R. C. Moss, the "Moose" as he called himself, from Georgia. Tom was a tall, handsome fellow of twenty-six or so with striking eyes and a classical nose. His lips were rather thin and his mouth a bit too small but his chin was firm and square, and his ears well shaped and close to his head.

Jones said he had worked his way through college by working in a funeral parlour in Olympia, Washington. Later he went in the Navy, married, and had to keep it a secret because it was against Navy regulations to marry without permission. He and Jack Newkirk had been stationed together, two years before.

R. C. Moss was as handsome as Jones, only on a small scale. He was always talking of the little girls back in Florida. At one time he had been a life guard at Miami Beach, and according to him, he knew everybody who was anybody from sixteen to sixty. He had been an adagio dancer and a sculptor's model before he went into the Air Corps. "Now, Olga," he said, "don't you tell anyone that I was a dancer. If it ever gets out, I'll never be able to live it down with this outfit."

The two of them decided to go on a tiger hunting trip. After talking to the Colonel about it, they made their preparations. The starting point of course, was our Indian house. They arrived one night carrying heavy rifles, jungle knives, flashlights and a few provisions. After getting information from the natives, they had planned on going to the lower Chindwin Valley region, not far from the famous ruby mines of Mogok, where, they were told, tigers were as thick as flies.

Toungoo Chapel during Armstrong's funeral.

Chaplain Paul Frillman reading the service for
Armstrong.

Jack Newkirk (with wrist watch) and other pall-bearers carry John D. Armstrong to the Christian cemetery, Toungoo.

General Wavell, accompanied by Colonel Chennault, inspecting the aerodrome and pilots, Toungoo.

(Photo by 1st American Volunteer Group)

The next morning early they left on the train going north to their happy hunting ground. They didn't see a single tiger, but Tom came back with a nice dose of malaria, and Moss with a touch of dengue fever.

I didn't see them again for quite sometime until one day I went to the hospital, a shack consisting of four rooms built in line, each with a door opening into the narrow veranda. The second room was the "ward room." There I found the two boys. The sun was burning in through the cracks of the bamboo wall. One ray of light struck Jones across his forehead and over his left eye. He was delirious and mumbling and all the time he kept rocking his head from side to side on the pillow. I plugged up the crack and his head stopped rocking. His eyes opened and he recognized me. He smiled, a thin, sickly little smile and said so softly that I could hardly hear:

"Don't let them write to her. My wife. Don't want her to know about this. I've always been so healthy. Don't let them, Olga . . ."

Suddenly, he began to shake and shiver. He looked at me pleadingly. I understood. He wanted more blankets—and the heat was unbearable! I found some extra blankets in the spare room and covered him with them and tucked him in as I would have a child. He went to sleep.

That's just one of the things malaria does to you.

One of the last to join our Group was W. H. S. Davis, known as "Daffy," an Irishman who had lived in China for twenty years. When the company he was working for in Hong Kong went bankrupt, Harvey induced the Colonel to sign him up. From Hong Kong, the Colonel ordered Daffy to Manila to buy supplies for the A.V.G. From there he went to Singapore, and one fine, hot day he turned up in Toungoo loaded with suitcases and boxes and an electric iron for me.

Although they worked sixteen strenuous hours a day it was no easy matter for the Old Man and Harvey to bring the boys up to the point where they could hold their own against the enemy they would soon encounter. Japanese tactical weaknesses were drilled into them constantly—and then drilled into them again. No phase of their training was neglected, including how to take care of themselves in case of forced landings in the jungle.

The characteristics of each Japanese airplane were studied repeatedly so each pilot knew exactly how to successfully attack any particular type. One great service the A.V.G. did for all Allied fliers was to explode the myth of the great superiority of the highly touted Japanese Navy Zero. Because they had been taught how to attack it properly and how to escape from it, the Zero was no tougher a nut for our boys to crack than any other Jap plane. As a matter of fact, some of our kids regarded Zeros as pushovers.

There were plenty of airplane troubles to be overcome—tires rotting from the humid heat, thrust bearings which had to be replaced, defective radio equipment, eccentric electric gun sights. Little by little by patience and profanity the difficulties were ironed out.

The three squadron leaders had been named: "Ole" Olson and Robert Sandell, who came to the A.V.G. through the United States Army Air Corps, and Jack Newkirk, an ex-Navy fighter-pilot. Gradually but certainly each unit acquired cohesion, smooth and skillful teamwork and enthusiastic squadron morale which was a credit to each squadron leader.

Whenever the starting time was going to be, the American Volunteer Group was just about ready for the opening kickoff.

When the British brass hats commenced to drop into Kyedaw I then began, for the first time, to form an opinion that the A.V.G. was beginning to assume a definite importance in the scheme of the war. Up to that time I had had my doubts.

About five-thirty one morning I went to the field with Harvey, although I was told I wasn't wanted as there were possibilities of one of those "bigwigs" arriving. They had expected him the day before but he hadn't shown up. I went out to Kyedaw frequently to see what was going on. I was afraid I might miss something. Good thing I went that morning, too. No one was paying much attention to me as I stood by the runway watching a plane come in. Suddenly, I saw four big ships circling over the field quite high. The field came to life and many cars began to scoot about. I asked Harvey what the fuss was about, and he said Air Marshal Sir Robert Brooke Popham was arriving.

The planes landed—four Hudson bombers with five guns on each wing. Out of one stepped the British Commander in Chief of the Far East. Harvey called me over and introduced me. While our planes were flying in review Sir Robert gave me advice as to how best to take pictures of planes in formation. The boys really put on a good show for him. "Popeye," as he was unofficially called, was very pleased.

Later we were visited by the air officer commanding the Far East, Air Vice Marshal Pulford, and Group Captain Bishop. They came from Rangoon by plane. Air Vice Marshal Pulford was the air officer in charge at Singapore. We all had dinner together at the Colonel's table. After dinner, Group Captain Bishop went back to Toungoo with us and joined a poker game. He took fifty rupees out of his pocket and laid them on the table. When they were gone, which didn't take very long, he quit the game, saying that the R.A.F. didn't get as much money as the A.V.G. Sandell was the big winner.

Sir Archibald Wavell was next to arrive—and we were also visited by several American generals including Generals Mac-Gruder and Brett. General Brett was not impressed. His only remark after inspecting our whole layout was "I never saw such a dirty kitchen in my life." He referred, I presume, to the Burmese flies which there is not enough Flit in the world to exterminate. I couldn't help but feel he was being captious, and overlooked, intentionally or otherwise, some of the Group's fundamental military qualities. We later demonstrated that while we perhaps weren't much at killing flies we were pretty good at killing Japs.

Although our existence was supposed to be a deep secret—not known, probably, to more than several hundred active Japanese spies and Burmese fifth columnists—newspaper correspondents began to drop in on us too. Among the more famous were Leland Stowe, Edgar Mowrer and Vincent Sheean. They snooped around and asked questions. Vincent Sheean was very interested in the story about the Nats. We saw more of Leland Stowe than of the other two. After lunch one day at the field, he gave us a comprehensive review of the war in Finland, Norway and Greece. It was very revealing, and I think it increased the morale of the boys—he indicated to them a duty they had to perform in the best American tradition. We all knew he was referring to a possible war with Japan. That night we put him on the train bound for Lashio.

On November 2nd, Soul's Day, the Burmese natives lit up all their temples, pagodas, and their own houses. Even the trees in the countryside and in the village were bright with little oil lamps covered with colored paper. The whole town looked like a Christmas tree. I walked to the Christian cemetery. It, too, was brilliantly lighted. I thought of our three graves, bare, the only ones without candles, so I went back to the bazaar and bought eighteen of the largest candles I could find.

I returned to the cemetery—walked along the path until I reached the spot where the boys were. I lit the candles and placed six at the foot of each grave. Suddenly I realized I was alone there, glanced at my watch and saw it was six o'clock. The whole graveyard looked weird with all of those flickering little lights, and I felt a strange tingling in the back of my neck. Hurriedly I left the place. When I got home several of the boys were there. They asked where I had been. I told them lighting candles. They looked at me in bewilderment.

Captain Boatner Carney, our finance officer, came up from Rangoon one day with an old Chinese friend of ours, Colonel S. M. Loo. Carney wasn't really a captain, but had acquired that title when training Chinese flying cadets under Colonel Chennault. When the A.V.G. was organized, the Colonel hired him—but he didn't stay long with us because the Chinese needed him as chief instructor at Yunnanyi.

Carney had a Chinese girl friend—Rose Mok. He said Rose would come through shortly on the way to Kunming with one of her own convoys and would I put her up for the night. I said surely as I had known Rose for some time and was very fond of her.

She turned up later with R. L. Hastey, a pilot, at that time acting as Assistant Transportation Officer, a job which he held even towards the end, although sometimes he joined his squadron and did some fighting. To Hastey, all women, white or brown or black, were the same, and he never lacked company.

Rose was a clever girl. She owned a transportation company of her own and was coining money. She intimated she was doing a bit of smuggling across the China border. No luxuries were allowed up the Road—only necessary food supplies, and war materials. But Rose had her own little way of getting stuff through. She had opened a restaurant in Kunming in anticipation of the arrival of the A.V.G. Another very profitable trick she had was buying cars in Rangoon, driving them into China as her own personal property, and then selling them there at a tremendous profit.

Rose told me to warn the boys about the girls in Kunming. She said that two years before there were two young, good-looking Chinese girls from Shanghai who had settled in Kunming and rented one of the best houses there. The fee for an evening's entertainment was 25,000 National dollars, and of course, they only catered to the wealthy. I asked her what had happened to those girls. "Oh," she said, "they are still there, but their price has gone down—it was found out that they had leprosy."

She left early the next morning to catch up with her convoy at Lashio.

It had been definitely decided that as soon as our training was completed we would move, as a group, to Kunming, across the China border where a field and adequate facilities were being prepared for us.

For some reason I didn't much care. My nerves were getting on edge. I could see no percentage living there and leading that crazy, uncomfortable existence. It was no place and no business for a woman. I told Harvey I wanted to go home. He was angry with me and walked out without saying a word. I almost called him back to try to explain how I felt, and then decided not to. In view of what happened the following day it was just as well I didn't.

Chapter IV

IF the Japanese had launched their December 7th morning blitz against Toungoo, Burma, instead of Pearl Harbor, they would have caught Olga Greenlaw sound asleep in her little bed. The telephone awakened me around seven-thirty, with Harvey on the other end babbling something about our being at war with Japan. I mumbled "Okay, okay" and hung up. For several seconds it didn't penetrate. Then it did—and I flopped on the bed and started to cry. The Nanny, hearing me, came in and asked what was the matter. I told her to get me a pot of hot coffee—right away.

So we were at war with the Japs—at last!

I wasn't surprised. I had seen it coming since the middle of 1938 when we were in the thick of those terrible Hengyang bombings, but now that it had happened I found myself stunned and heartsick. I knew from personal experience that Japanese warfare was cruel and brutal and utterly senseless. I suddenly felt very far away from home—and alarmingly unsafe.

I snapped on the radio and tuned in San Francisco's KGEI. There it was, coming through loud and clear—a running description of the attack on Pearl Harbor! I uncorked a few remarks which would have scandalized a Texas Ranger and spun the dial to Hong Kong!—Batavia!—Singapore!—My God! The Japs were bombing there too—and Manila! They seemed to be rushing up and down the globe like mad dogs, frothing at the mouth and biting everything in sight. The air waves vibrated with rumors and contradictory reports.

For some silly reason I tried to figure out whether the attack had been yesterday or tomorrow. There in Burma we were west of the Date Line—so today was yesterday—or was today tomorrow? I couldn't make up my mind.

The phone rang. Harvey was sending his car for me. Swell! I started to dress. The phone rang again—Harvey, telling me to bring him an overnight bag with a few changes in it. He was staying at the field from now on. He said I would stay there, too, where he could keep an eye on me.

I reached the airdrome about ten o'clock, in time to watch a C.N.A.C. Douglas take off for Kunming carrying the first part of the hospital staff and some of the sick, including Tom Jones. The field was buzzing in an atmosphere of expectancy. Morning greetings from the boys were punctuated with "Those God-damn Japs," "Monkey-faced little bastards" and similar tender sentiments. Consensus of opinion was they'd get their little brown ears slapped down in a hurry now that they'd been stupid enough to pick on the United States. We were very optimistic then, but not so optimistic later.

Everyone was togged out in side arms and steel helmets. Gurkha Guards with glinting bayonets walked their posts and pilots and planes stood ready to take the air at a minute's warning. All our cars were being hurriedly camouflaged with green and yellow paint. Burma was no longer a neutral country. Anything might happen now—without warning.

I was issued a helmet and gas mask along with all of the men—but no gun. I asked Harvey could I have one. His husbandly retort was: "There aren't enough for the men. Scram!"

I walked away haughtily. Harvey followed to ask if I had brought his bag and one for myself.

"From now on you're sleeping here at the field," he declared. "The town isn't safe. We expect to be bombed any moment—you'll be better off here. You can sleep in the hospital. Now run over to the radio tower and wait for orders."

Instead of going to the tower I headed for the headquarters office—vaguely wondering why the master military mind which was my husband's considered it so safe at the airdrome where a bombing was expected momentarily. There was no one in the pilot's room. In the pay office next door I found Wyke, the Group Sergeant Major, and Larry Moore, a clerk. Moore was a puny, sickly little fellow with straight blond hair and blue eyes that had the habit of winking at everyone behind his thick glasses. I asked was the Colonel in his office? They didn't know. I peeked through the crack of the Colonel's door and almost hit the ceiling when I heard: "Why aren't you working at the *Diary?* Take the empty desk in that room and get at it!"

I said: "Yes, sir" meekly, backed into Wyke, asked if he knew anything about keeping a *War Diary*. He said he'd been in the Army for six years and had a pretty good idea. We were seated at the desk drawing up a form when Harvey popped in.

"That's wrong," he said. Of course he *would* know exactly how to do it. "You post up your *War Journal* first; on that journal you base your diary. Collect the orders of the day, special and field orders, memorandums, hospitals reports and such. Here—like this—"

He wrote across the top of a page:

FROM: 0600 Mon. Dec. 8, '41 To: 0600 Tues. Dec. 9, '41

TIME In out	SERIAL No.	TIME dated	NOTES: Special Orders, Field Orders, Memorandums, miscellaneous	DISTRI-BUTION
0600	57	1200	SPECIAL ORDERS: Re: 6 pilots of 3rd Sqdr. temporarily relieved from duties and attached to Group Headquarters for training.	A
0600	40	0600	FIELD ORDERS: Orders issued from Group Headquarters for Squadrons to stand by.	S

And so on.

From this first page of the *War Journal* I based the first entry of the *War Diary:*

Monday, December 8th, 1941
POINT "A"

WEATHER: Sunshine, scattered cumulous clouds.

It was made known this morning at 7 o'clock that the United

States was at war with Japan. Great Britain also declared war an hour later.

Field orders were issued from Group Headquarters for all three squadrons to stand by: The Third Pursuit Squadron to be the Assault Echelon; The Second Pursuit Squadron to be Support Echelon, and the First Pursuit Squadron the Reserve Echelon.

All members of the A.V.G. authorized to wear firearms. No leave for personnel is granted. Orders were issued for an air raid warning system. Watch for enemy parachute troops. Telephones were installed wherever necessary.

British co-operating but rather slowly. Radio news: Japanese bombed Wake Island and Honolulu—results unknown. They also bombed Singapore but not much damage done there. The Hollanders also declared war on Japan.

Complete blackout tonight and alert crew standing by. The auxiliary field four miles north of Kyedaw was equipped with red lights marking runways and white lights marking boundaries of field while Kyedaw was kept in complete darkness.

This command is on the alert 24 hours daily and prepared to defy hostile actions of the enemy. Alert ships to be fully armed and kept ready to take off at any time.

Squadron Leader of the Third Pursuit Squadron, Arvid E. Olson, Jr. is designated as Group Commander in the air, and Squadron Leader Jack V. Newkirk, Second Pursuit Squadron, is designated as Deputy Group Commander in the air.

Which was the beginning of my official duties with the American Volunteer Group.

At noon I went over to the pilot's mess only to find it closed. I hooked a ride back to the airdrome and finally found all the pilots who were not on duty eating from bare board tables at the supply shack. When I walked in, Bob Little shouted: "Make you a bet, Olga. Twenty-five rupees the Japs don't come over tonight."

I took it—twenty-five that they did come over. The others wanted the same bet but twenty-five rupees was all I cared to risk.

The excitement of the morning had cooled down. In fact, the boys were disappointed that the Japs hadn't already attacked us. They were itching for trouble and impatient for their share of it.

Late in the afternoon I returned to the village and told the servants I was closing the house. Some of them cried and said they didn't want me to go—which meant they didn't want their nice fat salaries to go. I packed the few things remaining. My passport had disappeared. I asked the servants about it. They all looked innocent. Then I offered a reward of twenty rupees to the one who found it. That, to them, is a great deal of money. They promptly dropped everything and started to search. I knew very well one of them had it, so I went back to the airdrome.

R. C. Moss was sitting on the veranda of the hospital shack in his pajamas as I drove up. He said he was glad I was going to share their roof with them for a while. He followed me into the nurses' room and watched me unpack, make up my bed and hang up the eternal mosquito net. Finally he said:

"I'd like to talk to you."

I told him to go right ahead.

"Well," he started out hesitantly, "I owe you an apology and I'll tell you why. About two weeks ago Tex Hill and I were talking about you. I had you pegged as a cold-blooded, matter-of-fact wench, hard-boiled and tough. We figured you had to be that way to be able to take it out here the way you have for years—that you just didn't have any feelings—you're Russian, aren't you?"

I said: "Don't Russians have any feelings?"

"Well, yes, I suppose so—"

I said: "I'm not Russian."

"But you've got an accent—and your name is Olga—"

I said: "I am an American—" left him sitting there on the veranda and walked down toward the mess wondering who else had been saying what about me. Did all the boys think I was cold-blooded and hard-boiled?

After dinner Harvey told Bob Little to light all the kerosene lamps which were used as field markers during night flying operations and stow them away in one of the hangars ready for instant use should they be needed. Bob asked me to go with him. I did.

Driving over to the hangar through the inky black, Bob started to sing *Maybe* in a hushed, sweet voice. Then he drifted into *The Nearness of You*. The songs were familiar—they were on opposite sides of one of Bob's phonograph records. After a while I told him to hush up. A warm, starry night, romantic songs, a handsome man beside me—the next thing I knew I'd be forgetting I was the Chief of Staff's wife. He looked at me strangely with his dark violet eyes luminous in the darkness. Then he laughed, that soft, low laughter that came from somewhere deep in his throat.

It took us an hour to trim wicks and light the thirty-eight old-fashioned hurricane lamps, some with clear glass chimneys, others red. Finally we walked out of the hangar and closed the door. Light poured into the darkness through a dozen cracks. So we went back and moved everything to a small inner room where the boys kept gloves and goggles and helmets, covered the single window with an old straw mat and went outside again. No light showed this time.

Bob said: "Shake" and held out his hand. I offered him a cigarette. He lit it and gave it back to me. A Gurhka's voice with marked English accent came from out of the night:

"Please, no smoking. It can be seen from the air."

Bob dropped me back at the hospital and I went to bed quite tired. I didn't go to sleep for a long while—thinking about Harvey sleeping on that tiny cot in his office at the foot of the control tower. In case of a raid a direct hit there was quite possible but he said that if the going got too tough he could always run the fifty feet to the concrete pillbox the British had built.

For two or three days we lived in what might be called a state of increasing anticlimax. Elsewhere the war was spinning along like crazy but we apparently weren't going to be let in on it right away. Between the radio, the Rangoon papers and British and Chinese Intelligence we were able to compile a thoroughly inaccurate picture of what was going on.

Because office equipment was being boxed to move to Kunming, Harvey advised me to forget the *Daily War Journal* until we were settled again. I finished my personal packing and delivered the house back to the owner, but only with the assistance of Mickey Mihalko, one of our radio men. The Indian owner claimed one mattress was missing. I knew this was not so. He argued and I argued back. Mihalko arrived, by accident, just as the controversy was on the verge of unpleasantness and with the aid of a .38 Colt, gently persuaded the landlord to sign a receipt for the place and furniture. I was about to leave when the old sweeper handed me my lost passport. I looked at him fixedly. His eyes dropped. I didn't say a word but divided the twenty rupees reward between the five servants, which left them all, including the sweeper, quite satisfied.

On the night of December 10th, at three in the morning, a vaguely familiar sound woke me—like the sounds I heard in Hengyang in 1938. The siren! I jumped out of bed and looked at the sky. The moon was full and brilliant. What beauty! What a perfect target our runways must make! One of the nurses turned on a flashlight to find a shoe. I hissed, "Put that damn thing out." I was fully dressed by then as, expecting a raid, I had placed my clothes where I could find them in the dark—and in a hurry.

I went outdoors and wandered around until I found a hole— a nice deep one with steps. I returned to the hospital, rounded up a stray patient, led him down to the shelter and made him comfortable. He didn't look particularly ill. We sat very still —listening. Cars were moving about on the field. Planes roared off into the blackness. I wrapped Lucy in a blanket and placed her next to my box—the Elizabeth Arden make-up box which, in every emergency, I seemed to pick up out of habit.

I settled back and wrote a few pages in my diary, which

always seemed to steady my nerves. At four-fifteen the all-clear sounded. I listened to the planes come in—one—two—three—the fourth one landed badly. It sounded as if the wing had struck the runway. The fifth plane circled twice and then slipped in. That was all we had up. I helped my patient back to the hospital and into his cot. On my way out I asked Red Foster: "What's the matter with him?" Red grinned sardonically. "Venereal," she said. Luckily we had remarkably few such cases at any time.

After washing my face and giving my hair a couple of quick licks I went over to the mess for a five o'clock breakfast with the pilots. I sat next to Sandell. "Hm-m-m," he said, "you don't look bad for a babe that's been up all night."

I answered: "You don't look so bad yourself for a man who just landed on his wing-tip."

Sandy laughed. "That wasn't me."

To this day I don't know who made the bad landing.

My problem of the immediate future was how to get to Kunming. I wanted to go up over the Road with a convoy. I had never made the trip and was eager to try it. If I was to go that way, Harvey had assigned M. E. Ceder, an intelligence clerk, to accompany me as car driver and general protector. He was a thin, blond fellow of medium height, curly hair, blue eyes and a bushy mustache. His chin was rather weak. He said he'd rather go by road than by air as he couldn't endure flying. And he said for me not to worry, that he would take care of me. I told him that if Harvey would issue me one of those Colts I'd take care of myself. Durrall, another one of the clerks, came in carrying three .32's and two .38's. I reached for one and started threading the holster through my heavy pigskin belt just as Harvey entered.

"Take that thing off before somebody gets hurt," he commanded.

I protested this time. He compromised by promising to issue me a gun when I was on a truck ready to start for China.

Daffy Davis warned me: "Don't go by convoy, grandma." Daffy always called me "grandma." The road is dreadful—take you ten days just to get to Kunming."

On the way back to the hospital I met Bob Little bicycling peacefully along. He stopped. "Lost your bet didn't you, Sucker?"

I tried to protest that the Japs had come but failed to find the field, but got nowhere with that technicality so paid him from my purse. And then had dinner with him and Sandy at the mess. Afterwards we went to the tower to see Harvey. It was fun sitting there in the complete blackout, trying to pour coffee, listening to radio reports from everywhere. Harvey finally threw us out so he could get a little sleep.

We stopped at the First Squadron's alert shack. Outlines of the dispersed planes loomed out of the darkness—grinning red mouths and vicious white shark's teeth. I shuddered a little as I thought of those silent monsters that could vibrate with life and tremendous power at an instant's notice and spew more death from their nostrils than a thousand men with rifles. I always felt those P-40's were real, almost human, each one a part of the pilot who sat in it and became its brain. Number thirty-three was Bob's plane—Bob's wings. Number eleven, Sandy's wings. Somehow each took on the personality of its pilot. Or maybe I was going a little bit daffy.

While there was no fighting during these first days, several reconnaissance and photographic missions flew over Thailand and returned to report plenty of Japs were there. And in Indo-China, too.

On December 10th, the British requested we assign one of our squadrons to reinforce the R.A.F. defenses at Rangoon. Colonel Chennault preferred to keep all three squadrons together and fight them as a group. But there were insufficient facilities for three squadrons at Mingaladon, the Rangoon airdrome, and orders were orders, so on the 12th of December the Third Pursuit Squadron, under command of Squadron Leader Arvid Olson, Jr., headed southward. I wondered if they would all come back to join us in Kunming. Why did they have to go to Rangoon? What was the matter with the British, the Burma R.A.F.? Probably they had sent most of their planes to Singapore.

Our first daylight alarm came shortly after the Third Squadron had departed. I was busy compiling radio news with a clerk named Dudsick who was trying to get out a daily news sheet with indifferent success when the alarm signal cut loose with three long blasts—the first warning. Dudsick's face turned white. Outside, the Colonel's car streaked away toward the control tower. Trumble, another clerk, came dashing out of the Colonel's office, dashed back in, then repeated the manuever. All three of us went outside—just as a car came along. The Connells. They volunteered to take us away from the airdrome. As we drove off men were scampering all over the place—looking for shelter. The only cover was the drainage ditches along the roads, which weren't much good but better than nothing.

We drove through the gate and onto the main road. To stay in the field would have been folly. Mr. Connell stopped the car and we got out. The Connells were going back to Toungoo to join their babies. When I turned around again, Trumble was galloping through the bushes a quarter of a mile away. Dudsick and I located a nice, deep hole—a few inches of water in the bottom but protection in case the Japs came. We sat for a while but nothing happened so we went back toward the field. A lot of excitement for no reason, but I was beginning to find out who had guts and who hadn't. I made up my mind that no matter what happened I wouldn't leave the field again. One place was as good as another.

I was talking to Sandell when the Beechcraft landed. Eric Shilling, a tall lad of twenty-six who was so blond he looked almost "washed out," had flown it back from Rangoon. He said there had been a brief alarm there, everyone was in a dither and the native population was preparing to leave the city in case anything happened. Olson's outfit was keen and expectant and looking forward to early action.

I bumped into Red Probst and asked him what he thought of the alarms. Red pushed out his chest and said: "Just wait and see what I'm going to do to those little yellow bastards." I told him not to count his chickens before they were hatched. A funny little guy, Red. He always wore tight slacks which made his small, compact posterior protrude like a woman's. I made myself a bet that Red wouldn't shoot down a single Jap.

For several more days nothing much happened at Toungoo. I continued to wait for a chance to go up the Road which I still preferred to flying. Ceder bought a few cases of provisions in the bazaar in the event we should need them—and Daffy Davis continued to advise me not to attempt the trip. The little blue devils had Daffy because his fiancée, Doreen Longberg, was still in Hong Kong and wouldn't leave until she got her final divorce papers through the Danish Consul in Shanghai.

From my personal *Diary:*

December 15th, 1941.

Today we had a crash. Student Pilot Laughlin (one of the last arrivals) crashed north of Kyedaw in a paddy field but escaped unhurt. One less plane and we need them so badly. We can't even get spare parts.

Washed my hair and gave Lucy a bath. Put on a sunsuit and sat out in the sun near the young teak trees. Read a little and picked ticks off Lucy. Washed some clothes and hung them to dry on the branches. While I was doing this Sam Prevo, the doctor, came along. He said I was being very domestic. I said that after all I had to have clean clothes and now had no maid to do them for me. He asked if I would wash a pair of wool socks for him as the Dhoby ruins them by pounding them on the rocks— so I washed the doc's socks. Sam would be very handsome if he were not so fat. He weighs at least 250 lbs. I tell him to diet but he always has convincing arguments against it. I decided he was just plain lazy and told him so. He said exercise was bad for the heart.

Sam is quite young—about 32. I tried at various times to draw out of him his 'life story'—why he came out here, etc. Once he started to tell me about a girl nurse back in the States when he suddenly stopped and said: "And just why should I be telling you all of this, Miss Inquisitive?" I still suspect there is something in his past because why should a promising young doctor with a bright future come out to this God forsaken place? I think Sam and I are going to be good friends—but I am still curious about him.

Bill Pawley broke the monotony by appearing with a blond— she turned out to be his secretary.

The next morning just after Bill Pawley took off for Rangoon in his private plane the regular C.N.A.C. transport landed from Lashio. Everyone crowded around the pilot asking for news of Hong Kong. The pilot only knew it was being shelled to pieces. The C.N.A.C. was operating only as far as Chungking. Several of the planes were already making the run to Calcutta and getting acquainted with that territory in case Rangoon happened to fold up—which began to look probable in the not too distant future. So far, the Japs seemed able to do about as they pleased.

On December 18th Harvey sent Ceder over very early to tell me to bring my bags out to the tower. When I got there he asked me to go over and pack his and the Colonel's things. The Colonel came in and said I could go on the next transport with Frank Higgs, an old friend, or stay and leave on the last ship with Harvey. I preferred to go with the Colonel and Higgs as I don't like night flying—particularly over the mountains between Lashio and Kunming. Our pilots were checking their planes and preparing to take off at noon.

When I appeared at the transport with my bags, Higgs looked down and saw Lucy. "Now, look here, Olga—don't tell me you're taking that rat along?" I said I certainly was because where I went, Lucy went. Besides, she was good luck. Frank said we might need good luck at that as he had just received a report the Japs were bombing Kunming. I thought he was kidding, which he wasn't.

The P-40's took off at thirteen-thirty on the dot. One of the boys, Burgard, couldn't get his ship up quickly enough and nosed in at the end of the runway. Another hit a parked car—which put two more planes on the inactive list. The Colonel's reaction was an emphatic "Christ from Vicksburg!" which was one of his more picturesque expressions.

We, finally got away ourselves—twenty-three people, one dog, and one monkey belonging to a mechanic. A nice overload, but C.N.A.C. planes were practically always overloaded those days.

At Lashio the Colonel went into a huddle with British and American officers who met him. While we were having coffee, Higgs said he wasn't fooling about Kunming being bombed. "Raid's going on right now," he said. I asked what he planned to do. He said: "Oh! if they're still bombing when we get there we'll cruise around till they get through. I certainly won't try to stop them." He laughed. I didn't.

We landed at Kunming at five-forty. It was already dark. All our P-40's had arrived safely. The bombing raid had killed about 200 civilians. Nobody had made any arrangements for a place for me to sleep. Dr. Gentry, who met us, drove me through narrow streets and side alleys to the Hotel du Commerce. I told him to leave me there as I knew my way about with the Chinese and knew Kunming, too. As far as I was concerned, I was back home. It was bitterly cold, in marked contrast to the soggy Burmese heat we had just left. I remembered that Rose Mok, Carney's girl friend, lived at the hotel and as there were no more rooms available, asked to be shown up to hers. Rose was out. The room was very dirty I finally got a clean towel and a bucket of hot water. After I bathed, or rather, sponged myself with the hot water, I ordered a whiskey soda. "No soda" said the boy. I paid him forty National dollars for the diluted drink of whiskey, which was over $2 American money, and ordered my dinner. The food wasn't good but I was hungry. Rose returned about two o'clock and we talked until daylight—and finally went to sleep with Lucy curled up at our feet.

Chapter V

KUNMING, the ancient capital of Yunnan Province, is approximately the mid-point of the Burma Road between Lashio, its southern terminus, and Chungking, the heart of fighting China. Before the Japs infested Indo-China, Kunming's strongest defense had been its distance from the nearest Japanese flying base but thereafter, with Tonkin's border a scarce 150 miles away, it was a sitting shot for Japanese bombers who, above all other targets, love a concentrated few hundred thousand defenseless civilians. The function of the American Volunteer Group was, therefore, to protect the city and the road from Japanese attack.

The importance of the Road needs no explanation, but a quick geography lesson may help clarify events and movements which will follow. I can best explain distance and directions by comparing Burma-China with the United States. Taking Rangoon and New Orleans as common starting points, the corresponding cities in both distance and relative direction would be—Mandalay and Memphis; Lashio and Nashville; Kunming and Charleston, West Virginia; Chunking and New York. An A.V.G. flight from Kunming to Rangoon, for instance, would correspond to a hop from Charleston to New Orleans, a matter of some 900 miles.

Rugged 12,000-feet high mountains and plenty of them surround Kunming on all sides and the weather is sudden and violent, which made night attacks unlikely if not impossible. Of course, the mountains and weather were as tough on our boys as on the Japs—but we were defensive and could succeed simply by doing nothing while they, the aggressors, must press the attack.

I was up early the morning after my arrival, anxious to

learn if Harvey had come through on the night transport. The first person I saw was Tom Jones, who looked well enough but was suffering a recurrent attack of malaria. We found Harvey at the Number One Hostel, and he introduced me to enormous and jolly Colonel J. L. Huang, who looked like a Buddha and was in charge of all hostels, the head man of the War Area Service Corps. He had just ordered ham and eggs and coffee for me when we heard "*Ginbao!*" Being extremely hungry I said, "Damn those Japs!" Harvey had gone to the field so the Colonel drove me out of town to a house on a hill which was being occupied by General MacGruder, head of the American Mission to China.

Mrs. Huang was already there with her two little boys and baby girl. We waited until nearly noon—no food, no Japs. The Colonel and Mrs. Huang both talked at length about the work of the important New Life Movement, of which the Colonel was Secretary General.

We finally went back to the hostel where Harvey showed me the two rooms which had been assigned to us. They had previously been occupied by Colonel George of the United States Army, who was in Chungking but expected back soon. The rooms adjoined—and held great possibilities for an attractive suite.

Late in the afternoon Harvey drove me to the airdrome. We went through the main streets of Kunming and saw thousands of people carrying bundles and children returning to the city for the night. That was the daily routine—to escape from the air raids, most of the civilians spent the day in the country and returned in late afternoon when shops opened for business and the town came to life.

At the field, hundreds of coolies were working to complete runways. They all smiled as I passed. I smiled back and tried: "*Neehappa-how?*" They answered: "*How, how,*" which means "Very well."

The operations office was a shack at the far end of the

field. On the door to Harvey's office was painted "Chief of Staff—Executive Officer—Group Operations Officer." On a huge square table was a map covering the area of Yunnan Province, parts of Kwangsi, Indo-China and Burma. The center of the map was Kunming. Around it were drawn concentric red-ink circles, about one inch apart, each inch representing sixty kilometers. Dots and squares at regular intervals indicated the positions of radio and telephone stations. If an enemy plane crossed any of the circles—even as far as three or four hundred miles distant—the news would immediately be relayed to the field. It reminded me of a great spider web. This warning net system was still quite new, but was eventually to be conceded the finest in the Far East. This plotting room was nowhere near as elaborate as those at Singapore and Rangoon, but several hundred per-cent more efficient.

There were many other interesting features of the Kunming defense which I cannot reveal here as the field is still in active operation.

The last time I had seen Kunming was in February, 1939. It had changed very little except for the enormous influx of refugees, the strange daytime silence and the night-time bustle and noise which had increased a hundredfold.

The lovely old city by a beautiful lake was the terminus of the French railroad, the Michelin, which, in peace time, ran up from Hanoi bringing French merchandise of all sorts. Although the French influence was obvious, most of the French had departed. Almost no foreigners of any nationality remained.

The climate was supposed to be salubrious—but not for me. The air was dry and cold and very dusty.

It is unfortunate that tremendous events to which you look forward with vivid anticipation sometimes turn out to be deflating anticlimaxes. December 20th was certainly one of the great red-letter days for the A.V.G. and yet it wasn't completely satisfying. It started out badly for me. I got up about seven and barged right into serious bathroom trouble. At the end of the hall, in back of the officers' bar, was the community bathroom—three wash basins, two showers, one tub, three toilets—used by the staff. I was halted at the door and told I couldn't go in—several "masters" were inside. They remained inside a great deal longer than, to me, seemed necessary.

I returned to my quarters and puttered around trying to make the rooms look homey when I noticed cars dashing out of the courtyard. Wyke, the Group Sergeant Major, shouted it was another *ginbao*—looked like the real thing this time and I'd better come along with him. I grabbed a coat, Lucy, make-up box and my *Diary*. Besides Wyke, two clerks were in the car—Forbes and Larry Moore, the winker. We drove out toward where I had been the day previous, parked on a hillside and sat, twiddling our thumbs. Larry Moore was so frightened his teeth began to chatter. We could hear plane motors but couldn't see any planes. Moore kept saying: "Here they come, here they come!" I told him they sounded more like our P-40's than Jap bombers. I wasn't the least bit nervous —I had been through too many raids before.

We shot craps to pass the time, finally started back toward the city as the excitement seemed to be over. Presently we met Chinese officers. They waved cordially. At the field everybody was grinning from ear to ear. We drove to the First Squadron's alert shack and there found all the pilots jabbering like mad and simulating aerial maneuvers with their hands. Sandy saw me and came toward me. Even before he spoke I knew what had happened.

"Well, Olga, we did it," he said, trying desperately to be casual. "We met 'em and kicked hell out of them." He couldn't conceal the exultation in his voice.

Having no inhibitions I exclaimed: "Marvelous!—simply marvelous, Sandy!"

"First Squadron scored first," he grinned. "We met them and chased what was left of them right back where they came from. I was disappointed we didn't get all of them. I know we got three for sure, and maybe five or six others." He was very proud of his squadron's performance and not ashamed to express it. He put his arm around me and gave me a little squeeze. "That's just the beginning, my girl, just an appetizer."

I asked him for more details for the *War Diary*.

He said: "Jack Newkirk took off first, and his flight was to protect Kunming from the enemy planes by circling the field at 18,000 feet. My squadron was to act as assault echelon and fly to 15,000 feet, patrol the line from Iliang and Chenkiang and intercept the Japs if they came that way, that is, if they got away from Jack's flight. Well, we were cruising around 16,000 feet seventy-five miles northeast of the field, when we saw ten enemy two-engined bombers, single tail, aluminum construction—and that red sun on the wing tips. There was no mistake, they were the Japs. Two flights of four attacked from beam out of the sun, after overtaking them from rear; one flight plus two weavers remained above as reserve. Then our flight split into pairs, and singly after the first two or three runs, then we went on with co-ordinated attacks from all directions, that is, above and below, except dead ahead.

"After fifteen minutes of combat, reserve flight and weavers came into attack, and the pilots with jammed guns fell to the rear or turned back to the home base. Every enemy ship seemed to be smoking badly when we broke away to return to the field. At this time, we were about 175 miles southeast of the field. The enemy flew extremely good formation under heaviest of fire—a shallow V formation. They used the second ship from the left of the V formation as a decoy, flying about 300 yards ahead and a little above the squadron. The two end planes were shot down, and later the second from the right. I saw three go down for sure but I don't think more than six of them got back to their base."

Sandy had lost none of his pilots and only a few of his

fourteen planes had bullet holes. Jack Newkirk was fuming—his flight only had been able to make one pass at the Jap formation before it disappeared into the clouds.

We were more than jubilant. The long, tedious months of training and waiting had shown results at last. We had met the Japanese enemy, defeated him and sent him away in precipitous retreat. We had drawn first blood.

During my years in China I always felt that the Chinese people, especially the lower classes, were faintly antagonistic toward foreigners. But the day after Sandy's boys shot down their first Japs, a more cordial attitude was apparent. Even the servants were more cheerful and solicitous of our comfort.

Since the days of the 'Gypsy Squadron' in Hengyang, 1938, there had been no real air resistance in China, Therefore, it was easy to understand the change of feelings of the Chinese people toward us who were, more or less, their liberators. Because of the lack of airplanes, and anti-aircraft weapons, practically all Chinese communities were vulnerable from the air. Spring was the bombing season. In May the Japanese began their concentrated raids on Chungking. Before we arrived, there was nothing to prevent the Japs from bombing any city to a bloody shambles. The Chinese suffered stoically—and buried thousands of mutilated bodies. But there in Kunming, on the 20th of December, was evidence of deliverance come at last.

The grinning shark-faced P-40's, manned by a handful of heretofore unheard of American lads, had trapped and defeated the marauders a hundred miles short of their target. At last, although not enough, American planes and pilots had arrived to terminate the three year scourge of indiscriminate Japanese bombings in that area. The news spread like lightning to the farthest corners of Free China—its effect on morale was tremendous.

Two days later the Mayor, leading citizens, the military and the *belle demoiselles* of Kunming paid picturesque homage to our two squadrons which awaited, restless and shivering on the cold wind-swept airdrome. A band made noises which might have been national anthems with bits of *Dixie* and *Yankee Doodle* thrown in. Harvey, in command of the Group as Colonel Chennault was in Chungking, suddenly left, returned in haste and whispered something into Jack Newkirk's ear. I heard Jack's voice: "Men, man your planes!" The Second Squadron broke formation and scurried toward their planes. Sandy's men, nervous as cats, remained at attention and prayed the Mayor would snap up his long-winded speech. Hundreds of firecrackers were set off, which, because it was nearly dark, would have been clearly visible from the air. The Mayor decorated each one of Sandy's pilots with a red silk sash. Finally, it was over—and all of us rushed to the control room to learn that several enemy aircraft had been within fifty miles of Kunming, but had turned back.

As soon as I got our quarters comfortably furnished, they became the same transient hotel they had been in Toungoo—boys in the afternoon, boys for dinner, boys all hours of the night.

For a while, Harvey and I considered getting a house in town which would give us more room and more of a chance to entertain, and relieve what was, for me, the impossible bathroom situation. The only solution I had been able to find was to get up with Harvey at four-thirty, bathe and go back to bed. One morning I had to wait for some time—finally got in. When I came out a paper was pinned on the door: " DANGER —MEN NO COME INSIDE WOMAN INSIDE MISSY GINLAO."

The author was our own particular boy who always stood on guard at the bathroom door while I was inside. Everyone called him "Tugboat" because he had at one time worked on a China coaster. The name seemed to suit him; he was short and squatty with a round face and hair standing on end like a brush. He was very jealous of his position and disliked anyone else trying to serve me. I always had fresh flowers which he stole from the forbidden compound garden. When I asked where he got them. He said: "Me walkee, Missy—me catchum."

It was Tugboat who found me an amah, or personal maid— a tall gaunt woman who had lived in Hanoi for years, spoke French and was familiar with the demands of European ladies. As soon as the news got around, the boys started bringing their shirts for her to wash—to which I promptly put a stop.

The same day I employed her, December 23rd, I went to the field just in time to see Generals Wavell and Brett arriving in a big bomber. They held a long pow wow with Colonel Chennault and Harvey. By the time I arrived at the control room they had taken off accompanied by the Colonel. Later in the afternoon Harvey, Sandell, Jack Newkirk and I were sitting around gossiping when Bougie Baughman's voice came through the radio:

"Battle over Rangoon—one hundred enemy planes . . . . "

Harvey, Sandy and Jack stiffened. Sandy said:

"God a'mighty—Ole's on the hot seat now!"

Jack said: "Christ—a *hundred* of the little bastards!"

Ceder popped in from the adjoining room looking very pale. "Did you hear that, Mr. Greenlaw?"

Harvey said: "Write up a sheet and pin it on all the bulletin boards so the gang will know what's happening." Then he phoned through to the radio control. "Check up on this raid in Rangoon! Contact Lashio and Toungoo! Try to get Mingaladon from Toungoo!"

I felt weak and funny inside. It was the first battle for those boys down there, against dreadful odds. As if in answer to my thoughts, Jack said: "Hope the R.A.F. won't let them do all the work."

Earlier in the afternoon Toungoo had reported that three of our new CW-21's—interceptor fighters—had left at two-thirty and were headed for Lashio. Eric Shilling was leading the flight. I remembered the gossip about his having a jinx. At seven o'clock not a word had been received from Shilling, or further word from Rangoon. At last a message from Shilling: "Forced down. Merrit and Mangleburg arriving together." But they didn't arrive. We waited. Eight o'clock, nine o'clock —no planes. We had dinner. A message from Olson:

FIFTY FOUR BOMBERS ACCOMPANIED BY FIGHTERS BOMBED MINGALADON. THREE SHARKS DAMAGED AND TWO MISSING. SIX ENEMY PLANES SHOT DOWN. OPERATION BUILDING SUFFERED DIRECT HIT. CITY OF RANGOON BOMBED BADLY. ENEMY FIGHTERS STRAFED STREETS KILLING MANY CIVILIANS. PILOTS MARTIN AND GILBERT LOST IN COMBAT.

The full report of that combat, which I wrote in the *War Diary*, said:

No air raid alarm signal was given at Mingaladon. All ships were suddenly ordered off airdrome. No information of enemy prior to take-off was known. Three minutes after the take-off radio orders were given: "ENEMY APPROACHING FROM EAST" —No co-operation was given by anti-aircraft guns—pilots report that it was practically nil and very inaccurate. Fourteen P-40's and sixteen Brewsters (R.A.F.) joined the fight. There was no friendly support from nearby airdromes. There were two formations of enemy bombers. The second formation, about twenty-seven ships, was about ten miles behind the first, and about 3,000 feet above. The enemy flew a very close formation,—large V of V's. They were attacked by the P-40's and the Brewsters before they dropped their bombs. The enemy formation did not change its course or formation until after the bombs were dropped. When individual enemy bombers were shot down, the remaining bombers quickly filled in the key positions by means of fast executed cross-overs. Bombers put out a strong cross-fire from top of turrets, and air was filled with white tracers. The enemy aircraft is camouflaged brown and green on upper surfaces, and a light grayish green on the undersides. The red circles are painted on upper and lower wing tips.

That was the only time in the history of the A.V.G. that an adequate number of planes intercepted the enemy. Most of the Brewsters were badly damaged in the fight and others in landing. Some of them never left the ground again. Our ground crews worked madly night and day repairing the damaged Sharks.

We were disappointed that Ole's squadron hadn't shot down more enemy planes,—but then, they had destroyed more than they had lost. With Mangleburg and Merrit still missing it was a bad day for us. Three days later they found Mangleburg. His plane had crashed and exploded when he attempted a forced landing in a stream bed. Merrit had also crashed but was unhurt. I felt very sorry for Shilling as he felt responsible for Mangleburg's death—which he wasn't, of course.

Christmas Day didn't add up to much. We were all down-hearted—Martin, Gilbert and Mangleburg gone. I found Sandell in Harvey's office,—it was his day off. He asked me to take a day off, too. Harvey said: "Sandy, get out of here. You're cluttering up my office—Olga, you go with him."

In the open country surrounding the airdrome, were a number of hollow, man-built hills used for storing ammunition—some of them served as dugouts for the people of the field. Sandy and I visited several and even went inside to see what was in them.

After the inspection tour we drove to the First Squadron's hostel. Sandy suggested I might like to see his quarters. His was the first of a number of rooms in one long narrow shack; next to his were Bob Little's and Bob Neale's. It was a simple little room, quite orderly. A small army cot on one side, a wash basin, dresser and table. On the dresser was a picture of Sandy's mother—and another picture, clipped from a newspaper. The girl was pretty. I asked Sandy if she was the one. He nodded. We had lunch and then drove around the town until tea time. "Next time I have a day off," he said, "will you let me fix your hair?" I said I would—and he might practice on his own moustache in the meantime—it needed a little brushing and trimming.

It was already late on Christmas Day when I thought of Tom Jones—and went over to the hospital. He was very blue and bemoaning the fact that the Chinese Government had ꞅotten a bad deal on him, so far. I changed the subject—had he heard from his wife? Her picture was on the bedside table, a pretty young girl, smiling. Tom's eyes lingered there. "Isn't she beautiful, Olga—hair the color of yours and she's built like you—maybe not so tall . . . . " She had written she expecetd their baby on Christmas Day.

"I ought to be there," he said. "When a woman is going through that ordeal her husband ought to be with her."

I told him not to worry—she'd be well taken care of.

A message from Rangoon said Olson's twelve remaining planes had shot down seventeen out of seventy-eight attacking Japs, with the loss of two missing pilots. They showed up later. Colonel Chennault was delighted. "Those boys evidently have what it takes," he told Harvey. But the good Christmas tidings were mixed with bad, for we received the terrible news from Chungking that Hong Kong had fallen!

The morning after Christmas I went into the Colonel's rooms after he had left and placed on his desk a carved walnut cigarette box from Kashmir. On top of it was a dragon beautifully carved. The Colonel is very fond of dragons. He was so pleased with the gift that he suggested to Harvey that we have a dinner party at the Kwang Sing Yang.

This Cantonese restaurant was the high spot of our gastronomic activities. The entrance was through a typical Chinese grocery store—and such a store! Liquors and tobacco and candies, fat Yunnan hams hanging from the rafters, baskets of fruit covering the floor—and enticing Oriental smells. In the back was a courtyard with tables and small private rooms at the sides. The place was always crowded. We were met at the entrance by the smiling proprietor who led us upstairs to one of the best rooms. The farther up you go in a Chinese restaurant the more expensive the food. We sat down to a large round table and the boy came in immediately with clean table-cloth and the inevitable saucers of watermelon seed and pots of hot tea. The dinner was excellent—Cantonese cooking at its best and in all the world there is no finer. As the Colonel's tastes are distinctly New Orleans Harvey had ordered several different kinds of fish, prawns and shrimp. While we were eating, Mark Chen, the Colonel's Chinese secretary, came in with a dispatch from Rangoon that had just been decoded.

ALL PILOTS RETURNED AFTER BATTLE DECEMBER 25 SHOT DOWN TEN FIGHTERS NINE BOMBERS STOP BRITISH ACCOUNTED FOR SIX STOP LIKE SHOOTING DUCKS STOP WOULD PUT ENTIRE JAP FORCE OUT OF COMMISSION WITH GROUP HERE STOP HAVE ELEVEN PLANES LEFT STOP OLSON

The Old Man grinned. "The boys are going to town."

We drank a toast to the Third Squadron.

It took a little time for the Chinese to learn to trust the Americans to keep the Japanese away and Harvey had a hard time convincing the civil authorities that it was no longer necessary to evacuate the city every time a Jap plane was reported. The co-operation of the authorities was finally obtained and Kunming came to know a sense of security.

On December 28th I worked all day. At lunch time the Colonel dropped in sniffling—said he had a touch of the flu and was going to bed. I asked if there were anything I could do and he said, "No, I just wanted to see how you are getting along. Your rooms are looking pretty good—the feminine touch. How about fixing up my quarters some time?"

This is as good a place as any to present a few personal highlights of the Southern gentleman whose influence on the war against the Japanese has been, and I think will continue to be, considerable. For a year I knew him as intimately as a woman knows, say, her uncle or father-in-law with whom she resides.

General Claire L. Chennault is about five feet ten, muscular and supple. At fifty-five his hair is still black but greying at the temples. His features are coarse, rugged and seamed. He

Olsen, Chennault and Sandell in Kunming.

(Photo by J. E. Regis, 1st American Volunteer Group)

Chennault (fourth from right) and his staff, Kunming.

(Photo by J. E. Regis, 1st American Volunteer Group)

American Volunteer Group Identification.

Kunming interlude — Greenlaw, Williams, Chennault.

(Photo by I. E. Regis, 1st American Volunteer Group)

looks tough, determined and indomitable—and so far as the Japs are concerned, he is. He reads with glasses but has perfect long vision and is a remarkable shot. Fishing and hunting are his passions—particularly hunting Japs. He is a superior English student and exceptionally well-read. His ancestry is New Orleans French but he pronounces the final syllable of his name to rhyme with "walt" and not "Chen-no" as I have frequently heard it mispronounced. He speaks with a charming Louisiana drawl.

He is uniformly courteous—courteous to everyone. If he has one fault as a commanding general, this inbred courtesy may be it, although when profanity is justified his vocabulary is adequate and picturesque. Women like him. He has that God-given gift of knowing how to say the right thing at exactly the right time. He likes the feminine things about women—pretty clothes, flowers and fragrant scents—and he can be as charming and gallant as only a Southerner can. I realize now he is definitely opposed to women on a fighting front—and how he managed to put up with me I never will understand. While he was too polite to ever even suggest it, he must have considered me a nuisance and a pest.

When he is bearing down on his work he hates interruption. He writes most of his letters in longhand and takes a great deal of care with their composition. He will not answer a letter addressed to him with his name misspelled. He has a violent temper which, somehow or other, he manages to suppress. The effort of suppression sometimes makes him ill. He used to delight in deliberately heckling Harvey until he got mad. Then he'd say, calmly: "You have a very bad temper." I always thought he did this to flatter his mastery over his own violent disposition.

Generally after lunch he takes a nap. He smokes incessantly, cigarettes and pipe. He dangles a cigarette from the corner of his mouth and can talk without removing it even though the smoke gets in his eyes. His many years of flying and power diving have made him quite deaf, but like so many similarly afflicted he too frequently hears things not meant for his ears.

His personal courage is beyond reproach. He is a bad loser and plays all games to win—which surely must be a military virtue. If he happened to get behind in a poker game he would play all night, if necessary, to get even again—and always did. At cribbage, his favorite card game, he was practically unbeatable. He believes in the value of service sports and was, in China, a better than average soft-ball pitcher. He is inclined to be absent-minded about his papers, personal and official, and was always looking for things which were frequently right under his nose. He was constantly losing his glasses. True to Southern tradition, he prefers good bourbon whiskey to all other spirits but I never saw him take more than two drinks in an evening.

He is by no means a spit-and-polish general who might, for example, think it necessary to exterminate flies before starting to exterminate Japs. It was my personal belief that he was too lenient about the use of liquor, particularly with the men, and that the Group as a whole would have benefitted by a bit more iron-handed discipline. Then I would look at the magnificent record his command was building up and decide I had no business to criticize such brilliant success. Apparently he knew how to turn out fighting airmen.

The General was always reluctant to inconvenience anyone or, for personal reasons, take advantage of his military position. I recall one time when he was quite worried about his son, Jack, who was in the United States Air Corps. He hadn't heard from or of his boy in months, didn't know where he was. I am sure Washington would have been glad to tell him, but the General refused to ask. Harvey finally did—and received a prompt answer.

He is a man of high principles and great sincerity. He had confidence in his men. They knew it—and therefore had confidence in themselves. He sent Olson and the Third Pursuit

Group—youngsters who had yet to fire their first "for keeps" shot—down to Rangoon with his blessing and permitted them to run their own show without interference—which they did magnificently. He was not afraid to delegate authority and placed a premium on personal initiative.

He must surely know more about how to kill Japs in the air than any one other American. While all other A.A.F. brass hats were learning the art second hand, or through reading meager newspaper reports of Jap air raids, General Chennault was four years in China dodging Japanese bombs, observing and studying, and devising tricks and tactics to stop them. He knows every strength and weakness, every quirk and eccentricity of Japanese minds and Japanese machinery and how to use this knowledge to the greatest advantage.

He thinks Huey Long was a great man—and can prove it! He is tremendously popular with the Chinese who admire his courage and ability and appreciate his courtesy and thoughtfulness. He hates Japs!

Later in the day Larry Moore came by to ask if I cared to go shopping with him. He wanted to buy some comfortable chairs for the room which he shared with Sanger, a radio man, who was in Rangoon with the Third Squadron. Moore kept on telling me that Ken Sanger didn't like such bare rooms— Ken liked comfort. This struck me as funny. I looked at him closely. Moore was wearing a pale blue sweater with queer trimmings and resembled an adolescent girl with his pimply face and girlishly slim figure.

About seven Harvey returned from the field with Jack Newkirk. They said hello and went into the Old Man's quarters. Jack was to have a chance at the Japs and was very happy about the whole thing as he had never forgiven himself for missing the boat on the 20th. I thought then, that Jack was going to be one of our best fighting men and his record subsequently showed that I was right—he shot down eleven Japs!

The next morning I went to the airdrome with Harvey to watch Jack and the Second Squadron take off for Rangoon to relieve Olson. I wished all the boys good luck before they took off at nine-thirty. Jack had eighteen planes. His crew chiefs and the rest of the ground crew had taken off at seven in a C.N.A.C. plane. After they had gone I again suffered that unhappy feeling of wondering how many of them, and who, wouldn't come back.

I don't know what we would have done without C.N.A.C. as we had no transport planes except the old decrepit Beech-craft. C.N.A.C. was always moving our men and equipment from one place to another, sometimes making as many as three round trips a day. Their pilots were never too busy to do some-thing for the A.V.G. Their office in Calcutta was of ines-timable value in slashing customs and other red tape, to get the important spare parts and equipment so sorely needed, and never would C.N.A.C. land at Kunming without a load for us. This airline had a great influence in the lives of the Chi-nese people as it has been the only means of communication and transport from the interior.

In the chaotic last days of Hong Kong, despite the lack of co-operation from British authorities, they did heroic work in taking out evacuees during bombings. Those pilots were all our friends; Chuck Sharpe, chief pilot, a small stout chubby fellow, one of the best airline pilots in the world. He had been in China over ten years and knew the country like the back of his hand. Woods, twice shot down by Japanese planes and still flying. W. C. MacDonald, who had been chief flying in-structor with Colonel Chennault before joining C.N.A.C. Frank Higgs, "one-eyebrow Higgs," the original of *Terry and the Pirates*. Bob Angle, another one of the old instructors; Royal Leonard, an old student of Harvey's and a master navi-gator; Hal Sweet, who always had some new scheme or ven-ture in mind; Kessler, a steady, fine pilot who was always on the job; DeCanzo, a lad from Australia who had joined recently; Emil Scott, another ex-instructor; Bob Shuler, a beginner; Moon Shen, a Chinese pilot who could fly a board if it had a propeller. The exploits of this gallant band were legion and too much cannot be said for them.

Sandell stood by me as Jack's eighteen planes took off. He said: "When I take off with my squadron, will you stand here and watch me, too?"

I answered: "Of course."

We walked over to his squadron's alert shack and right into a poker game. I played for some time but quit when I had lost about three hundred Chinese dollars. When my luck is out I don't believe in sending good money after bad. Sandy made fun of me and said I was losing my technique.

As I played cards, I listened to all kinds of rumors. Maybe that was why I lost—didn't have my mind on the game. It had been sometime since Jack had left and no word had been received of him. Some of the fellows said he was trying to "shoot the moon" and make a record flight. I left them and went into Operations to find out the truth. Harvey said: "No reports yet. You know we keep radio silence on these flights. Keeps the Japs from hearing too much. Newquack is okay, probably found a tail wind and knows he can make Toungoo without refueling at Lashio."

In a few minutes a message arrived from Toungoo: "All Sharks landed for food." I went to the alert shack to tell the boys. Rumors were still rampant: the two missing pilots reported in the battle of December 25th over Rangoon were C. E. Smith and Greene. The boys said that Smith had run away from the fight and landed in Pegu and that Greene had shot two Japs off Smith's tail and had been shot down himself and almost killed when the Japs fired at his parachute. One of the boys said: "Smith won't fly again—if he has his wind up. The Old Man will probably make him Adjutant."

I don't know to this day whether or not Smith had "his wind up"—but he didn't fly again while I was there and the

Old Man appointed him Adjutant, a position very much coveted by the Group Sergeant Major, Wyke. This was the beginning of a feud between Smith and Wyke. Smith, an ex-Marine pilot, was one of the oldest men of the Group. The boys never did take to him.

Entering my quarters I met Colonel Huang. He said he had organized a dinner party for that night at the hostel and I was to be hostess. It was a problem finding something to wear. I decided on an old white dinner dress with gold embroidered jacket I had bought in Hong Kong two years before. The embroidery was rather tarnished since the dress was a reminder of happier days when we used to dress for dinner. After the amah had pressed it, it didn't look so bad, after all. I found some Kleenex and with it tied my hair in knots to curl it. I was sitting in front of a charcoal pot trying to dry it when Wyke came in. When he saw me he laughed and said: "You look like Topsy." I went on with the business of drying my hair and asked him what he wanted.

He said: "I brought you some flowers for the party tonight." He produced a small bunch of white cherry blossoms. He blushed a little and added: "I got them from the British cemetery."

The only coats I had were a camel's hair and a leather fur-lined jacket, such as the pilots wore. I compromised and decided to freeze. After the dinner we went upstairs to the auditorium. Long-winded speeches by the Chinese. I looked around for some signs of the Colonel and Harvey.

At last they appeared. The Colonel, still suffering from the flu, had just gotten out of bed. Colonel Huang came down from the platform and led the Colonel to the seat of honor. After more speeches, Colonel Huang unwrapped an ornate bundle wrapped in red silk and handed a beautiful Chinese sword to Colonel Wang, who after a speech, presented it to Colonel Chennault. A sword like this had never been given to a foreigner before—it was an honor seldom accorded a foreigner.

The Colonel, who was wearing a Sam Browne, solemnly hooked the scabbard to his belt, strode to the center of the platform and drew the sword. He then made a short dramatic speech—so dramatic it would have sounded ridiculous from any one less sincere. I knew that every word he said came from his heart.

The meeting broke up soon after and I was glad to get back to my warm quarters. The Colonel followed: "How did I do, Olga—all right?" He always worried about his speeches.

The next day was miserable and cold. A C.N.A.C. plane came in with the crew chiefs and two pilots of the Third Squadron, all with startling stories to tell.

Rangoon was a mess and a madhouse. The Indian population had moved out; many had started the long walk to India. Most of the whites were gone. The lepers and the insane had been turned loose. Rioting, thieving and looting were going on. The police had lost control over the natives. No one was safe on the streets at night.

The boys said there was still plenty of food left on the Rangoon docks that customs hadn't cleared. The stupid customs officials were still trying to maintain their usual red tape even though they were in danger of being bombed every minute. Millions of dollars of Lend-Lease equipment was rusting on the docks.

Charlie Sawyer, who is now a major in the A.A.F., had been playing with hard luck. At Toungoo, while testing a new gun sight in a power dive he had broken an eardrum. He was grounded for a long period and then in the fight on December 20th he again injured his ear which thereafter was always conspicuously decorated with red mercurochrome. He was a splendid pilot and always eager for a fight. One day toward the end of December, Sawyer, J. J. Dean, an ex-Navy boy, and Red Probst were given a photographic and reconnaissance mission to Indo-China as there were several airdromes that needed looking into. Their orders were to turn back if they ran into an overcast, as the weather threatened to be nasty.

Over Indo-China they hit the overcast but they didn't turn back. They broke formation and lost one another. Result: Probst and Dean made crash landings miles from nowhere while Sawyer, using his head, squeezed back to Kunming safely on his last gallon of petrol. Two more ships gone and no replacements in sight: and one was the very important photographic ship.

Olson and the Third Squadron arrived from Toungoo. The boys were dog-tired but jubilant. They reported that after the first bombing on the 23rd of December all of the house boys and cooks deserted, taking with them most of the food supplies. A direct hit on the mess buildings reduced the menu to bread and cheese. On Christmas Day Bill Pawley rounded up all of the food he could and sent it out to them—or they wouldn't have eaten. Crew Chief Quick, who had been a garage mechanic, took care of the feeding of the gang and did a tasty job of it.

The crew chiefs got busy painting little Japanese flags on the bullet-ridden ships of the Third Squadron's aces. Duke Hedman had shot down five in one day. Charley Older, of Beverley Hills, California, also had five flags on his ship.

I was very busy trying to get the stories of the different pilots. Ed Overend, an ex-Marine pilot from Coronado, California, told me that on the 23rd he shot down one Jap plane and that on Christmas Day he shot down two more, was shot down himself, but was not injured.

Bob Brouk, of Cicero, Illinois, later to be killed in a collision in Florida, was the engineer officer of the squadron. He was a very nice chap, always smiling and happy. He was standing by his plane when I saw him. We both sat down on a box near by and he said:

"I'll tell you a little story, don't go to sleep. . . . On December 23rd we were running patrols and going up on false alarms. About eleven o'clock we intercepted the Japs about ten miles south of Rangoon. I made several passes and shot down one of the bombers which were in close formation. It was an Army 97 twin-engine bomber."

I interrupted him: "Tell me, Bob, how did you feel when you were up there fighting—were you scared? Did you want to murder the Jap—did you feel anything?"

Brouk laughed: "Hell no, that's not the feeling at all—you sort of become part of your plane. You just don't figure that you are fighting man to man—it's plane to plane. You see, if you don't get the other plane first, it will get you. . . . On the 25th I knocked down a fighter. I closed in on him until I was very close and then shot him down in flames. He never knew what hit him. After that I kept on with the daily patrols but had no more fights. Wasn't lucky."

I asked another one of the boys, "You don't want to go back, do you?"

"You bet your boots I do," he replied. "Just as soon as I rest up a bit—have a score to settle with those little yellow so-and-so's."

New Year's Day was cloudy and dismal. I was in a gloomy mood. The Colonel was still ill in bed. I too, was ill and as I lay in bed I thought of the boys we had lost in December. "You can't fight a war without somebody getting killed."

Harvey came in from the field to see the Colonel. It was one of the few times he had been in the hostel during the daytime and he stayed long enough to have a cup of coffee. Tom Jones he said, had gone to Rangoon to join Jack's squadron. I didn't believe it possible as only a few days before he had been in bed in the hospital. Harvey said that Jones wouldn't fly, but could be useful helping the ground crews.

On January 2nd, Bill Williams, the tall, slim communications officer, came with two radio men and put up a very high aerial for the twelve valve Philips set we had purchased in Toungoo, a very good set especially for the tropics. After they left, I tried out the radio and wished I hadn't—Manila had fallen! What a shock! Those Japs who had been so badly underestimated—I was sick at heart thinking that if we only had had more airplanes and equipment and co-operation, the Japs could have been stopped in their tracks. If we could only hit them near home, Indo-China, Hainan, Formosa, Japan itself! I had listened to the Colonel and Harvey talking about what they could do with the proper equipment and more men. . . .

Early that same morning Probst and Dean returned from the scene of their crack-ups. I asked Red how he had spent his New Year's Eve. He said: "Gosh, I was lucky enough to crash near a Catholic mission and the Priest was a hell of a fine fellow. He and I drank the Old Year out and the New Year in. That Father sure had a good stock of booze. . . ."

His face suddenly became serious. "The Old Man and Harvey are sore as hell at me and blame me for getting lost. I have to go up before a board of inquiry. I'm not too worried though, as I have a good excuse—my radio wouldn't work."

I said: "Red, why don't you stop making alibis and cut out this kid stuff. You will find out that you would get along with the other fellows better then. . . ."

Harvey never left the airdrome until dark, consequently it was seven o'clock when he appeared at the hostel. It was his practice to clean up and then go to the Colonel's quarters for a review of the day's happenings and to discuss any problems, of which there were many, that had arisen. The United States Army was all for the induction of the A.V.G. into the United States Armed Forces, but Harvey was definitely against it at that time and was continually fighting it. Sometimes, when the Colonel was annoyed at infractions of discipline, he would be in favor of immediate induction and Harvey would argue him out of it. The shadow of induction hovered over the Group as but very few of the men wanted to change their status. They thought they could do more to help the common cause by remaining as they were—the A.V.G. was an elastic mobile unit not trammelled by miles and miles of red tape.

After discussing the problems, the Colonel suggested a game of cribbage which was a passion with him, so he and Harvey started the game. I could not understand why they liked that silly game so much. I soon got bored and started to leave, but the Colonel called me back.

He said: "Sit down. I'll have this whisky-drinking, poker-playing, evil old husband of yours beaten in a few minutes—there's a bottle of Bourbon on the table. Why don't you pour us a drink?"

The Colonel preferred Bourbon straight, but I never saw him take more than two drinks. The game finished, with my husband on the losing end, as usual. The Colonel cleared his throat as he always does before speaking—he has a bronchial affliction—and said: "Olga, you have been working on the *Diary* since December 8th, haven't you?"

I answered: "Yes, Sir."

"Have you received any pay yet?"

"You haven't authorized anyone to pay me."

"I'll be dogged—Harvey, why haven't you taken care of it?"

Harvey said: "That's your job. . . ."

The Colonel said: "Well, Olga, we'll give you one hundred and fifty dollars a month from now on. See the Finance Officer and have him make out a contract. Is that all right?"

"No, Sir," I answered. "That's not enough money to pay me for my trouble in getting material for the diary, but money hasn't anything to do with it. I want a copy of the *Diary*—that will be my pay."

They both laughed. The Colonel said: "You may have a copy of the *Diary*, but you must promise not to use it until the A.V.G. is dissolved. However, I am still going to give you a salary as I want you to be an official member of the A.V.G."

I started to protest but he said: "As a *bona fide* member of the Group you have reason to live here in the hostel. Then too, if we are inducted, Harvey will have to stay here and they would send you home, but if you are on the payroll you will stay with the Group—let's have some Chinese chow, I am hungry."

We picked up Troy Perkins, American Consul at Kunming, and took him along with us. Mr. Perkins told us amusing stories of the old Governor of Kunming who was dead and had been succeeded by the present Governor Lung, who now peacefully administered the people of Yunnan Province under the Generalissimo's orders.

Mr. Perkins promised to ask us for dinner soon but bemoaned the fact that there wasn't much food to be bought in the markets of Kunming. I told him to remind me to give him a bean recipe that I knew for his dinner.

On January 10th, several transport planes landed at our field. About eleven o'clock Bill Pawley and his brother, Ed, arrived—on their way to Chungking. Higgs was the pilot, and the co-pilot was Shuler, a fairly new man, but in another two months, he told me, he would be a full-fledged pilot. Late in the day, Emil Scott arrived from Chungking with Colonel Chennault. It was like old home week, all together again, just like the days in Hong Kong.

I was particularly fond of "Scotty." He and his pretty young wife, Betty, spent their honeymoon with us in our villa in Doson, French Indo-China, in December, 1940. That Christmas we invited the "American gang" in Kunming to a party. They chartered a C.N.A.C. plane and came down *en masse*. Some stayed for a week or so. By the time they left, Betty was ill—the first symptoms of a blessed event.

Betty was a Honolulu girl. Scotty had met her there, and immediately fallen head over heels. The last time I had seen her was in Hong Kong when we joined the A.V.G. She went from there to Honolulu with their baby girl, left her there and returned to Manila to be near Scotty. And now she was at the mercy of the Japs.

Scotty said: "You know, we still talk about that party of yours in Doson—we had so many laughs and were so happy. . . ." His face clouded as he added: "I'm worried sick about Betty. I can't contact her at all. They tell me the Japs are sending the Americans to Shanghai and I hope she might have been sent there, too. What a swell girl—my Betty! God knows what's happened to her—but if she gets to Shanghai I'll borrow a C.N.A.C. crate and get her out of there. I've got it all planned—know just how to go about it ... look ... want to see something beautiful?"

From his brief-case he took out two large photographs of Betty, showed them to me, proudly, kissed them both and returned them to the case. "She's the last thing I see when I go to sleep at night—and the first when I wake up in the morning."

He had me blinking back the tears. Betty had been one of my best friends and I knew how dearly these two loved each other. Scotty had heard nothing about his baby in Honolulu, either. My heart ached for him.

"Come on, Scotty," I said. "Let's go into town and see what we can pick up."

We joined Higgs and Schuler, then met Greg Boyington and Adair and asked them along, too. We went to the Thieves' Alley, a market place where one could find almost anything, from bracelets to a pair of trousers, mostly stolen.

We looked around for leopard skins, but found only two. I offered 500 Mex (about $12.50) for the pair but when I wasn't looking, Boyington bought one of them for 350 Mex. That made me mad. I asked him: "How do you expect me to get the price down when you go and pay the asking price?" But the damage was done. I couldn't get the price of the other one down. When we got back to the car Boyington said he had bought the skin for me for a delayed Christmas present. I was reluctant to accept it but he insisted, so I did. I knew I could go back and get the other one, but decided to send one of my Chinese friends who would buy it for me at no more than 100. Later, my Chinese friend bought two more for me, with which I covered the sofa.

I went to bed thinking of Scotty's problem. Poor Scotty!

Poor Betty! The next morning I had breakfast with him and drove to the field to watch him take off. He waved good-by from the cockpit and promised to bring me some medicine from Loiwing for my bad cough. He said he had seen a bottle there in someone's quarters—some stuff the Navy used. He would beg, borrow or steal it if necessary and bring it to me. He returned the same afternoon about six and sure enough, had the cough medicine.

He said: "When I come back from Calcutta I shall bring you one of those Max Factor eyebrow things—if I can find one."

I wondered how many eyebrow pencils I was going to get, as I had asked all the pilots to bring me one, in case one of them forgot about it.

There was talk of sending reinforcements to Jack Newkirk in Rangoon. The First Squadron was drawing tickets, numbered, out of a hat, to see who the lucky fellows were who would go. In the afternoon, Boyington came to see me. He sat around a long time without saying a word while I kept on with my work on the typewriter. Finally, he said:

"You don't like me, do you?"

"What makes you say that?" I asked.

He answered: "I don't know. I just thought you didn't. The other night with the C.N.A.C. pilots I had a good look at you—the way you talk to them, so freely. But then, they are your old friends. I felt sort of out of place with them."

I said: "You are younger. Those fellows are more my age, you see?"

"What do you mean younger? I'm almost thirty—I have two kids—or did you know?"

I said I didn't.

"Yes," he said slowly— "and a wife I divorced—or rather, she divorced me. It's kind of tough, I guess, for a young, attractive woman to be married to a Marine. I was no bargain to get along with."

He arose and went over to the radio. On top was a photograph of my sister Alicia's two little boys. Boyington picked it up and looked at them. "Your children?" he asked.

I said: "My sister's."

Boyington said: "My kids are as pretty as these although maybe you wouldn't believe it?" He stood there for a long time looking at my nephews' picture. I could see the longing in his face—longing for these two little ones that were his. Was this one of the reasons he had joined the A.V.G. and come out to China? I didn't want to ask as I thought I might open old wounds.

It was time for tea, and I offered him some. He sat very quiet again, drinking his tea. When he finished, he said: "I am going tomorrow with a flight to join Jack's squadron. I wish to say a parting word—you won't take it wrong? You are the only bright star in this place—does a man's heart good to look at you."

Before I could say anything, the door was closed, and he was gone. Queer bird, I thought. Still, I felt sorry for him, not knowing why. Lord only knew what drama his life was. Why, I wondered, would a young fellow, a captain in the Marine Corps, with a fine record, suddenly give it up and come out here?

It was Monday when they took off. I went to the field to see them—eight pilots of the First Squadron leaving for Rangoon to help Jack. Amongst them were Bob Little, Bob Neale, of Seattle, the Vice Squadron Leader; Greg Boyington, Flight Leader, and Bill McGarry, of Los Angeles, whom everyone called "Black Mac." As usual, I stood there, watching the planes until they disappeared. It always made me feel sad, thinking—will I see them again? Who will come back?

Chapter VI

D URING the ten years that I knew General P. T. Mao,
Chief of Staff of the Chinese Air Force, I never saw
him without his hunting dogs. On January 14th he turned up
at Kunming in his own plane accompanied by two colonels—
and two pointers.

I hadn't been to the field that day and, although the mess
room was only two doors from our quarters, I didn't feel like
eating with the rest of the gang. I put on a black chiffon Chinese dress, black embroidered Chinese slippers and waited for
Harvey to come home. When he did, General Mao was with
him. He complimented me on my appearance saying that few
foreign women could wear the Chinese dress as they usually
had such broad hips, but that I looked all right because I was
slender. Need I say I was flattered?

General Mao asked about my sister Alicia and her husband,
Jack Schweizer, who had been one of the instructors in Hang-
chow. I told the General they had two baby boys. He said:
"We now have six sons and the seventh *en route.*" I said,
"Don't you wish this one would be a girl?"

He answered: "Another boy will be all right—another
fighting man for China."

I congratulated him and asked about Mrs. Mao, who my
sister and I liked very much when we were in Hangchow. We
used to go horseback riding with her, and she and the General
frequently came to our house for American dinners. We talked
about the old times and the General said: "Olga, it does not
surprise me to find you here. This is where you belong—you
are a part of China. We think of you as Chinese." That, indeed, was a great compliment, and I felt very happy about it.

Early in the morning of January 17th, I went to the field with Harvey. I had a hunch something important was going to happen and wanted to be right there in the operations room if it did.

At nine-thirty Harvey was preparing to send off a photographic and reconnaissance flight of four planes headed by McMillan. The other pilots were Eric Shilling, Older and Haywood. All were veterans, except Shilling, who hadn't yet been in a fight. The orders were to get pictures of Japanese airdromes at Hagiang, a town on the Indo-China border. The flight was just warming up when the "net" reported loud noises crossing the border at Hokow.

Harvey ordered the flight to take off immediately for Mengtze, 124 miles south, flying at 12,000 feet. In a few minutes the "net" reported three Jap bombers flying toward Mengtze. The information was relayed to McMillan's flight. About two minutes later, Sasser, the radio operator at Mengtze, said three Jap bombers were over the field. Almost immediately thereafter McMillan made the interception and the first bomber was down in flames. In a few minutes the other two played follow the leader.

General Mao and Colonel Chennault appeared at Operations right after the first bomber had been brought down. Harvey explained he had been too busy to call them. General Mao was very pleased with the interception, as was the entire city of Kunming.

Was I glad I had come to the field! I listened to the whole thing on the radio. The victorious flight returned an hour later, buzzed the field, and each one did a victory roll.

On January 19th we received the following message from Rangoon:

ALARM LAST NIGHT FOUR BOMBERS DID NOT REACH OBJECTIVE BOMBS DROPPED IN JUNGLE STOP WRIGHT TOOK OFF TO ATTACK ENEMY STOP UPON RETURNING DEVELOPED PRESTONE LEAK BLINDING HIM WHILE LANDING RAN

OFF RUNWAY AND HIT CAR DEMOLISHING BOTH STOP MER-
RIT SLEEPING IN CAR KILLED INSTANTLY PETE WRIGHT
OKAY END NEWKIRK.

Poor Merrit—his time was up, no doubt. His crash at the
time of Mangleburg's death, was a preliminary—I was thinking
that the only survivor now was Shilling, when Shilling entered,
looking a little pale. He said: "Did you hear about poor Merrit? Maybe I'm next." I told him not to be a fool, that he was
one of the best navigators and pilots we had. "Yes," he said,
"but Merrit wasn't even flying—probably had been on
duty all day and was tired out and went to sleep in the car.
I'd hate to be in Pete Wright's shoes—he must feel pretty bad
about it. . . ." He stayed for a few minutes. "I just came in to
see if you knew about it," he said as he left.

One of the ground men who had shrapnel wounds arrived
from Toungoo with new reports and stories. He said that on
the 18th of January, Frank Lawlor, of Coronado, California,
had told them about his experiences for the day:

"At ten in the morning Rossi and I escorted six Blenheims
on a mission from Mingaladon to Tavoy. We flew across the
Gulf of Martaban to the opposite shore and turned south until
we reached Tavoy. Rossi got lost, so I found myself the only
escort of the Blenheims. The Blenheims were going over to
evacuate people. Before taking off I was told that if a white
cross was on the field, Tavoy was still in British hands. If not,
the Japs had it. I looked down and saw no white cross. I looked
up and saw six Jap fighters. No sight of the Blenheims. Evidently the Japs didn't see any Blenheims, either, so they concentrated in chasing me all over the sky. I shot one down and
then proceeded to prove the theory that he who fights and
runs away lives to fight another day."

Later I saw Lawlor and he verified the story. I asked him
what he thought of the enemy fighters. He said: "Enemy fighters are inferior in quality but superior in quantity—and I do
mean quantity."

General Mao remained with us for several days. About four o'clock one afternoon he told me he was going hunting around the lakes south of Kunming. "I think," he added, "tonight we will have a duck dinner."

Right after he left, Trumble, the Colonel's secretary, came in. "Do you know where the Colonel keeps his shotgun? He's going hunting with the General."

I went to the Colonel's quarters and found his gun—a Winchester pump, behind a wardrobe, and finally located the shells in a box under his bed.

A duck dinner sounded good to me. I was getting a little bit weary of pork chops and beans. Sure enough, about seven in the evening the Old Man knocked at my door, peeked in and said: "When Harvey gets home, you two come over to my quarters—duck dinner!"

The dinner surpassed my expectations. We started out with fresh oysters!—unheard of in Kunming. MacDonald, of C.N.A.C., had flown them from Calcutta for the Colonel. General Mao and the Colonel together had shot thirteen Burmese geese. A bottle of good French wine appeared on the table—a remnant of the days when traffic was open between Kunming and Hanoi.

After dinner the Colonel, Harvey, General Mao and some of the pilots went into conference for several hours. I wasn't invited—there was no reason why I should have been—so I couldn't find out what was going on. As I look back I am consistently amazed at how, under the stress of war, you come to know a great many things almost instinctively. Out of no specific information whatever, I managed to put two and two together and get a good idea of what the conference was about. When General Mao took off in his own plane for Changyi it confirmed my idea. However, I had to wait until the next day to really be sure I was right.

That day was windy, with drifting clouds at about 8,000 feet. I went to the field early, so I wouldn't miss anything.

When I arrived, ten leering sharks were warming up. I saw Red Probst's flaming hair blowing in the breeze. Further away I recognized Sandy and one of his wingmen, Cross. And Boyington, which I thought strange. He was supposed to be in Rangoon.

I went to the operations hut and asked Harvey: "Are the fellows escorting the Russian bombers?"

He gave me a dirty look. "You are the nosiest damn woman!"

I answered: "I just figured it out—General Mao went to Changyi—that's where the bombers are, isn't it?"

"You ask too many questions," he said.

I went outside to see the planes take off. They disappeared toward Mengtze. On the desk I saw some maps of the territory with lines drawn from point to point giving the course of the flight. Kunming to Mengtze, 157°; Mengtze to Hanoi, 137°. So they were going to bomb Hanoi! At Mengtze they would refuel and join the bombers.

As radio silence was maintained throughout the flight we didn't hear anything until the boys returned at four o'clock. Sandy jumped out of his ship, slipped off his chute and made straight for the operations hut. I followed him, notebook and pencil at the ready.

Harvey asked: "What happened, Sandy?"

Sandy said: "What *didn't* happen! Eighteen Chinese pilots in those damned S-B3's flew all over the landscape—it was twice as crazy because they flew in two formations of nine each. Right after we joined them their second flight dropped back and remained a mile behind the first. We couldn't decide which ones to escort.

"I don't know what they were aiming at but they dropped their bombs about twenty miles east of Haiphong because I saw one hole through the clouds that was over the Gulf of Tonkin. I saw some explosions but don't know whether they were the bombs or ack-ack. When the leader turned for home he increased his air speed from 140 miles an hour to over 180 and they were scattered from hell to breakfast. We came back to Mengtze over solid overcast—hit it right on the nose. Probably Hanoi was under broken clouds but we passed about fifty miles northeast so I couldn't tell."

The fellows thought one of the bombers had been shot down but none could verify it. Our planes were too fast for the bombers and by the time they cruised back and forth trying to stay with them they had practically run out of gas.

"If we'd met any Japs we'd have been dead pigeons," said Sandy.

Up until January 24th, our group had shot down sixty-two enemy planes and destroyed eleven on the ground, a total of seventy-three destroyed in thirty-five days, during which period we lost three men in action and two in accidents. Those were confirmed victories—no maybe's or perhapses. We thought that the combat ratio, in the air, of better than twenty to one wasn't at all bad.

On this same day some of the boys, with Olson leading, escorted the bombers for a second time—with the same unsatisfactory results. Ole reported the bombers wouldn't stay in formation and made it impossible for him to properly escort them. However, they all returned safely. Olson said: "If we'd gotten into a scrap or slipped up on our navigation we'd never have gotten back to Mengtze. The bombers unloaded into the overcast somewhere southeast of Hanoi." Later we learned that the raid had done some good. It had lowered the morale of the Indo-China civilians and given the Japs something to think about. But Harvey said: "You can't beat 'em simply by giving them something to think about."

I had been at the airfield all that morning. I was still in Harvey's office listening to the talk about the mission when Sandy arrived, all dressed up in his United States Air Corps tunic, with his American silver wings. "I have been looking for you all over," he said. "It's my day off again. How about going to the Y.M.C.A. to see the Chinese Art Exhibition?"

I left with Sandy. On the way we stopped and bought some

French cigarettes smuggled in from Indo-China—"*Cotabs*" they are called. They were perfectly dreadful but since we were running short of American cigarettes, we smoked them and saved the good ones for special occasions. A lot of Chinese were already at the Y.M.C.A.—we were the only foreigners.

The walls of one large room were completely covered with pictures, some in water colors and others, pastels. I liked one very much—a tiger about to leap out of jungle grass. Sandy said: "The figure is too large for the size of the paper. But if you like it, I'll make you a present of it." The price was $800 National. I thanked him and told him that I didn't like it so well, either. We left without buying anything and returned to my quarters.

Tugboat immediately made his appearance. "Wanchee tea?" he asked.

"Yes," said Sandy, "and bring four egg sandwiches. We plentee hungree."

It didn't take the boys long to learn pidgin English—and they loved it.

Sandy said: "How about me fixing your hair? Last time I had a day off you told me that the next time I could fix it. It looks pretty rat's-nesty. Got a pair of scissors?"

I sat on the floor and he on a chair above me and clipped my hair here and there, gave it a good brushing, then dressed it. Exercising a barber's prerogatives, he talked—about a lot of things but mostly about that wonderful country around San Francisco. "It's beautiful, Olga. Me for that—and a nice little farm or ranch or whatever they call them up there. Cows and chickens and a whole flock of little Sandells. Yes, sir, the minute this mess is over with."

When he finished he said: "Stand up and take a look at yourself."

To my surprise, it was very becoming. He, too, was pleased with it. "I've always wanted to try that sometime," he said.

We were having our tea when he got up suddenly. "I'll be right back," he said. He returned in about an hour—very excited and smiling all over his face. He started to remove his tunic.

"What's all this, anyway?" I asked.

He said: "Catch!"—and threw the tunic to me.

I caught it and still wondered what it was all about.

"Just had a long talk with the Old Man. I'm going to Rangoon tomorrow to relieve Jack Newkirk. What do you think of that? You are always talking about wanting a coat like this—so here's your chance. Put it on—let's see how it fits." I put it on and Sandy said: "Fits like you'd been poured into it."

"Sandy," I protested, "I can't do that. I will keep it and have the tailor copy it. How's that?"

"Well, all right," said Sandy, "but maybe—I won't come back." That made me angry. Sandy laughed. "Calm yourself," he said. "Have you got that leather jacket? Let me have it. I'll wear it." I took the leather jacket out of my wardrobe and gave it to him. "Listen," he said, "I have to go back to my quarters so that I can tell the fellows and draw lots to see who is going with me. Too many men and not enough planes, see? I am going to have my three carpets rolled up. As soon as I take off tomorrow, you go to my quarters and get them. If I don't come back—you keep them. I want you to have them because you helped me pick them out, and I know you appreciate them more than anyone else. I have a couple of books that I like—kind of silly, isn't it? Tomorrow I'll bring them to Operations. You will be there to see me off? Oh, another thing, send a wire to Gross National Bank, San Antonio, Texas . . . No, don't. Just send a wire to some friends of mine. Have you got a pencil?" I gave him one and a piece of paper. He wrote: "Allen Guiberson, Dallas, Texas."

"Sandy," I said, "you are acting damn silly. What's come over you, anyway?"

He didn't answer: He came close to me, put his arms around me and gave me a tight squeeze. Softly he said: "Good-by, Olga. Take care of yourself—think of me now and then."

He left me standing in the middle of the room, feeling dazed.

I began to cry, not knowing why. All I could say was, "Oh, Sandy. Dear, silly, Sandy!" I still had his jacket on. I touched all the buttons—the Air Corps buttons with the eagle. My hand drifted to the left-hand pocket. Above it I felt the wings —Sandy's first wings—large, silver wings. "Hell," I said, "this will never do." I went into the next room and washed my face with cold water. Then, I went back to my desk and got to work. I picked up a message that was on top, and read:

CHENNAULT: RAID ON 1030 SEVEN HEAVY BOMBERS AND TWENTY FIVE FIGHTERS STOP SEVEN AVG AND TWO HURRICANES AND FOUR BUFFALOES TOOK OFF STOP ENEMY INTERCEPTED STOP ALL ENEMY BOMBERS SHOT DOWN IN FLAMES AT LEAST TEN FIGHTERS SHOT DOWN STOP OUR LOSSES ALLIED OO STOP HAVE TEN PLANES IN COMMISSION TEN SUFFERING FROM LEAD POISONING STOP END NEWKIRK.

Sunday morning was beautiful. Scattered clouds and sunshine. I went to the field very early as I didn't want to miss Sandy. At the entrance of the first alert shack I met "Cokey" Hoffman, the oldest of the pilots—tall, slim, with a devil-may-care look in his face. He was already dressed in his flying suit and helmet—and the goggles pulled up above his forehead.

"Good morning," I said, "you look cheerful."

"I am," said Cokey. "I have been looking forward to this for a long time. Now it's come, thank God. I don't like waiting around much. That's why I came over—to get into good fights. For the hell of it."

"Doesn't you wife worry about it?"

"Oh," he said, "I guess she does, like all women do. But she's a good sport. I talked it over with her before I came out here. She didn't like it, but then she knew I was keen on it, and didn't raise any fuss. She's a great gal. I sure miss her and our kids."

I wished him luck. "Well," he said, "if anything happens to me, she'll know I'll go the way I want it—fighting. My wife will understand. . . ."

The way these men talked gave me the creeps. I walked into Operations. There I found Sandy and the other pilots studying the huge map that covered the table.

Sandy came over to me. "I got the books here. Don't forget them. When we take off, I'll leave the flight and fly low over this hut. I'll waggle my wings—that's a good-by to you. When you can't see the planes, go over to my quarters and get the carpets." He went back to the map.

Red Probst came in. He signaled to me and went outside again. I followed him.

"Hold out your hand," he said, "keep it for me." He placed his large gold ring with a two-carat ruby in the palm of my hand. I looked at him. "If I don't come back," he said, "take it home with you and send it to my mother." He handed me a piece of paper with her name and address on it. Then out of his pocket he pulled out another piece of paper. "This," he added, "is a list of the fellows, and how much they owe me. Will you collect for me? They are all poker, bridge, black-jack and crap debts. We have been keeping books. Now, I want these fellows to pay up. So, you collect from them. Except Olson. If anything happens to me, I know he'll pay it into my account with Finance." I glanced at the paper. A lot of money was involved.

Red was scared, I thought, plenty. And he had been talking big to me of how he was going to shoot so many Japs. I wondered. His usual red face was a pale pink that morning. He shook hands and went off toward his plane. I went back into Operations.

The pilots were filing out, going to their planes. Sandy stayed back. There were six clerks in the office, and Harvey. Sandy shook hands with Harvey, said "So long, fellows" to the clerks and at the door shook hands with me. I kissed him. He blushed like a young girl, and all the fellows smiled.

I walked up to the little observation tower and, with the aid of field glasses, watched the boys get into their planes, taxi, and take off. It was nine fifty-five. Six P-40's took off. They got into formation, and one plane pulled out, made a circle and dove over the operations shack, pulled up and made another circle—flew low over the shack again and tipped its wings. Sandy was saying good-by.

I went back into the hut and picked up the books Sandy left. One was *The Anatomy of Revolution* by Crane Brinton. I opened it. In it I found a piece of paper—a plan for movement of the First Pursuit Squadron to Burma. I read the list of pilots: "R. F. Sandell, Squadron Leader; Prescott, Kuykendall, Hoffman, Liebolt, Wolf, Probst, Dean, Boyington, Brown, Smith, Bond." Then a list of ground men. It was addressed to the "Commanding Officer, A.V.G., and signed, R. J. Sandell, Squadron Leader, Commanding." The date, January 20th —five days before. A card fell out. I picked it up and read: "Robert James Sandell," and in the right-hand corner: "Lieutenant Air Corps, United States Army." The other book was a biography of Mozart. What a queer combination of books, I thought.

The remaining six P-40's of Sandy's squadron took off at ten thirty-five, Boyington leading. I didn't see Boyington before he left. I went over to Sandy's quarters. One of Sandy's clerks had the carpets already rolled up. Wyke, who was with me, helped him put them in the station wagon. We went back to our hostel.

Ole had dinner with us at our quarters. He and Harvey left soon after to go into town. I stayed alone playing with the radio. From the BBC I learned that Thailand had declared war on the Allies. What cheek, I thought.

When Harvey returned, he gave me a little parcel. I opened it and found a lovely gold bracelet. I had been wanting one for some time. I told him I was going to invest all my salary in buying gold bracelets—like having money in the bank—and that bank wouldn't close. Had he heard from Sandy?

He nodded, "They all arrived safely at Mingaladon." I asked if Jack Newkirk and his squadron were coming back now. He answered: "No, not yet. Sandy's squadron will support Jack's. About six of Jack's pilots will come back, those with disabled planes."

I asked again: "Is Sandy going to command, or Jack?"

"Jack is still in command. When he leaves, Sandy will take over."

Late the next day Harvey handed me a paper. "Read that," he said. I read:

CHENNAULT STOP COMBAT WITH TWENTY ENEMY PUR-SUIT AT 1100 STOP SHOT DOWN THREE ENEMY PLANES STOP HOFFMAN SHOT DOWN AND DEAD END NEWKIRK.

Cokey!—and I was talking to him only yesterday. How tersely Jack wrote his messages: "Hoffman shot down and dead...."

I wondered about Cokey's wife—"She's a good sport—she'll understand."

Before long the reports from Rangoon for January 26th arrived—the day Hoffman was killed. Jack's report said: "Twenty to thirty enemy aircraft seen—I-97's. Allied aircraft, seven. I took off with six other planes. As my RT was out, I turned the lead over to the next section led by A. L. Probst of the First Squadron."

I was at the field when two P-40's landed—George Paxton and Petach. They were sunburned, full-bearded, dirty and tired—they looked like the devil. They were both slightly wounded—their planes were badly damaged and unfit for another fight, so they flew them to Loiwing for repairs. From there they flew up to Point "X" (Kunming).

They brought a lot of mail and wild stories about the fights with the Japanese. Paxton said that Sandy had had a narrow escape. He told us the story in detail:

"On the 28th (January) Sandy had been up in a fight and shot down two Japs and damaged another one, which Sandy reported as smoking badly, but he did not see it go down.

After shooting at this third plane, Sandy's ship began to get hot—the prestone temperature went to 150°, and the cockpit filled with smoke. Sandy made a forced landing on the field, without power, and with the right tire punctured by gunfire. Immediately after he landed, a Japanese fighter, probably the one that he had damaged, appeared over the field. The Jap knew he was a goner anyway and figured he might as well take a P-40 with him. He circled the field slowly, dove straight into the tail of Sandy's ship, machine guns blazing, and demolished all the movable tail surfaces. Sandy jumped out and got into a trench just in time."

That was a narrow escape for Sandy I thought. I felt kind of sorry for Sandy's plane—Number 11. It probably would take a long time to fix up.

The next day the old Beechcraft staggered in—loaded with sick and wounded pilots of the Second Squadron: Jones, Pete Wright and R. C. Moss. Hennessy, who was flying the ship came into the operations hut saying that the "damn-old" Beechcraft could hardly pull up over the high mountains. He always said that when he came in and swore he would never fly the thing again—but he kept on doing it until the very end.

They all sat down and began to tell their stories. Jones hadn't been able to get into a fight at all—right after he got there, the malaria kicked up on him. His eyes were glassy and yellow. Harvey asked them if it were true that they had a new radio direction-finder in Rangoon, and if adequate warning was given of the approaching Japanese aircraft. Both Jones and Moss said that was a misstatement of fact, as during the last two or three weeks there had not been more than ten minutes' warning given to the A.V.G. before any attack.

Harvey said: "The lack of communications is evidently as bad as ever."

Pete Wright said: "It's pitiful—the R.A.F. had hardly any at all. We were in a bad way 'til we put in our own station."

Jones laughed: "You know? The British officers still take Sundays off, and all of them take time off for tea. They lack organization, starting from the bottom. I don't know what's happened to them. Guess they are waiting for the Australians or the Canadians to come and help."

I interrupted: "Maybe they are under the illusion that God and/or Franklin D. will provide more Americans!"

They all laughed and Harvey said: "Now, Olga, that's enough out of you."

Pete Wright said: "The British are losing a hell of a lot of planes—they have hardly any left.

"Well," said Harvey, "we've learned one thing—that Americans can adapt themselves to anything, or any circumstances. You kids are certaintly proving that."

"You said it," said Moss. "We have taken matters into our own hands. When the damn cooks and coolies left us at Rangoon, we did the cooking ourselves. We went into stores—if there was anybody in, we bought—if it was empty, we took. Guess that comes under the head of looting, but what the hell, we had to eat! Some of the British women still there took some of us in and put us up. They were pretty good sports, but when their cooks took a runout powder they didn't know what to do. They had plenty of stores in their cupboards, but weren't on speaking terms with a frying pan. That's where we pitched in."

At night we received a message from Jack:

COLE KILLED ON RECONNAISSANCE HOP OVER MOULMEIN 1200 TODAY JANUARY 30 STOP FLEW INTO TREES STOP MOULMEIN FIELD OCCUPIED BY GROUND BANDITS THIS MORNING STOP SIMPLE BASIC FLANKING MOVEMENT AND ARMY JUST WATCHED IT HAPPEN STOP JAP POSITION NOT STRONG OR BY ANY MEANS PERMANENT ADVISE STOP END NEWKIRK

Another death! How many more? I was not going to enter this one in my dairy, but on second thought, decided to do so. But it would be the last time. Perhaps, I told myself, if I stopped writing and thinking about these fatalities they might cease.

At three o'clock in the afternoon of January 31st, Colonel

M. S. Wang, Chinese Chief of Staff, presented our pilots with Chinese Air Force wings, with appropriate ceremony. He awarded one to Harvey first, then Squadron Leader Olson, and all the pilots of his squadron. The remaining wings he put away, awaiting the arrival of the pilots in Rangoon.

I liked Colonel Wang very much. I knew him in Hangchow when everybody used to call him "Black Wang" and "Bear Wang." He preferred the latter because he always admired the bear. He thought he looked like one,—short stature, husky, very dark skin and thick black hair.

The boys were very proud of their new wings. One of them put up both, the Chinese below the American—but was told he must wear one or the other, couldn't wear both. Since they were all part of the Chinese Air Force, the Chinese wings were more appropriate.

In January we lost five men: C. D. Mott, missing in action, Thailand; K. Merrit, accident, Mingaladon; Christman, in action, Rangoon; Hoffman, in action, Rangoon; T. J. Cole, in action, Rangoon. FIVE! But we still had hopes for Pilot Mott. The Jap radio reported he was in Tokyo. A broadcast was made supposedly by Mott—but all who heard it said it wasn't his voice.

Two days later, around cocktail hour (ours being between 6 and 8) R. C. Moss came over to ask me about leopard skins and to tell me about his "lovely new teeth" and how Dr. Bruce had fixed them. A little later, Olson, Pete Wright, Jones and the American Consul came in. They all wanted something to drink, so I rang for Tugboat. He rushed in shouting: "Drunks? Drunks?"

"No," I said, "not drunks—drinks, six of them."

The topic of conversation was induction—none of them wanted it. The boys in Rangoon also were against it. Harvey had been fighting it tooth and nail and the Old Man, too, was against it.

The situation in Burma looked bad—nothing could stop the

Japs unless a miracle happened. I went through the pile of papers on my desk and found a letter from Jack Newkirk to the Colonel. The Colonel had given orders to Jack to return to Kunming with his squadron as soon as possible. Jack was doing all he could to delay his departure—evidently liked it there too well. Here is an excerpt from Jack's letter:

We will have to leave all planes behind, that is, as follows: 1,—25 planes can be put in commission. 2,—6 planes need major repairs at Rangoon. 3,—2 planes will be flown to Kunming by us for overhaul. 4,—all other planes are write-offs.

Of the 25 planes mentioned in "1", 17 are now ready and in use. Five are being repaired in Toungoo. There is quite a battle going on at Moulmein and the Japs have two divisions in there. The air work these days consists mostly of offensive bombing and an occasional fighter sweep on our side, and no effective activity by the Japanese. . . .

Even Jack's letters were curt and to the point—like his messages.

A radio dispatch said:

OUR FIGHTERS FAILED TO INTERCEPT ENEMY AS ADE-QUATE WARNING IS AT PRESENT IMPOSSIBLE.

"Adequate warning is at present impossible"—that made me sore. I remembered when we were in Toungoo, about the middle of September, our group repeatedly warned the authorities, civil and military, that their warning nets were insufficient—there weren't enough of them, and those in existance were no good. At that time, we had no communications with the R.A.F. headquarters, except through our station in Kyedaw which had to call up Rangoon on an 1850 model telephone, said service taking all the way from thirty minutes to two hours.

And this in time of war! I remembered too, how on arrival at Toungoo, Harvey requested that a machine-gun butt be constructed so that our guns could be sighted properly. After interviewing the C-in-C of the Far East, the A.O.C., and finally the Governor of Burma, the P.W.D. engineer was finally ordered to construct an embankment—which he finally did three months later. Colonel Chennault repeatedly asked the military and civil authorities to build auxiliary airdromes—but gave up in despair.

The British were bringing in a few replacements of planes to Rangoon by February 2nd,—but not enough. Sometimes these planes got to their destination, and sometimes they didn't. On one occasion, eighteen R.A.F. planes left Calcutta for Mingaladon—all crashed into the mountains in the northern Shan States. Seven pilots bailed out but couldn't be found in that dense jungle. The pilots of these eighteen planes had been given instructions to land in Mingaladon at night—there was no radio beam and no lights. At no time had the R.A.F. in Burma ever co-operated with the A.V.G. in giving us weather reports, arrivals and departures, or other vital information.

When Pilots Bacon and Swartz arrived from Toungoo, Bacon said the Japs had bombed the airdrome twice. On the second raid they completely demolished the operations building, one hangar, and destroyed one Blenheim bomber on the runway. There were three P-40's close by, but these were not damaged. No one was killed or injured. There had been absolutely no warning—most of the personnel were still in bed asleep. Lucky thing they did not hit the barracks.

The two pilots said that in the beginning of the raids on Rangoon, the British usually failed to tell them the Japs were coming. The first thing they knew about it was when they saw the R.A.F. taking off. Mihalko, one of our radio men, got the idea of getting into the radio and telephone office. He would wait around, and when the phone rang, he would jump up and answer it quickly before the British had a chance to get at it. The moment the receiver was picked up, a voice would say, "Enemy planes approaching from the southeast. . . ."

Mihalko then would hand the phone over to one of the operators. Then he would go to the radio that controlled all planes and say: "Go get 'em, cowboys!" The British didn't know what that meant, but our boys did.

Bacon said: "We sure did turn the tables on the R.A.F. Before they used to get off the ground first, but not after 'Mickey' got into that control room. When we got the signal from him, the British didn't know what the hell he was talking about—they don't understand American slang. Well, for that matter, we couldn't understand the Limey's either, that's why they put an American in the control room. 'Mickey' said that many times they got alarms, and instead of telling him about it, they notified their pilots first."

Wyke came into my office to show me a special order. It was a dishonorable discharge for Larry Moore and Ken Sanger. They couldn't take it. Sanger had been nervous ever since he came back from Rangoon with Ole's squadron, and afraid he would be sent back there. Ole told me he couldn't get Sanger to stay on the field or out of the trenches. Sanger then was sent to Lotze—one of the stations of the Net—but remained there only a week. When he returned he told Harvey he had promised Moore's mother he would take good care of him. Harvey talked to the Colonel about it. The Colonel shrugged his shoulders and said that it was a problem, all right, and that it was better to get rid of them. When the two boys put in their resignations, they were gladly accepted, but they got dishonorable discharges just the same. Everyone said: "Good riddance. We don't want that kind of guys here with us."

However, their dishonorable discharges didn't seem to do them any particular harm. They hastened back to the States and sold a few hair-raising stories about their exploits with the ferocious Flying Tigers and then penned a slightly fantastic but still very successful motion picture.

That same day, February 5th, Harvey came home fairly

early with General Denys and his aide, Lieutenant Baird. I liked the General and was glad to see him. Tall, pink cheeks, grey hair—a well preserved man in his late fifties. He brought me a present—a bottle of Scotch. We hashed over what had happened to all of us since we had last met. The General admired my Karenni drum and said I was lucky to have been able to fly it out of Burma.

"Yes," I said, "otherwise the Japs would get it and make shrapnel out of it."

He laughed, "Apparently you think the Japs are going to take all of Burma."

I said I couldn't see who was going to stop them. He was going to Lashio on official business and expected to be back in Kunming in a week or two en route to Chungking.

A message arrived that same evening—Sandy's first:

FIRST SQUADRON UNASSISTED BAGGED SEVEN ENEMY FIGHTERS AND FIVE PROBABLES STOP ONE BULLET HOLE IN ONE WING STOP END SANDELL

The morning of Saturday, February 7th, was warm and sunny. I started to work quite early, right after breakfast. About eight o'clock I thought I heard someone come into my room—someone whose steps were very familiar. I turned around and looked, but no one was there. I thought it rather strange, resumed my work and forgot about it. Sometime later Wyke came in and said there was a telephone message for me from the field. Suddenly, I had a sickening feeling in the pit of my stomach. I asked Wyke, "Do you know what it is about? Did something happen?"

He didn't know. I ran down the hall into the personnel office, picked up the telephone and said, "Hello."

It was Harvey. He said: "We have bad news—from Mingaladon."

I interrupted him: Don't tell me. I know it. It's Sandy. He's dead!"

Harvey said: "What do you mean? Who told you? He is only seriously injured."

I said: "He's dead."

"I hated to have to tell you, Olga."

I said: "Did it happen this morning,—about eight o'clock?"

"Yes," said Harvey. "About eight. I'll send you the message right away. He spun in while testing his plane."

I ran back upstairs. My throat felt tight. I couldn't cry. Wyke was still there.

"What happened?" he asked. "You look terrible—have a cup of coffee."

I took the coffee and asked him to leave. I sat alone in that room—thinking. Sandy was gone. Yet, he wasn't. I looked at the chair where he had sat when he brushed my hair. One of his rugs hung on the wall in front of me. Only the day before I had written him a letter telling him how pretty it looked, hanging on the wall. "You will see, Sandy, when you come back." But Sandy wasn't coming back. He would never see that rug again, not with his mortal eyes.

I went back to work and was still working past lunch time when Ceder came with the messages. He looked at me closely but I couldn't face him. I was afraid I would cry. Ceder knew how much I cared for Sandy. I read the first message:

SANDELL SPUN IN AND KILLED TESTING PLANE WITH REPAIRED TAIL END NEWKIRK

I said aloud: "The plane the Jap flew into when he made his suicide landing. Sandy's plane—Number 11." The Jap accomplished something that time—he took one of our best men.

Ceder didn't say anything. He only stood there looking at me. I read the other message.

SANDELL'S PLANE COMPLETELY DESTROYED STOP ONLY PARTS SALVAGED TAIL WHEEL AND RIGHT WHEEL STOP CRASH 0810 STOP RESULT OF INVERTED STALL AT 2500 FEET

NO MECHANICAL FAILURE NOTED STOP ENEMY FIGHTER
SWEEP HERE THIS AM 37 ARMY I-97 STOP THREE ENEMY
PLANES DESTROYED STOP HEAVY BOMBING LAST NIGHT
END NEWKIRK.

Suddenly, I remembered what Sandy had said: "If anything happens to me, go to my quarters and put away my
belongings. When they make an inventory, you be there, will
you?"

I asked Ceder to take me to the field. On the way over
Ceder said: "Do you remember that day just before Sandy
went away to Mingaladon, when his squadron presented him
with a paper?"

"Yes," I said, "I remember—Sandy was too strict for the
fellows. He tried to keep men and pilots apart. He didn't
believe in their mixing. I remember the time in Toungoo
when he bawled me out for playing games in the alert shack
with pilots and a few of the men. He didn't like it. He was
the only real soldier we had in this outfit—besides the Colonel
and Harvey."

Ceder said: "The pilots of Sandy's squadron decided to
ask for another squadron leader. They wrote out a petition,
and asked all the members of the First Squadron to sign it.
They all did, even those Sandy thought were his friends.
When they all had signed, they took it to Sandy. He read it
without saying a thing. Then, he took out his pen, signed at
the bottom of the list and gave the paper back to them."

"Yes," I said, "that's true. And after he signed he went into
Harvey's office. I was there when he told Harvey about it.
Harvey asked him, 'Well what are you going to do? Lose
your squadron?' 'Yes,' said Sandy, 'if they want it that way.
Maybe they will be better off with someone else as Squadron
Leader,—Bob Neale, for instance—he would make them a
good one.' "

Ceder said: "Funny thing is, when the fellows saw what a
hell of a good sport Sandy was, they tore up the paper. Sandy
never said a word, just kept on as usual."

We met the Adjutant, C. E. Smith, at Sandy's quarters. I went in first. The room was as Sandy had left it, but covered with dust. I walked over to the dressing table and picked up his mother's picture, wrapped it in a piece of paper and laid it back on the table. I did the same thing with the picture of his girl, the girl who thought she was too good for Sandy. If she only knew, I thought.

It took us about two hours to itemize the things and repack them. We found a bottle of whisky—poured ourselves a drink and made a toast to Sandy. Afterwards, we stood there silently, each one with his own thoughts.

"What are you going to do with these things?" I asked Smith.

He said: "The same as we did with the things of the other fellows—Hoffman's, Mott's, Christman's—store them in the attic of the hostel. Guess we will auction off Sandy's phonograph records, maybe some of his clothing, too. No use sending that stuff home."

I said: "Send everything home. I have Sandy's tunic and wings. I will keep them and send them to his mother when I get back to the States. I am sure he would want Little and Neale to have the records. They were roommates."

I went back to the hostel with Smith and worked the rest of the afternoon. After dinner, they held an auction in the auditorium upstairs. They always did after a pilot was killed. I never went to them. It seemed to me as if we were vultures, picking up stuff when the men got killed. I didn't like it at all. I was reading some papers when I heard the shuffling of many feet coming down the stairs—some went on down the hall to the bar or recreation room. Talking, laughing,—there was always fun at these auctions, so they told me. The dead man was forgotten—life went on.

I went outside my door and saw Dr. Gentry. He was carrying a large bundle. "What did you buy, Doctor?" I asked.

He said: All of Sandy's records for sixty-six rupees."

I closed the door and went to bed. Harvey came in with

a telegram for me from Red Probst from Rangoon telling me about Sandy and asking me not to forget to send the message to his friends, the Guibersons of Texas.

Early the next morning I went into town to the telegraph office to send the message. "Allen Guiberson, Dallas, Texas. Sandell killed Rangoon February 7 testing plane after inflicting heavy losses personally upon Japanese." And signed it, Olga Greenlaw.

Back in my office, I found on top of my desk a copy of the message the Colonel sent to Bob Neale:

BOB NEALE MINGALADON STOP TERRIBLE SORRY LEARN SANDY'S DEATH STOP ENTIRE GROUP SENDS DEEPEST SYMPATHY TO FIRST SQUADRON STOP YOU ARE APPOINTED SQUADRON LEADER EFFECTIVE THIS DATE STOP CARRY OUT INSTRUCTIONS ALREADY ISSUED FOR SANDELL STOP RECOMMEND DEPUTY LEADER FOR APPOINTMENT END CHENNAULT.

Later in the day, more messages arrived. One was from Neale:

COLONEL CHENNAULT STOP HAVE APPOINTED GREG BOYINGTON VICE SQUADRON LEADER SUBJECT YOUR APPROVAL END NEALE.

That was good news. Boyington deserved it.

Another, from Jack Newkirk to the Colonel, read:

MOVEMENT OF PACKAGES POSTPONED 24 HOURS DUE SHORTAGE OF PILOTS HERE STOP REQUEST I REMAIN HERE FOR A WHILE STOP ONE PLANE SUFFICIENT FOR PACKAGES FROM RAILHEAD TO X END NEWKIRK.

The "Railhead," of course, meant Lashio. "Packages" meant men, "X" meant Kunming.

Thinking about the messages got my mind away from work. I got up and started to look for Harvey's pipe cleaners. These were expensive items, almost impossible to buy in Kunming. I couldn't find them, so I went to the Colonel's quarters and found a package on top of his desk.

I went back to my office and settled down on the sofa. I took out two pipe cleaners and proceeded to make dogs. It was a habit I had acquired a long time ago. In Hengyang when Harvey was testing planes, I would get nervous. I would take out the pipe cleaners I carried with me and start to make little figures. That's what I did that day,—I made all kinds of dogs—dogs that looked like Lucy, or like Joe, the Colonel's dachshund,—like bulldogs and some that looked like wire-haired terriers. These were the best ones. Then I painted eyes, nose and mouth with black pencil. I placed them on the Karenni drum. One dog had his leg up so I placed him against the vase—it really looked like a real dog near a fire plug—I laughed at myself and thought that I was getting childish.

Chapter VII

WHILE we were in Toungoo we had no difficulty keeping up with the news of the world, as the Rangoon English newspapers arrived daily on the "Up Mail." Of course you had to dig around the inside pages to find the headline stories but they were there if you had the patience to ferret them out. The Kunming press, however, was exclusively Chinese and no help to our boys at all. For quite some time Colonel Chennault had been contemplating the publication of a daily tabloid which would present a digest of what was going on in the world—which at that time was plenty. One effort to do this while we were in Toungoo had fizzled out so the Colonel had suggested that I take a try at it.

Consequently on February 9th, he called me in and said I'd better get busy and start writing and printing a newspaper. I promised to do so the next day. He said: "Bring me the first copy to see how it looks." I asked if it would be all right to run a little column and call it "A.V.G. Gossip." He answered: "Yes, but keep it clean. I just want a plain little paper that will tell the fellows what is going on in the outside world. See to it that a copy is put up on each of the bulletin boards, send me one and distribute one or two in each of the recreation rooms. And don't forget—let me see the first copy."

The next morning, I turned on the radio to KGEI, San Francisco. Then I tuned in on the BBC, and a fine Spanish broadcast from Uruguay. I got Rome and Berlin,—broadcasting in Spanish for the Latin American countries. I thought it would be a good idea to tell the boys what Berlin, London and Tokyo were saying, and then let them figure it out for themselves—this paper was going to be different,—no censorship.

The most important news of the moment would be headlined across the page. Below, in narrow columns, the lesser news. This all would have to be done on the typewriter, as we had very few stencils and a limited amount of mimeograph paper—enough only for the official orders. I headed the paper like this:

"THE AVG NEWS"

POINT "X"   Monday, February 10, 1942

HEADLINE NEWS

Instead of "Headline News," it would be: "SINGAPORE DOOMED," and below that again in large letters: "BRITISH TROOPS HEROICALLY DEFENDING ISLAND." Something like that, I thought, would be fine.

At five o'clock I completed the first issue, took one copy to the Colonel's quarters and sent the rest to the Adjutant's office for distribution. At the end of the third page, I wrote: "WAR OR NO WAR CUPID STILL AT WORK." I didn't mention any names, but everyone would know that I was referring to Red Foster and John Petach.

About noon, Petach and Red had come to see me. Pete hemmed and hawed. Red tried to keep calm and couldn't. They wanted to get married. I told Pete to go and talk to the Old Man. Pete went out, falling all over himself. He was only twenty-two years old, and I could well understand how he would feel facing the Colonel with such a problem. We all knew the Colonel thought they should wait and that time of war was no time for wedding bells.

Red was a bit nervous waiting. She told me she and Pete had been contemplating marriage for some time, but were afraid of the Colonel. I said: "Don't be afraid of him. He understands young people—has eight kids of his own."

Red felt better after that. "Do you think he'll give his consent?" I assured her he would.

It was quite a while before Petach returned, but when he did, he was smiling and one thumb was up. We cheered appropriately.

They left and I got back to work on the paper.

When I took the first copy to the Colonel, he read it slowly, carefully, then he said: "That's fine. You made a mistake here."

"Where?"

"In this paragraph—grammatical error."

"No it isn't," I said.

The Colonel said: "Goddamit, girl, I know what I am talking about. I used to be a professor of English."

I said: "Professor or not, you're wrong." We both started to laugh. He took out a pencil and wrote some sentences. "Now, do you see?," he said.

I said: "No, Sir, but I'll change it to please you."

He looked at me and said: "Don't you ever do that. If you think it is right, and are not convinced it is wrong, then don't change it. Never do a thing until you are absolutely convinced that you are right."

"You said it was wrong."

"Dammit," he said, "never mind that."

After the paper was out, we received a delayed message. The Colonel told me to make copies of it and put it up on the bulletin boards. It was:

TODAY (February 6th) THE FIRST AMERICAN VOLUNTEER GROUP DESTROYED ITS ONE HUNDREDTH JAPANESE AIRCRAFT IN THE DEFENSE OF RANGOON STOP I TAKE THIS OPPORTUNITY OF EXPRESSING TO COLONEL CHENNAULT THEIR COMMANDER SQUADRON LEADERS SANDELL NEWKIRK AND OLSON AND TO THE FIGHTER PILOTS AND MAINTENANCE CREWS THE DEEP ADMIRATION OF THE RAF BURMA FOR THIS REMARKABLE PIECE OF AIR FIGHTING STOP THE AMERICAN VOLUNTEER GROUP BORE THE

BRUNT OF DEFENDING RANGOON FROM UNRESTRICTED
JAPANESE AIR ATTACKS DURING THE PERIOD OF THE
OPENING WEEKS OF THE CAMPAIGN STOP IN DISCHARG-
ING THIS TASK THEY DID THEIR DUTY STOP THE HIGH
COURAGE SKILLFUL FIGHTING AND OFFENSIVE SPIRIT DIS-
PLAYED MARKS THE AMERICAN VOLUNTEER GROUP AS A
FIRST CLASS FIGHTING FORCE AND THEIR EQUIPMENT
SUPERIOR TO THAT OF THE ENEMY STOP WITH SUCH
AMERICAN PILOTS AND SUCH AMERICAN EQUIPMENT
FIGHTING SIDE BY SIDE WITH OUR HURRICANE SQUAD-
RONS I AM CONFIDENT THAT WHAT CAN BE DONE WILL
BE DONE TO DEFEND BURMA FROM THE ENEMY AIR AT-
TACK STOP

It was signed by Air Vice Marshal Stevenson, C.B.E.,
D.S.O., air officer commanding the Royal Air Force, Burma.

One of the boys said: "When a Britisher admits that Americans are good, then we are good,—by damn!"

They all were elated, but not all was going smoothly—
there was trouble amongst the men—petty jealousies, dis-
agreements between pilots and men. The Colonel talked to
Harvey about it. Harvey suggested we have a provost marshal. Most of the trouble seemed to be the way the men were
acting in the city itself—they were getting drunk, acting dis-
orderly, beating up some of the Chinese civilians, insulting
women,—they even tried to break into the Y.W.C.A.! Luckily, the offenders were only a few,—not more than three or
four. All kinds of reports were coming in. The Colonel approved Harvey's suggestion. Harvey talked to me about it
and I said: "How about Ceder? He would make a good one—
he is quiet, sensible, and is well liked by the men." Harvey
thought it was a good idea, so he made Ceder the Provost
Marshal.

We were running short of supplies, such as cigarettes,
chewing gum and liquor, when a convoy arrived from Lashio.
Daffy Davis arrived with it. The first thing he said to me
was: "Have you heard anything from Hongkong? I am

awfully worried about Doreen. What a fool I was not to have sent for her before the trouble started."

The Colonel suggested a Chinese dinner at his quarters to celebrate Daffy's arrival. The Colonel, being very fond of green peppers, had taught his boy how to pickle them. I wondered how in the world he ate them as they were so hot. When I asked him, he said: "I like hot food—like Louisiana food." Harvey bet him that he could make better pickles than the Old Man could, and with that the war between them as to who made better pickled peppers started.

We were all feeling quite gay and happy. The Colonel was very proud of his boys down in Rangoon.

The dinner was about over when Wyke came in to say there was trouble in the men's barracks. Harvey went with him to investigate. When he returned he said:

"I had the men come up to my quarters. There were only six out of the fifteen who were causing the trouble. I told them if they wanted to resign to make out their resignations and give them to me right away—that we were anxious to get rid of people who didn't want to stay, and who couldn't take it. They were all very definite in their statements that they didn't want to resign at this time. Then I picked out individuals and told them their various shortcomings, and why we would be happy to get rid of them, which put a new aspect on the situation. The men were mostly clerks. As you know, they are always talking too much. It all started because I made Ceder Provost Marshal and gave him a raise. They want a raise, too, but I told them that they didn't merit it, yet."

The Colonel laughed: "And who is going to give you and me a raise?"

Harvey said: "I wish I'd thought of that."

"By the way," said the Colonel, "Jack Newkirk finally left Rangoon. He had to go to Calcutta to get the plane to fly over here. Sam Prevo went with him. Now Doc Richards is in Rangoon taking care of the boys."

I said: "Funny about Jack,—he certainly hated to leave Rangoon. He likes fighting too much."

"Yes," said the Colonel, "but it's about time he was leaving there. I want to see what Bob Neale can do—now that he took Sandy's place. I am interested in Boyington, too. I want everybody to have a chance. Neale is a good boy. I think he will do all right. Too bad about Sandy. He was a fine fellow."

In the Burma theatre of war since December 23, 1941, to date, February 12, 1942, the number of enemy planes our group had encountered were: bombers, 464; fighters, 371. At least one third of these had been destroyed by our squadrons, although not all of them had been confirmed. Our losses, so far, were comparatively insignificant.

The Japanese Army was moving closer,—they had occupied Martaban. The British were hurriedly sending inadequate reinforcements.

We were all confused by the increasing number of American officers that were arriving. No one seemed to know who they were, where they were going, or where they had come from. Almost every day some of them dropped by on their way to Chungking. The men of the A.V.G. felt they were intruders and resented their presence. General F. I. Brady and his aide, Captain Box, stayed two days. A little later Colonel Mayer arrived. He was military attaché to China.

We certainly needed help, and since the British couldn't hold up much longer, we hoped for American Army support. There was talk of an American Expeditionary Force coming to Burma to help the British. But, if the British would let the Chinese Army into Burma before it was too late, maybe it wouldn't be necessary for the Americans to step in. All the Chinese needed were supplies and more supplies. Man power? They had millions—what with 18,000 to 20,000 Chinese coming of age every day. The thing was supplies.

I liked Colonel Mayer very much. He, too, was of the opinion that the Chinese should be supplied with guns, ammunition, airplanes, bombs, and all the other innumerable things needed to combat the Jap menace. With the coming of so many American army officers, the boys were certain we would be inducted. That, they didn't want, and for that reason they resented the presence of the American Army officers. I didn't. I thought we needed the moral support of the American Government and liked to see the interest that was being taken in our group.

February 14th was the ending of the Chinese New Year. I didn't see many celebrations, as I had seen a few years back. The streets were quiet and not brightly decorated as in other days. Still, the familiar *"Kung Hsi Fa Tsi"* (wishing you prosperity and fortune) was heard—voices, young and old, were shouting it. The Chinese Government was trying to do away with the Chinese New Year and change it to Spring Festival instead, but the Chinese people didn't take to it, and Spring Festival or not, they continued to celebrate the New Year.

Early in the morning I woke Harvey. He said it wasn't four-thirty yet and wanted to sleep a little longer. I gave him a cup of tea and said, *"Kung Hsi Fa Tsi."*

Harvey said: "What in the hell are you talking about?"

I explained it was something like "Merry Xmas" or "Happy New Year." "Can't be," he said. "Christmas is gone, and so is New Year's. Go back to bed."

That morning Sam Prevo and Jack Newkirk returned. Jack looked thinner than ever. I noticed there were flecks of gray in his dark hair. He said: "What's the matter, Olga, lice?"

"No," I said, "gray hairs."

"Could be," he said, "that was no picnic—but it was a lot of fun."

In the evening Jack and several of the pilots who were going on a ferry mission to Cairo, dropped in.

Shilling came over to me with a glass of beer in his hand.

"Drink a sip of this," he said, "and wish me luck. I'm going, too. Hope that jinx doesn't follow me over there."

I took the glass and had a little drink.

Shilling said: "I'll bring you some perfume."

Newkirk wasn't going with them, but he too, joined in drinking a toast to the success of their ferrying mission.

Early in the morning of February 16th, after drinking my usual three or four cups of coffee, I turned on the radio. A Tokyo broadcast announced Singapore had fallen at five o'clock the day before. That was the headline of my paper. What a blow and what a menace to Burma! It would only be a matter of days before they would overwhelm Rangoon.

The Chinese were still trying to get into Burma. The guerrillas, considered as part of the Chinese Army, were already established all around northern Burma, only waiting for the word from the British to come in. It was rumored that the British didn't want to antagonize the Burmese by bringing in the Chinese—that the Burmese were waiting for the British to give the word—that it was up to the British. No one knew just what was what. There was tension everywhere.

We, in Kunming, felt shut off from the rest of the world. We all had been thinking we were just an obscure group, of which the world knew very little. But evidently news of our activities was getting out. Although the Colonel was against publicity, I noticed how pleased he was when he received clippings of newspapers from Louisiana about himself and the A.V.G. He would hand them over to me and say: "Write that up in your paper—the boys will like it."

I was hard at work one afternoon when I heard a timid knock on my door. That was strange. The gang usually hit that door with a bang, or more often didn't even bother to knock—just walked in. I was curious, and instead of saying, "Come in," I got up and opened the door. A tall, slim, young fellow with a lot of hair and blue eyes, holding a notebook in his hand and a gray overcoat thrown over his arm, stood there, a thin smile on his lips.

He said: "I tried to get into the field to interview the Colonel and Mr. Greenlaw, but those two won't talk. Can you tell me anything? I want a story. My name is Karl Eskelund."

I said: "I have heard of you. Haven't you already been writing stuff about the A.V.G.?"

He smiled: "Yes, some things, but not enough. I represent—well, I work for United Press. Sometimes I free-lance a little. I want to know about Mr. Greenlaw. He is the man who interests me most. I want to tell the people who he is. To me, he is the man who is running this show—that's what a lot of the pilots say, too."

I said: "Colonel Claire L. Chennault is running this show."

"Yes," he said, "I know that, but I mean that Mr. Greenlaw is the Colonel's right hand—the man who carries out the Colonel's orders and instructions, tells the boys what to do. He is the only real Army man in this outfit, isn't he?"

"The only West Point graduate," I told him.

Before leaving, he said: "I'd like an interview about you, too. People back in the States should know about the woman with the Flying Tigers."

We both laughed and I told him that I was of no importance—just a "drop in the bucket!"

A report came from our men in Rangoon that the Governor General of Burma had already evacuated to Maymyo, without notifying civilians who thought he was still there. Maymyo became the capital of Burma. The people of the Baptist Mission in Rangoon had done the wonderful work of evacuating children in a limited number of cars. They were depending on the Government to help them with trucks, but at the last moment, those trucks were commandeered to get liquor and supplies out of Rangoon for the Governor's use in Maymyo. It was incredible, but that was the way things were down there.

Everybody was happy because the boys down in Rangoon were doing great work. They were all saying: "If we only had more planes, those Japs wouldn't get to first base." The Colonel thought that the score of the A.V.G., so far, was a blazing record in the history of aerial warfare. "No one can equal us," he said. We weren't being modest about it then. We had the record to back us up.

The tactics indoctrinated by the Colonel into those pilots were certainly showing results. The pilots were great—and so were the ground crews, who made such success possible. One of them, Harry Fox, had been down in Rangoon since Jack Newkirk's squadron took over from Olson. He should have come back, but he was such a valuable man and so willing he was allowed to stay in Rangoon.

And these ground crews really took it on the chin. They had been bombed, strafed, and scared out of their wits, but they still carried on—working day and night to keep those planes flying. There were many others like Fox, such as Frank Jacobson, Harrington, Carter, Overly, Mihalko—in fact, nearly all of them.

Jack Newkirk was sent back to Rangoon with a special message, but he returned soon. He was awfully tired when he came into my quarters and wanted to lie on Harvey's bed. I told him he was welcome, and asked what was wrong with his own quarters. He laughed and ran his fingers through his hair. "That damn place of mine is filthy, and the guys there are too noisy."

I took him into the bedroom, and showed him where the shaving stuff was, gave him one of Harvey's clean shirts, and told Tugboat to bring some hot water. I went back to my work. An hour later Jack emerged. I was glad because I wanted to talk to him and hear more about Rangoon. He sat in the most comfortable chair and stretched out his long, thin legs, spread out his arms and leaned his head on the back of the chair.

"In a way," he said, "I am glad to get back here. What a

hot spot Rangoon is—but all the fun is there. Now, our task is mainly defending the city, although we have been carrying out some strafing missions on the Sittang front. The odds are so great. I don't see how we do it—guess we are just plain lucky."

I asked: "How far away are the Japs?"

"Pretty close. Their bases are now only about half an hour from Rangoon. Doubt if we can hold out much longer."

I asked: "Why did the R.A.F. move up while we stayed behind?"

Jack grinned. "Somebody had to cover their retreat."

"Did you get into any fights this time?"

Jack said: "I went on one strafing mission—Sittang canal. The Japs were crossing their columns on small rubber boats. They are clever fellows, those. We flew low and machine-gunned them. Some of them fell over-board, scattered like rats and began to swim toward shore. We made several passes until we ran out of ammunition. If we only had more planes! We could have held them up for a while, at least, until the armies get organized."

He stopped talking, and I sat there silent, not daring to disturb him. I tiptoed across the room and looked down on his face. He was asleep. I watched him for a while, noticing how his mouth twitched, and his lids fluttered; his nostrils were distended, like an old war horse's. Tired Jack—even in his sleep he was restless, his nerves taut as an E-string. Suddently, he sat up straight in the chair.

"What was that?" he exclaimed.

"The six o'clock whistle from the girl's school," I said.

"Oh," he said, relaxing. "I thought it was an air raid alarm. When I woke up I expected to see my plane right there beside me. Funny how a fellow gets used to things. . . ."

By the end of February the field at Mingaladon was a mass of bomb craters. Supplies were running short. The R.A.F. had moved up to Magwe. Our own A.V.G. was so badly in need of repairs and replacements that it was too difficult to operate from that point. They too, moved to Magwe. By the first of March the whole First Squadron was there,—waiting to be replaced by the Third, which was well rested and fresh. A.V.G. was still defending Rangoon, but it was only a matter of a few days before its fall was expected.

The Japs had crossed the Sittang and were near Pegu. The Chinese armies were still in the north on the Burma-Yunnan border and along the northern Shan States, waiting for the word to move southward. Our men had completely evacuated Toungoo. Kyedaw airdrome could no longer be used as a repair base. It was a constant Jap target. The Japs had ceased bombing Rangoon. The only work out pilots were doing was strafing the advancing Jap columns around the Bilin and Sittang rivers. A number of British troops had been cut off in that district.

Chapter VIII

CERTAINLY one of the most interesting and important women in the world today is Madame Chiang Kai Shek. Luckily for me, Harvey's years of participation in Chinese aviation gave me several opportunities, which few American women have had, of observing her at close range and through personal contact. Even more significant and revealing were the opinions of her which were freely expressed by my many intimate Chinese women friends.

It seems to me that this remarkable woman's ultimate place in history is going to depend not on how far she has been able to sway this statesman or that government to China's eventual advantage, or even the tremendous help and inspiration she has been to the Generalissimo, but rather on the quality and quantity of her permanent influence on the more than two hundred million women of all classes of her native land. Chinese women are powerful and important. Regardless of certain ancient customs which may seem to place them in the background, the women run the family—and the family is the backbone of Chinese life.

All of us at Kunming were thrilled and excited to learn on the morning of February 28th that we were to be the guests of honor at a dinner to be given that same evening by the Generalissimo and Madame. They had arrived the previous night in a C.N.A.C. plane from a lengthy visit to India where they had conferred with the ranking Indian leaders. According to the Chunking radio, the Generalissimo had expressed himself in favor of India's political freedom and had urged the Indian people to stand and rally with the democracies against the totalitarian aggressors. Madame, as usual, had charmed everyone with whom she had come in contact.

We knew in a vague way when the Generalissimo, almost always accompanied by the Madame, would be passing through —but we never knew the exact hour or day and sometimes not even the exact week. With the Japanese in control of the skies—or at least they had been until the advent of the A.V.G. —complete secrecy as to their whereabouts was essential to their safety. The C.N.A.C. pilots who had flown them thousands of miles on countless trips to all parts of China told me that never until they were safely aboard and the plane was airborne was the pilot told where he was going. The Japs would have given Tojo's neck to know exactly where China's foremost citizens could be reached by high explosives at any hour. Even as it was, they miraculously escaped severe bombings on numerous occasions, some of which were plainly the result of accurate espionage and lightning communication.

The boys of the Second and Third Squadrons—which were at Kunming while the First was watching the final death throes of Rangoon—suddenly got quite steamed up over the affair. They were properly impressed with the high tribute which was being paid the Group by the two great leaders of the Chinese nation. All during the day they drifted into my quarters by twos and threes to ask questions, particularly about the Madame. What sort of a woman was she? What did she look like? Just where did she fit into the A.V.G. picture? And what else did I know? "Come, Olga, give us the low-down!"

First, I explained that we, and the English-speaking Chinese, always spoke of the First Lady of China as "Madame," using the French pronunciation. The word was used as a title, as one would speaking of a queen. Then, I told them as best I could of the part Madame had played in the development of the Chinese Air Force and recalled, as I did so, the first time I had met her.

That had been on a blustering winter day in 1933, at the training field at Shien Chiao, just outside of Hangchow, in Chekiang Province. The occasion was the graduation exercises of the first class of Chinese pilots to complete their training under the newly established American mission headed by Colonel John H. Jouett. This was, incidentally, four years before Claire L. Chennault emerged from retirement on his farm at Water Proof, Louisiana, and went out to China to fulfill his destiny as one of the great modern strategists of the air.

Harvey was one of the original instructors with the Jouett mission and several of the graduates of that first class had been his personal students—but he had a rather dismal time that day on account of a pair of luscious black eyes—which he lamely attempted to explain had been given to him by his darling young bride when he too suddenly aroused her from a nightmare—which was exactly what had happened. Even if no one did believe it.

The Chinese fledglings were preening their wings in spectacular formations and maneuvers, flying in what were at best a lot of obsolete second-rate American, British and Italian planes. Madame watched them from a small raised platform at the edge of the field, her sharp black eyes taking in everything. Although I stood next to her on her right I can't for the life of me remember whether this was before she abandoned hats—which, to the permanent enhancement of her beauty, she did about that time.

For a long time Madame watched, silently and intently. Suddenly she turned to me and said:

"That is what China needs—what China must have! Thousands more like these boys—and thousands of airplanes for them to fly and to fight with!"

Perhaps those weren't her exact words but that was their meaning. What was going on inside her head I could only guess. Madame's outward expressions do not always mirror the processes of her mind. It would be interesting to believe that at that particular moment China's ghastly suffering and humiliation from aerial inferiority were being revealed to her through some power of mystic Oriental prophecy. But I am sure Madame was only speaking as a practical visionary. The Japs were already ravaging Manchuria; their aggressions against China had begun. It took no celestial seeress to foretell the unhappy fate of a China unable to defend itself against aerial attack.

While I was conscious of the compelling force of this attractive woman's personality I don't remember being otherwise particularly impressed, although I appraised her as an intense and intelligent woman, passionately patriotic and entirely sincere.

Two years later, in 1935, I met her again at the same place and under almost identical circumstances—another performance by another graduating class of pilots. She remembered me immediately and we chatted some more about flying. It was not a particularly happy graduation. The Jouett mission had completed its contract and was returning to the States—and China's aerial fortunes were to be badly kicked around for the next year or two.

Not having seen Madame since that time I naturally wondered how she had changed—and was understandably curious to learn if she would remember me and our earlier meetings at Hangchow.

As to her connection with the Flying Tigers, which the boys wanted to know about, I could only give them my version of the situation, which was this:

Several persons have been given, or have attempted to take, credit for the origin of the idea of a voluntary force of American pilots fighting under the Chinese flag—to which credit I personally do not think any of them are entitled. It is my belief that the American Volunteer Group was first conceived in the mind of one person and one only—Madame Chiang Kai Shek. China was desperately in need of help from a lethargic and partially isolationist United States—and had no hopes of getting any from Great Britain. Something had to be done to make the people of the United States and their representatives in Washington, China-conscious. The First Lady of China is extremely astute and foresighted—and essentially dramatic. How better to arouse America than through the exploits of a colorful American Volunteer Air Force—fine, clean-cut young men who would be ready to give their lives, as some of them assuredly would, for a free China and for the cause of Democracy everywhere? Maybe somebody else figured that one out but until I see proof to the contrary, my vote goes to Madame Chiang Kai Shek.

I didn't forget to remind the boys that, although only a few of them knew of it as many had been at Rangoon when it happened, the Madame had already graced the Number Two Hostel's mess with her presence—to her own amusement and the considerable embarrassment of two of the pilots. What had happened was this:

Late one afternoon three weeks before, she and the General-issimo had landed at Kunming en route from Chungking to India. Just about that time Ed Leibolt, a ruddy-faced young-ster from the Army, and "Mickey" Michelson, an ex-Navy lad, were cruising idly across the airdrome in a station wagon when they spied what they immediately and jointly realized was the answer to every lonesome Flying Tiger's dream—a beautiful Chinese girl. Not only was this one beautiful but she was unattached, alone and appeared to have nothing of importance on her mind.

Attractive girls were difficult if not impossible for the A.V.G. boys to catch in Kunming. There just weren't any— not an eligible American or European girl in the town or the Province—and the better class of Chinese lassies were not only wary but conventions forebode easy association with the American lads. For example, they still adhered to the custom of dating the American boys with the proviso that their Chi-nese boy friend would trail along—and to a man the A.V.G. still held to the old-fashioned belief that three is a crowd. So under the circumstances the boys divided their time between searching the skies for Jap planes and searching the ground for possible girl friends.

Ed and Mickey shoved the station wagon into a full power dive and rushed at their beautiful discovery. I would like to be able to quote the dialogue verbatim, but unfortunately Ed Leibolt returned to the Rangoon battle a few days thereafter and was reported missing after a dog-fight over Moulmein.

Ed said maybe they'd better match for her and Mickey said it might be a good idea if they first found out if she'd even speak to them. Ed suggested they invite her to tea—she certainly couldn't take offense if they asked her up to the mess to tea. So they eased alongside her and Ed bowed politely and saluted and asked: "Going our way?" Mickey said: "Can we take you up to the mess for a spot of tea?"

She staggered them by accepting their invitation in flawless English and then suggested perhaps she'd better tell her husband where she was going but the boys said never mind him— he'd be there when she got back and where did she learn to speak American like that? She said she had gone to college in the States—a long time ago—and they told her not to give them that "long time ago" stuff—she wasn't as old as all that. In fact, she was just about the prettiest thing they'd seen since they left San Francisco—

It went on like that all the way to the hostel and even for a moment or two after they entered the mess. And then came the denouement. Ed Leibolt even blushed when he told me about it.

After the boys had cleared out, Mrs. Huang dropped in. She, too was eagerly looking forward to seeing the Madame. Although Mrs. Huang was the active leader of the women in Kunming and carried out the Madame's wishes and plans it was not very often she saw her. To Mrs. Huang, and I think, every woman I knew in China, Madame Chiang Kai Shek was a symbol of all that was fine and courageous, unselfish, gifted. The women had rallied to her personal support and to the support of her many humanitarian projects such as Red Cross work; preparing medical kits and bandages for the soldiers; and operating canteens where thousands of poor, ragged, hungry women and children from occupied China were cared for and fed. They collected truly impressive sums of money for War Orphans, which is the Madame's favorite charity. They espoused the cause of wider and better education—the reduction of illiteracy. They were gradually learning to look toward the future—toward China's reconstruction and rennaissance. To accomplish a number of their worthy purposes many of them made great sacrifices. And in all of these movements, Madame was, and is, the inspirational leader. Wherever she leads, the women of China are willing and eager to follow.

As far as I was able to discover, the secret of Madame's success with her own countrywomen is that she, like the Generalissimo, practices what she preaches. I recall distinctly that back in 1933 several Chinese women who were my good friends and neighbors in Hangchow, were more or less indifferent to the dainty little woman who had been rather widely known as Mei-ling Soong but was now wife to the man who was apparently—but not yet certainly—rising to the position of indisputable Chinese leadership. The possibility that she might powerfully influence their individual lives seemed extremely remote at that time. But soon she did begin to exert an influence over them—slowly at first and then at a quickly increasing pace.

Madame's appeal was, I think, by example. She captured the Chinese feminine imagination because she did worthy, beneficial, compassionate and always practical things for China— for the poor, the homeless, the sick and wounded—and for thousands and thousands of helpless children orphaned by the Japanese aggressions. She was at all times sincerely concerned with the needs of her people. The Japs would devastate a district—Madame would appear almost instantly, as an angel of mercy—and with practical, hard-hitting plans for relief. She raised money. She arranged reconstruction. She brought comfort, solace and order—she gave unsparingly of her own physical strength and her moral faith in the future of Free China—and of freedom everywhere. She lived simply and modestly and remained calm and unafraid in the face of repeated danger.

Madame doesn't sit around and talk about things—she goes out herself and does them—and hundreds of thousands of other Chinese women, inspired by her example, are going out and doing things, too.

There was rushing and hustling going on all day. We were not having our meals at the regular mess rooms as the house boys and coolies were busy preparing for that night's great function. The front of our hostel was decorated with potted plants, borrowed from everyone's house in Kunming. American flags and Chinese were flying gayly. The walls of the hall downstairs were covered with silk embroidered banners.

Coolies were carrying chairs and tables, curtains, banners, and hundreds of yards of narrow strips of colored crepe paper upstairs to the auditorium. I went up and found Colonel Huang supervising. He smiled as he told me he was building a small stage at the end of the room to be used for a Chinese play, adding that the actors were all children and he hoped the boys would enjoy it. I was sure they wouldn't, but didn't say so. He then went on to explain the seating arrangement. The large table was for the Generalissimo and his staff. Leading from it were six rows of tables, at the heads of which would sit the Squadron Leaders and the Vice Squadron Leaders.

I went back to my quarters struggling with my eternal problem—what to wear. I wanted to look my best for Madame and because several Chinese ladies were to attend. I settled on the old white dinner dress. It was the best I had. I knew Harvey would be too busy to escort me so I decided on Colonel George, who had just returned from Chungking, and sent him a note.

When Harvey arrived, I was already dressed—but as usual, he didn't even notice it. He was in a hurry to get himself cleaned and dressed. He wore, like the Colonel and the rest of the pilots, the uniform of our American Air Corps, but with brass Chinese buttons with the Chinese twelve-prong star. Above the left breast pocket rested the Chinese wings. On the shoulder straps I sewed two wide blue stripes and a gold one in the center, the insignia of the Chief of Staff. The Colonel's was the same, only bright red instead of the gold. The Squadron Leaders wore narrower blue and gold stripes. Sewing insignia on uniforms was one of my little jobs.

I had just finished helping Harvey dress when Colonel Chennault appeared. "Better look me over—do I look all right?" He stood in front of my large mirror. I straightened his tie, pulled his coat, smoothed it out until there wasn't a wrinkle left, and told him he looked as if he had just stepped out of *Esquire* and that regardless of age, he had the best figure for a uniform of any man in the outfit. He smiled, winked happily at Harvey and left the room abruptly. The Colonel was very proud of his figure, almost vain about it, and many times reminded us that he exercised constantly to keep in shape, which he certainly did.

Practically every pilot ran into my office for a last look in the mirror, all were acting like young, bashful bridegrooms waiting for the bride. They too, wanted to look their best for the Madame.

I was about to leave when Colonel Huang rushed in. He said: "May I borrow some of your pretty pillows? I would like to place them on the chairs that the Generalissimo and the Madame are going to use." Some Chinese ladies arrived and Colonel Huang took them upstairs to show them their places.

After they left, I studied myself in the mirror. "Too white," I thought. Remembering I had a large, bright red chiffon scarf I began a search for it. Yes, that was it. The red looked well against the white dress. I joined Colonel George in the recreation room. He was a dark man, not very tall but carried himself well. He made a little mock curtsy and said: "Your escort, Madam. A pleasure."

The room was crowded and the boys restless. The bar was closed and the phonograph machine silent for a change—the A.V.G. was on its good behavior. The Adjutant came in and boomed, "Everybody upstairs and find your places!"

We filed out in orderly fashion, which was indeed surprising. Upstairs, we began to search for our place cards. I couldn't find mine anywhere. "No," I thought, "it can't be—" but Colonel George said: "Here you are, Olga, at the Generalissimo's table, and I am next to you on your left."

We all sat down. The babble of voices increased, then suddenly hushed as the doors were opened wide by two of our men, smartly dressed in brand-new uniforms. Jack Newkirk strode in with lugubrious Jim Howard on his left and Arvid Olson on his right. He called the room to attention. We all stood up. The Generalissimo and Madame Chiang Kai Shek entered, followed by Colonel Chennault, Harvey, Colonel Huang, Hollington Tong and several Chinese Generals and officials, and took their places at the table, the Generalissimo in the center, and on his right, Madame. Next to Madame was Colonel Chennault, then Harvey and Dr. Gentry. On the Generalissimo's left was Hollington Tong; then Colonel Huang and General Chow, whom I had known in Hangchow; two other generals, and the Minister of Education. I sat at his left.

Jack Newkirk, Olson and Howard, took their places at the head of the tables directly in front of the Generalissimo and the Madame. I looked around the room and noticed that two places were empty and hoped that the missing boys were not getting into any mischief. That a party of this importance could go off without a hitch was a bit too much to hope for.

We went on with our dinner—everything was quiet, but the boys' eyes were on the Madame. They watched every move she made. With dessert, Colonel Huang briefly introduced Colonel Chennault. The Colonel bowed to our illustrious hosts and then to the rest. He made a short speech mostly about contribution of money by us, the A.V.G., to carry on relief work in China, another one of Madame's "babies" and one in which I had played a small part.

I had a notebook and pencil with me as I knew there would be speeches and wanted to quote them in my newspaper. I took notes on the Colonel's remarks. When he finished, there was applause which immediately died down as the Madame stood, stretching her small figure to full length. She wore the conventional Chinese dress: the color was green, the material a very fine silk, and the buttons of the finest jade. She wore a jade bracelet on each arm and a jade ring on each third finger. Her hair was combed straight back, exposing the tips of her ears, which were also adorned with jade. I noticed that her eyes were heavily made up—a dark black line drawn under the lower lashes and extending beyond the eye itself. She used powder but no rouge, and her lips were rosy enough.

A great silence reigned—Madame threw back her head slightly and narrowed her eyes. She spoke:

"Colonel Chennault, Members of the A.V.G., and other friends: As your honorary commander, may I call you 'my boys'?" She spoke at great length of the life and death struggle of China. "And now, you have come here to vindicate us. We have always resolved to fight until final victory is ours; but we lacked the air arm which you are now providing. For this reason, I wish to thank you."

She nodded in the direction of Jim Cross and J. W. Farrel, who had been wounded in a fight over Rangoon and had been in the hospital in Yenangyaung, the oil field. They had arrived that same day for treatment at our hospital. Referring to them she said:

"They who have braved death in the air, forgot themselves because they knew that although they might have to pay the final sacrifice their comrades will carry on the great work which the A.V.G. has set for itself. This spirit, I feel, is the secret of the A.V.G. successes.

"I was asked a little while ago by one of my officers: 'Madame, some of the A.V.G. pilots are shooting down so many planes that we won't have room enough on the wings for all the stars which they merit. What shall we do about it?' I told him, 'We will have to provide an additional pair of wings.' And this is what we will have to do if you all keep up the score." Her last words drowned in cheers, applause and more cheers.

She spoke to us of discipline—"Without discipline, we can accomplish nothing, and I, as your honorary commanding officer, am going to din more discipline at you. I will go further than our Colonel Chennault. I mean discipline of your inner selves. . . . However, I am not going to make you little plaster saints, [laughter] and I'm quite human enough to like interesting people. But I do want you boys to remember one thing, the whole Chinese Nation has taken you to their hearts, and I want you to conduct yourselves worthily of the great traditions you have built up for yourselves. I want you to leave a true impress on my people of what Americans really are. Perhaps I should tell you, 'Boys, you are just grand. You are little angels, with or without wings' . . . [here everybody cheered—even the generals who understood little English were smiling.]

"You are my boys. I can speak to you freely. And I know that you will understand when I say that I hope every one of you, whether in the air, or on the ground, will remember that you are China's guests, and that everything you do will have repercussions upon the country which I love next best to my own—America!"

There was the nub—"Repercussions on America!"

There were more cheers, and at that point, the Assistant Adjutant quietly left the table. I wondered what was going on outside, thinking of the two missing boys. Madame continued:

"Now for just one final word. War is not only a matter of

equipment, artillery, ground troops, or air force. It's largely a matter of spirit—of morale. When I came into this room—I consider myself a very sensitive person—I felt tingling in the air—how very keyed up you are. Now that you have been fighting for a few months, you are all full of enthusiasm and pep. That is a great thing, but the greater thing is to gather momentum as each day goes by, and not let yourselves be discouraged, no matter what happens. As you soar into the skies, you are writing in letters of flame on the horizon, certain eternal truths for the whole world to see. First, the indomitable courage of the Chinese people. Second the indestructible spirit of the Chinese Army, and third, the deathless soul of the Chinese Nation. . . ."

There was an interruption. The Assistant Adjutant reappeared, went to Harvey and whispered something in his ear. Harvey rose and left the room. I wondered what had happened—I was worried thinking about the Japs and what a wonderful coup it would be for them if they dropped a single solitary bomb on the hostel.

"I would like all of you to get up and drink a toast to the two great sister nations on both sides of the Pacific. These two sisters have now a bond of friendship and sympathy which serves us well in the crucible of war, and which will serve us equally well when victory is ours."

Everyone stood, raised his glass, and drank. The glasses contained cold water. There was silence again. Everyone was seated but the Generalissimo remained standing. He spoke, and Hollington Tong translated sentence by sentence. His speech was short and to the point. He stressed the necessity of defeating Japan before Japan went on further with her conquests and rooted herself in the conquered lands. He spoke of the sacrifices that China had made trying to stop the advancing Japanese armies at the time when China was alone and getting help from no one—at the time when other countries wouldn't listen to China's pleas. He said that his gratitude to the American

Generalissimo and Madame Chiang Kai Shek.

(*Acme Photo*)

Chinese girl fighter — propaganda poster.

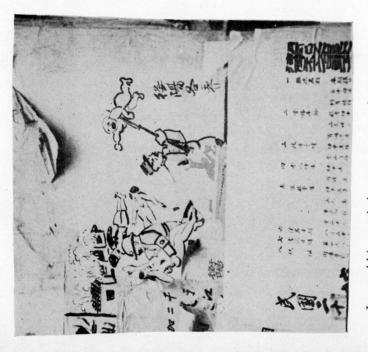

Jap stabbing a baby — propaganda poster.

Volunteer Group was infinite. He said this with such sincerity, with so much fervour, that my eyes filled with tears.

His dynamic personality commanded the attention of everyone. Madame listened intently to every word he uttered—looking at him with great pride, and in complete accord with what he was saying. His serene face suddenly changed—a smile played about his lips. He spoke again: "I am very pleased to present you boys with the five hundred dollar bonus for every plane shot down from the air. But, I shall be pleased also to give you a bonus for each plane destroyed on the ground as well." He sat down still smiling, while the crowd cheered.

Two of the Chinese ladies got up and went to the little stage. They played and sang three numbers. As luck would have it, the two missing pilots arrived. They were both high as kites and made a lot of noise trying to locate their seats. Fortunately, their seats were on the outside of the table near the door. They fell all over themselves as they fumbled with the chairs. I looked at the Madame and noticed that she barely glanced in their direction, only for a moment. Our bad boys began to applaud heartily, interrupting the singer. I was so upset about it, I was tearing my red scarf under the table.

The singing over, Colonel Huang explained to us the meaning of the play before it began. No one understood it very well. The boys wanted to smoke, but didn't know whether they should or should not. One of them took out a package of cigarettes and put it back in his pocket. Nothing escaped the Madame—she noticed it. She turned to Colonel Chennault and graciously asked him for a cigarette. As if it were a signal, everyone began to smoke.

During the intermission I glanced at the Madame thinking of the time I had last seen her and wondered if I would have an opportunity of speaking with her. Just then Colonel Huang left his seat and came toward me. He said: "Madame Chiang would like to speak with you."

I immediately rose and followed the Colonel. The Generalissimo had moved to Colonel Huang's seat. On close inspection I noticed how beautiful Madame looked, how the seven years that had elapsed had not changed her any, although she had been through some very trying experiences. Like every beautiful woman, she had a certain amount of vanity—no matter where she was, whether it was a remote village or in a soldier's camp, she was always well-groomed and beautifully dressed. She always wore the Chinese dress, but used exclusively foreign shoes—American preferred. Her fur coats, too, came from America.

She said: "Sit down, Mrs. Greenlaw. I am glad to see you again."

I sat down beside her and answered: "You do remember me? It has been a long time since we met."

"Yes," she said, "a long time—Hangchow. But I have a good memory. You were very young then, but time has treated you kindly. You look the same. And I?"

I answered: "You don't look a day older—a little thinner perhaps. I could almost say I had seen you yesterday. . . ."

"Thinner? And I think I am a little heavier . . . I wish to thank you for the work you have done collecting funds for my War Orphans during Christmas week. I hear that you are working hard on the *Diary*, and also that you take care of the newspaper. That is fine. We all work hard—we have a tedious road before us."

At that moment she looked tired. I would like to have stayed longer talking with that woman—the greatest woman in the world. But, I knew that everyone wanted to meet her and I felt I was keeping them away from her. I thanked her for inviting me to chat with her, and said that I was very pleased and happy to have seen her again. When I left my seat, the Generalissimo rose. He smiled as he extended his hand which I took and gently pressed.

Suddenly—the rumble of motors overhead—plane or planes? The Generalissimo and the generals and Madame exchanged glances. I listened carefully and distinguished the sound of more than one motor. Then I remembered that the C.N.A.C. plane was due in about that time. My fears calmed, I smiled to myself.

The Minister of Education said to me: *"Qu'est que c'est, Madame?"* I answered: *"C'est l'avion C.N.A.C., Monsieur."* He and I had been speaking in French. We had tried English but decided that his English was worse than my French—we settled it by speaking French. Word soon spread that it was only a C.N.A.C. plane and there was a sigh of relief in the room.

At that moment I thought of the hundreds of armed guards that had been posted outside the building, outside the compound and guarding all the entrances. For, although the Generalissimo is the acknowledged leader of the Chinese people, it is a well-known fact that he has many enemies, and there are many traitors amongst them who wouldn't hesitate to fire one fatal shot. I felt my blood run cold as I thought about it.

The play continued until almost midnight. The visitors left first, and after that there was a scramble—all headed for the recreation rooms.

The next morning I wasn't able to do much work because of the many interruptions. A lot of noise was going on outside my quarters. I found out that Colonel Chennault and Colonel Wang were entertaining the Generalissimo and Madame at a private luncheon party.

About two o'clock Colonel Huang came in. He seemed a little breathless as he said: "Mrs. Greenlaw, have you a copy of the Madame's speech? One of the clerks typed it out without corrections and put it on the bulletin board downstairs. When the Madame came in to attend the luncheon party, she saw it there and was rather annoyed. Will you make a copy right away and correct it?"

He took out of his pocket the guilty paper and handed it to me. "This is it," he said. "You can use your notes and this one and rewrite it. When you have finished, will you send it to my office?"

I glanced through the paper and said that it was just what she had said and asked him what was wrong with it. He said: "Madame says that it doesn't look like the speech she had prepared."

Alone, I read it over carefully and although the contents of the speech were correct, I realized why Madame had been displeased. Instead of flowing smoothly as she had delivered it, the transcript was full of repetitions, disjoined sentences, and too many "my mind's eyes."

Madame usually prepared all her speeches, going over them carefully, correcting them—then she memorized them. I recalled how now and then she had paused in her speech, like someone who is choosing the right word to fit in at the moment, her eyes half closed, face lifted. Very seldom does she use notes. She knows exactly what she is going to say, as the words she had written came from her soul—pure, strong, truthful words.

Three days after the dinner, the Generalissimo and Colonel Chennault left for Lashio. They were going to meet General Wavell and Marshall Foo of the Chinese Army that was entering Burma. General Stilwell was also to be there, I was told.

An American Army transport, a DC-3, flew in from India bringing Generals Sibert, Hearn and McGruder. There were also some colonels; Colonel Bill Wyman, who had been a classmate of Harvey's at the Point, and another whose name I didn't understand so didn't write it in my *Diary*. He had a "horsy" face and I figured he was a cavalry man. When he was introduced to me I asked him if he were one, and he said "yes." In addition there were fourteen other officers, from lieutenants to majors, all part of General Stilwell's staff.

I was out of my office early in the morning to have breakfast with the two colonels and General McGruder. I met General Stilwell for the first time—he was having breakfast with Colonel Chennault who brought him over to our table and introduced him. I liked Stilwell's looks instantly—a middle-age, quiet looking man of the farmer type, but a splendid soldier.

About noon a note came from supply office, saying they had received a phonograph and recording machine from Calcutta for the Chief of Staff. I went down to look at it. It was one of those "Chicago" machines. I sent it up to our quarters and tried to set it up. Not understanding the mechanism, I put it away until Harvey returned from the field. The bill staggered me—1,400 Rupees. There were twenty blank records, and only one small needle for them. I wondered what Harvey wanted the thing for. I had a good radio and whenever we wanted to play records, the boys brought along their phonographs.

R. C. Moss heard about the machine and came to look at it. He sat down and talked for a while. He said he liked a little privacy and had been looking for a place to rent. When I asked him how he had fared, he said:

"I finally found a swell place out of town while I was walking about this morning. It's right off the railroad tracks at the foot of the hills where the graveyards are. There is only one gatekeeper at the gate of the place which is enclosed by a high, white-washed wall. There are two brick rooms. One of them is used by the caretaker, the other one is empty. I made him a deal and said that I could use the empty one. I was thinking of taking over a mat for the floor. It would be a fine place to spend the afternoon, people could squat on the mat and play poker, for instance. Or shoot craps. It is a nice clean place, very quiet. Would you like to come over with me and look it over?"

He sounded so innocent-like and wistful. I began to laugh. "Moss," I said, "the place sounds great. But, you don't happen to be referring to the British cemetery, are you? It's a swell place, as you say. I don't know about your friends—they might like it there. But I wouldn't go in on a bet. Can't you just picture those suave British ghosts objecting? Why, they would come out of their graves and haunt you! Do you know what that empty room is?"

He said: "No, just an empty room, I guess."

I said: "Wrong. I'll tell you what it is. When someone dies, after the body has been embalmed, they take it to the cemetery; since there are no funeral parlors here, they place the body in that empty room. In China it is known as the 'Death chamber,' and the body lies in state there for three days. Then it is buried."

"Gosh," he said, "I didn't know that. . . ."

"Or, maybe you did," I said. "You are just a plain rascal, Mr. Moss. Get out, I am busy."

By March 5th part of the First Squadron had returned and most of the Third had taken over at Magwe. Some of the crew men still remained in Rangoon loading trucks with a few supplies that had been left there. After resting a bit, Bob Little come to see me. First thing he did was to give me orders—he wanted good, fresh coffee right away. The boys took it for granted that I was there to serve them, regardless of what work I might have—I was supposed to drop everything and attend to their whims.

"Go on," I said to Bob, "start talking. I have been waiting for you to give me the correct story."

He said: "Nothing to report."

"What do you mean, 'nothing to report?' Surely there must be a lot happening down there. Let me hear about it."

"About the Japs, you mean?" He smiled. "All right, General. First, I will tell you what I think about them. The Japanese tactics in Burma are very clever. They travel only at night, and I mean travel, not crawl. Their armies move about thirty miles a day. They attack usually at dawn. They have a clever system of making a hell of a lot of noise in one place to attract attention, while they attack at one spot where the main force is secretly moving."

"What about the British troops, what happened to them?"

"The number of foreign troops down there is discouragingly small, so the Japs carry out their blitz practically unhampered."

"And the wounded? British and Indian troops, I mean?"

"You know, it is a strange thing. I haven't seen any wounded British soldiers. I don't think there are any of them. If there are, we never saw them, and I happened to be in several of the towns near the front. About the only resistance the Japs are encountering is the A.V.G. When I left Magwe, the Japs were already in the outskirts of Rangoon. But when they get there, they won't find much. Rangoon was a flaming mess when I saw it last, about three days ago when I flew over it on a mission. Some of the evacuees that I met near Magwe said that when they left, over half of the city was destroyed. Nothing left but looters and rotting corpses."

"Did you see any of my friends—the Robins?"

"No," he said, "I didn't see any of your friends. I guess I wasn't looking for them. Besides, they all seemed to look alike —haggard, tired, hungry, and scared to death. The center of evacuation seems to be Magwe. I guess you heard that the R.A.F. is using the Blenheims for evacuating the British civilians—the A.O.C. of Burma, Air Vice Marshal Stevenson, was directing the show. Civilians that have cars and gas are trying to get to Lashio. They think they will have a better chance of getting a ride to India in one of the C.N.A.C. transports."

"How did the Burmese people feel toward the A.V.G.?"

"They felt very friendly toward all of us. Still, I wouldn't trust them. They are stabbing white men on the back. . . ."

I said: "Then the whole Burma situation is an awful mess?"

"Yeah." Bob stared at the coffee pot. . . . "That's enough about Burma. How about giving me a manicure?"

I refused, saying I didn't even have time to fix my own nails. When he said, "Oh, be a sport, Olga," I went to the bedroom and got the manicure set. I sat on the floor beside him, cleaned his nails and filed one. He looked at it and said:

"How do you expect me to pick up things? Look at it—no nail left. As a manicurist, you're a bust."

I told him to fix his own damn nails.

After dinner several of the pilots gathered in our quarters, they wanted to try out the new phonograph machine. George Paxton brought some bottles of rum he had brought from Rangoon. He appointed himself the official bartender. Tugboat supplied him with hot water, sugar and cinnamon. Colonel Chennault and General Sibert arrived a little later and joined in the merry-making. By the time the boys had the second drink, they were in a singing mood and Harvey experimented with the recording machine. He acted as master of ceremonies and held a little "mike" in front of the singers. He said:

"General Sibert, will you make a little speech, please—why the A.V.G. should not be inducted into the Army. . . ."

General Sibert cleared his throat and said: "Well, well— This is not going to be recorded, is it?"

"No, oh, no!" said several voices.

"The A.V.G. should not be inducted into the United States Army Corps. I think they are doing well enough as they are. Beside, the United States Army can't afford to pay them the same salaries. . . ." General Sibert ended weakly.

A small voice in back said: "That's off the record, Harvey."

I turned around and saw Colonel Chennault. The lines of his face deepened with laughter.

Everyone said: "Speech! Speech! Colonel Chennault will now speak. Step up to the mike, Colonel and say something."

"No," he said, "I have nothing to say. You boys sing."

He picked up the mike and said: "I always remember those days when I used to fish in the bayous of the Mississippi. But that's a long time ago and has nothing to do with tonight's gathering. I want to introduce the singing six of the A.V.G.: Arvid Olson, better known as 'Ole,' Jack Newkirk, Petach, Bob Little, C. E. Smith, and George Paxton. Take it away, boys!"

Before the Colonel was through with his little speech of introduction, the boys cut in, "Someone's in the kitchen with Diana. . . . Someone's in the kitchen, I know. . . ."

Olson took over the mike and said: "And now, Ladies and Gentlemen, little Bob Little will give us the news as they have developed in the last week or two—and a small dissertation on the Rrrrr . . . Aaaaa . . . Ffffff . . . Speaking up, Mr. Little."

Harvey cut in: "Coming in the Pppppppp-40."

Little: "Rrrrr, Rrrrr, swish, swish, swish. . . ."

Olson: "They have stopped the au-ro-plane."

Little: "Pft, pft, swish, swish . . ."

Olson: "The motors are going yet. But speaking up, Mr. Little, what is the latest dope?"

Little: "No dope, no dope."

Olson: "We have been given to understand, Mr. Little, that lunatics, lepers, criminals and the A.V.G. is all that's left in Rangoon?"

Little: "True."

Olson: "What is the latest retreat that the R.A.F. has completed?"

Little: "We haven't caught them yet to find out."

Olson: "Tell us, Mr. Little, of the wonderful 12-gun Hurrrrrrrrr-i-cane!"

Little: "They won't even taxi fast . . ."

Olson: "But shooting—what a marvellous weapon!"

Little: "No good."

Olson: "Heil Hitler!"

Little: "Yeah, me too."

Everyone joined shouting: "Hurrah, hurrah!"

George Paxton said: "I mixed the concoction tonight that will knock the eyeteeth out of a mule. Do you like it?"

Colonel Chennault said: "That wasn't for the record, was it? All that stuff about the R.A.F.?"

Harvey said: "Hell no, Colonel. Of course not."

General Sibert looked most uncomfortable. "I think perhaps I'd better go. It wouldn't do for me to be here—remember, boys, the British are our Allies."

"Hurrah for the British—Hurrah! Hurrah—and a Tiger!"

All right—maybe it doesn't sound funny in print, or perhaps I have reported it badly. But it sounded funny then and it sounded funny on the phonograph record. Or maybe it was the rum toddies.

The next morning Little took off for Magwe to take some spare parts that were needed there. Olson took off, too, with the rest of his squadron. Little returned a day later with several of the pilots of the First Squadron who had remained there waiting for Olson's replacements—Charlie Bond, W. D. McGarry and two others. From hearing them talk, one would have thought that they hated to leave Magwe. They said they were having fun trying to do the best they could with the battered equipment they had. They said the R.A.F. had the place in confusion. No one seemed to know where the gasoline was kept! The R.A.F. had told the A.V.G. that they had a warning net all fixed up, but much to the amazement of the boys, they found that the warning net was a Blenheim bomber that went out on a sort of a reconnaissance flight eighty miles south of Magwe. It flew so high that nothing of the enemy movements on the ground could be seen.

A.V.G. boys slept by their planes to be right on the spot. They took turns sleeping so as not to be caught unawares. They figured if they got at least ten minutes' warning, they were lucky. They said that the field at Magwe was dustier than that of Mingaladon and camouflaged after a fashion. The First Squadron came back covered with glory and was proud of the fact that they had to their credit forty-four air victories!

Black Mac said that he had eight Japs to his credit. Bob Little had increased his to six; Burgard had seven and Bob Neale had twelve. Most all of them had more than two. That was a good record!

On Monday, March 9th, Rangoon fell. The Japs cut the roads leading to Toungoo where the Chinese Army had one division. Another Chinese division was stationed at Lashio, but part of this one was being moved to the Yenangyaung oil fields. General Alexander, British general in charge of British, Indian and Burmese troops, was reported to be somewhere in the Irrawaddy Valley where the situation was critical. A Chinese vanguard pushed south of Toungoo, a later report announced.

A message from Chunking stated that Generalissimo Chiang Kai Shek had conferred, posthumously, the rank of Lieutenant Colonel on Robert J. Sandell, and the rank of Major on T. J. Cole. The rank of Captain on A. B. Christman and Hoffman.

I was over at Operations when a phone call came through from Changyi. Daffy Davis answered it. He said: "Harvey, it's a woman, and she's asking for you. That's strange."

Harvey took the phone from Daffy, spoke into it and said: "Hello, Doreen! How did you get there? Wait a minute, hold on . . . Daffy, it's for you, it's Doreen!"

The amazement on Daffy's face is hard to describe. He was probably thinking the same as I was—how could it be possible for Doreen to get out of Hong Kong? How did she manage to get to Changyi?

Daffy finished his conversation and turned toward us. He could hardly speak. Harvey said: "That's all right, don't say it. You can take my car, if you like, and go right now and pick Doreen up."

Daffy didn't have to be told twice. I drove with him to our hostel and packed some of my clothes, cold cream and lipstick, knowing she wouldn't have any.

"What does she want all this stuff for?" Daffy inquired.

I said: "What does any woman want all this stuff for?"

I hadn't seen R. L. Hastey since December. He stayed in Toungoo with the detachment and then went on to Rangoon as transportation officer, his same old job. He managed to get into a few fights and had some Japs to his credit. The last report we had from him was that he was coming up the Road with a large convoy, the last one to leave Rangoon with supplies for us. He had remained in Lashio for quite some time, but finally turned up at Kunming on the morning of March 13th. He came to see me. I asked him what else he had brought up besides supplies for us.

He leaned back in the chair and laughed: "I brought two for me and four others."

I said: "Two what?"

"Two females. Two gals. You don't think I was going to travel all the way up that damn Burma Road in a convoy just to bring supplies, do you?"

"Are they white?" I asked.

"White? Well, yes and no. But they don't look bad. They are Anglo-Indian. A couple of them are Anglo-Burman."

I said: "You can't put them up in the barracks, and the European hotels are full up. What are you going to do with them?"

He said: "Put them up in a Chinese hotel, the Taho Hotel. From now on it will be, officially, the Number Three Hostel."

Chapter IX

A NIGHT or two after Doreen arrived, we all got together for dinner at the Kwang Sueng Yuang. Doreen,
who spoke Chinese fluently, ordered all sorts of strange and,
for the most part, delicious native dishes. The party broke up
early.

We had no more than gotten to sleep than someone knocked
on our door. Whenever anything happened, no matter what
the hour, they always came to see Harvey about it. I heard a
strained and excited voice:

"—C.N.A.C. plane crashed and burned—haven't got the
exact location—not far from the field—"

Instantly I was wide awake.

Scotty!

I jumped out of bed. Harvey was peeling off his pajamas.
"Goddamit! It had to be Scotty!" His face was grim, pained.
"He took off at eleven-fifteen—it's midnight now." He was
scrambling into his uniform. "Colonel George was aboard,
too, and General Denys."

I asked where he was going. He said: "Out to find them—if
they're still alive!"

Oh, God—Scotty!

I said: "I'm going with you!"

Harvey shook his head: "It's no place for you. If they're
crashed and burned it'll be a hell of a mess. You stay here. I'll
be back soon."

He rushed out of the room. I could hear his running foot-
steps down the stairs, then the car's motor starting, gears shift-
ing. I listened until I couldn't hear the car any more. I didn't
go back to bed. I couldn't. "Crashed and burned."—a miracle
if Scotty had escaped alive. I thought of Betty, in the clutches

of the Japanese in Manila; his baby in Honolulu. Why, why, dear God, did it have to happen to them? So young, so utterly in love. I remembered what he told me: "If anything happens to Betty, I want to die." But of course, Scotty didn't know what had happened to Betty. He hadn't heard of her since December. For Scotty to die this way was a terrible cost in human lives. Seventeen passengers in that plane, many of them very important people.

At four thirty in the morning I heard the servants moving about preparing breakfast. The door opened, and Tugboat appeared. "Tea, Missy?"

"No, Tugboat, no tea. Bring me two pots of very strong, hot coffee."

He looked at me and said: "Missy no sleep. Missy have got trouble? Yes?"

"Yes, Tugboat, plenty trouble. I think good friend get killed."

At five o'clock there was a commotion on the stairs and Harvey staggered in almost carrying a tall man in his forties, a complete stranger. His American uniform was torn to shreds, his trousers burned and blood-soaked. His hair, eyebrows, and even his eyelashes were scorched. I led him to the sofa and placed him gently amongst the pillows. The man could not talk. I was afraid he had lost his reason.

Harvey said: "This is Colonel Edwards, Olga, United States Army. Get some whisky." It wasn't an introduction, just a statement of fact.

I poured a stiff drink and held it to the Colonel's lips. He gulped it down. I followed that with several cups of coffee. Suddenly he burst into tears. "It was terrible, terrible!" he sobbed.

"Don't talk now. Just take it easy."

I took a pair of scissors and ripped his trouser legs open up to the knee, removed his muddy, bloody shoes and cut off the socks. Tugboat had already brought two pails of hot water. I washed the Colonel's feet and legs and dried them carefully. There were several nasty cuts and burns, but none were severe. He was suffering from mental shock. He was like a child, very quiet as I attended him. Harvey helped me take off the rest of his clothing. Then we dressed him in a pair of Harvey's silk pajamas and a wool robe, put him on Harvey's bed and soon he was asleep.

Harvey and I tiptoed out of the bedroom and went into the office. "Tell me, what happened?"

Harvey hesitated an instant. "Evidently Scotty turned over the control to Shuler, his co-pilot. The ship was overloaded, as usual. It got off okay but then one of the motors conked out. Probably Scotty tried to take over the controls from Shuler, who, by the way, would have been a full pilot after this flight. They cracked up about six kilometers from the field. The plane was headed back towards the field, but couldn't make it and crashed into those high trees. They were all killed except Colonel Edwards, two Chinese he dragged out of the fire, and Fogarty." Mr. Fogarty was the English Commissioner of the Northern Shan States.

"Harvey, tell me, did Scotty die instantly?"

He snapped his fingers. "Like that! We found his body—what was left of it, pinned underneath a motor. Everybody was burned so you couldn't tell what was human and what was airplane. Ceder is still out there trying to salvage some of the stuff."

I felt faint and ill.

Harvey said: "Tell Tugboat to fix up one of the guest rooms and have Colonel Edwards moved in there. He'll need plenty of rest. I'll send Dr. Gentry to look him over."

About noon I went to see Colonel Edwards. He wanted to talk about the accident, and I let him because I thought it was good for him to get it off his mind. I poured him a cup of hot tea, lit a cigarette for him and sat on the side of his bed.

"Olga, whenever you fly in one of those over-loaded air liners, be sure you get a seat near the tail. That's what saved my life. Before the ship took off, I was asleep. The next thing I knew was a terrific bang. The impact woke me up for an instant, then I passed out. When I came to I was hanging from a low branch of a tree, still strapped to my chair. How I got out of it, I don't know. I started to run, then turned back realizing maybe I could help someone in that blazing hell. I pulled out three bodies. I don't know who they were —Chinese, maybe. I don't remember much after that. A Chinese and your husband picked me up and brought me here. I don't know how to thank you. You have been very kind to me."

"What did the doctor say?"

"No broken bones. Just shock, I guess."

I tucked him in, opened a window to get the charcoal fumes out, and promised to come back later.

Ceder was waiting in my office, looking very pale. "God," he said, "after seeing that mess out there, I'll never get on a plane again."

"Did you get Scotty's body out?"

He shuddered. "In pieces—little pieces. There wasn't much left of him. Harvey gave me something for you."

He handed me a large manila envelope. I poured out the contents. Buttons, buckles and a metal miniature propeller. All were blackened and not one had a speck of the polished brass. I picked up a piece of cardboard and turned it over— the picture of Betty that Scotty had shown me a few nights before. It was all burned around the edges. Only the face was left. Some of the buttons were the American Army Air Corps, others British. I thought, buttons of Colonel George's, Scotty's and General Denys' uniforms. Poor darlings! I wrapped them up again and put them away. Ceder watched me all the time without saying a word. When I dropped the envelope in one of the drawers, he said:

"I had to post a guard. By the time we got to the wreck, coolies were looting the bodies—pulling clothing off the corpses, searching pockets for valuables or money. One coolie was trying to wrench a finger off to get the ring, an American Army ring. It made me so ill I had to vomit. I fired my gun right into them and even then they wouldn't scatter. Damn vultures! When all five of us began firing, they scattered."

"Please, Ceder," I said, "don't tell me any more . . . . What did you do with the bodies?"

"What we could salvage we wrapped in blankets and ordered Chinese coffins to put them in. We took charge of Colonel George, Scotty and Schuler, Mr. Fenimore Lynch and a young Signal Corps lieutenant who was going up to Chungking—five Americans. The British Consul took charge of two King's Messengers who were aboard, and General Denys."

I knew Mr. Lynch well. He was financial adviser to the Central Bank of China. He would not be buried in the Chinese military cemetery with Scotty and the others.

Ceder left me with my thoughts. I had lost two of my best friends within five weeks—Sandy and Scotty.

The funeral was at four o'clock the next day, March 16th. Our chaplain officiated. There were four deep holes in a row, Chinese wooden coffins suspended over them, draped with American flags. In front of the four graves were four tables loaded with rice, pastries and flowers. Colonel Huang and other Chinese officers stood back of the tables. It was a strange combination Christian and Chinese service. Taps sounded. The crowd dispersed silently. I walked back to Scotty's coffin and placed upon it two white carnations I had found in the hostel garden. I breathed a short prayer and said almost aloud: "Scotty, these flowers—one from Betty and one from me. God bless you!" I walked away without glancing back.

I stopped at the flower market and bought all the flowers I could find to make a large wreath to send from the Group to the British Consulate for General Denys, whose funeral was to be at the British cemetery the next day. As I worked with the flowers I thought how strange it was that four Americans should be buried here in a foreign country. And I found myself wondering which of my friends would be next to go—and how soon.

I sent Wyke to deliver the wreath to the British Consulate and was feeling about as depressed as a woman can feel when the door opened and Daffy and Doreen bounced in, holding hands and their faces radiating happiness.

"Olga," said Doreen, "we are to be married tomorrow."

Daffy only smiled. He couldn't say anything. I congratulated them. They really deserved this happiness. They had waited so long for it. I asked: "Did you find a ring?"

"No," laughed Doreen, "we didn't. Have you got an extra one?"

I had a ring that only fitted my small finger—an alexandrite, about two carats, set in gold. Doreen tried it on. It fitted. I said: "It will do for engagement ring until Daffy can find one."

As to what the bride should wear—Doreen had salvaged a black suit and a white satin blouse. "I should wear a hat. Have you one?" she asked.

I was fresh out of hats but had a piece of white silk jersey we could make into a turban. She could add some white cherry blossoms. Daffy said he always had admired Doreen when she wore one of the things. So we got to work on the turban.

Strange, I thought, as I sewed, how life goes on. One light is suddenly snuffed out—another flames and burns brightly.

St. Patrick's Day was the day of the wedding. Early in the morning my amah arrived loaded with white lilies, white cherry blossoms and pale pink peach blossoms. How lovely they were. They filled the room with their perfume. We arranged all the vases and had to borrow more from Colonel

Huang. I expected a large crowd that night after the wedding ceremony, so I fixed the bedroom up, too, covered the beds with embroidered silks, spread Persian carpets on the floor and rearranged the chairs. We borrowed some small tables from the guest rooms and placed flowers, cigarette boxes and ash trays on them. Tugboat and two coolies left the rooms sparkling after much cleaning, dusting and polishing of furniture and floors.

Bob Little came in. "What's cooking?" he asked. "You certainly have the joint fixed up."

"A wedding," I answered.

"You and Harvey getting hitched again?"

I explained about Doreen and Daffy, and added: "Have to fix the auditorium, too. Colonel Huang is already building an altar there."

" Am I invited?" asked Little.

"Sure. But I don't think any of you roughnecks will be asked to the wedding. One of you might start giggling which might get me started, and I have to be serious. I'm going to be the matron of honor."

"Who gives the bride away?" he asked.

"Colonel Chennault. And Harvey is going to be best man."

At six o'clock Doreen arrived, already dressed in her black suit and white satin blouse. She pinned the white flowers on the turban and a small corsage on the lapel of her jacket. Her black eyes sparkled. "Do I look all right?" she asked.

I said she looked beautiful, but that she needed gloves. White gloves. I remembered a pair of new ones I had never worn—they were from Paris. They would be too large for her, but she could carry them. I found them in my old wardrobe trunk, and a black pair for myself. I got myself together in a still good print dress with a plain black crepe coat.

Doreen said: "Just like the days in Hong Kong. Remember? Dressing to go to a tea party."

Daffy and Harvey arrived. For a change Harvey admired

us and said the bride looked very pretty. Daffy wore his uniform—khaki-colored gabardine with Chinese buttons and R.A.F. wings.

Next to appear was the Colonel, in his newest uniform. Then, the Chaplain, Paul Frillman. He said: "Well, children, let's go upstairs and 'tie the knot.' " He winked at Colonel Chennault.

Looking at Doreen, the Colonel said: "I was a little over seventeen, I think, when I had the first one."

"The first what, Colonel?" I asked.

"The first child. A boy. You people seem to get started a little bit late, to my way of thinking."

Harvey said: "Keep it clean, Colonel. Keep it clean."

As we filed upstairs to the auditorium, a pleasant picture greeted our eyes, a white altar on the raised dais, four large candles twinkling merrily, flowers everywhere; at the edge of the dais, two silk brocade pillows. Doreen squeezed my hand—her fingers were ice-cold.

We were finding our places when our own cameraman came and with him Charles Fenn, the Associated Press correspondent. Both had cameras and flashlight bulbs.

"Who giveth this woman away," said the Chaplain.

The Colonel answered: "I, Claire Chennault."

Harvey fumbled with the ring, in the accepted best man tradition. Finally, the ceremony was over, and Daffy and Doreen were man and wife. The Colonel was the first to kiss the bride, then Harvey. Both of them took their time. Poor Daffy said: "When is it my turn?"

When we got back, our quarters were crowded—the Petachs, Bob Little, Colonel and Mrs. Chung, Greg Boyington, Williams, Adair, Mr. and Mrs. Turner, (British custom's official) Jack Newkirk, George Paxton, and most of the pilots.

They all stood up when we entered. Everyone had glasses in their hands, and they all shouted at once: "A toast to the bride! The bride, the bride! Bottoms up!" What confusion, and what a lot of noise. The electric phonograph was going full blast. I tried to tune it down, but Jack Newkirk wouldn't let me.

"Leave it alone," he said, "we like it that way—the louder the better. Mind if I take a flower?"

"No," I said, "but it doesn't go too well with a uniform."

"Oh, I forgot that," he said, "but I'll keep it in my pocket —it smells good."

About an hour later we all drove to the Chinese restaurant. Thanks to Mrs. Chung, I had been able to order a fine dinner the day before.

I was still wearing the black gloves. I took them off and gave them to Bob Little. He caressed them with his fingers and brushed them against his cheek. They were very fine French kid, which I had bought in Hanoi. "I think I'll keep these," he said slowly, "and carry them in the pocket of my flying suit for good luck. Oke?"

"No," I answered, "it isn't oke. That's the only pair of black gloves I have—and besides, black isn't good luck."

"Don't be superstitious," he said. "You are as bad as the Burmans."

We left it at that, and he kept them. We all had too much to eat and too much to drink and were boisterously happy. It was two o'clock in the morning when the party broke up.

I kissed Daffy and Doreen good night. Harvey and I went with the Colonel in his car. The streets were still brightly lighted. No blackouts. People were still moving about, some already starting out to their fields to work. They didn't seem to ever rest or sleep.

As I was drifting off to sleep I knew, vaguely but surely, I should not have let Bob Little keep that pair of black gloves. Not for good luck—not to carry when he was flying. Black was unlucky—everybody knew that—unlucky—the color of death.

By March 19th, the whole of the First Squadron was back

in Kunming, Point "X." I saw Bob Neale in the morning when I went to the field and visited Harvey's office. Tall, brown curly-haired Bob, looking thinner than ever, his skin tanned to coppery-red. I noticed how restless his hands were, how shifty the look in his eyes. Bob was still on the alert, his nerves strained, keyed-up and ready for action. Good thing he had come "home" for a rest.

He was saying: "When we finally pulled out of Mingaladon, warning of Jap attacks was all we were getting. The last thing we heard on the radio was, 'Sixteen to twenty Japs over Rangoon.' We kept on going, looking over our shoulders expecting at any moment to see some of the bastards dive on our tails. We were only six on that flight. The others had been moving up north in pairs and some solos. Our job was to see that the truck convoys got through with our stuff."

I had heard most of the story from Bob Little and other pilots, so I left.

A C.N.A.C. plane arrived about ten o'clock that night. I didn't see any of the passengers of the pilot because I went to bed too early. But when Harvey left the next morning, he said: "I wonder where in the hell we are going to put all the visiting firemen. We have four generals here in the guest rooms, but there are a lot of lieutenants, majors and colonels that we had to double up with the pilots." He didn't tell me the names of the generals or of any one. Well, I thought, I'll have to find out for myself.

After breakfast, I went to the field to the chief of staff's office—and what a strange thing Harvey was doing for a chief of staff, executive officer, group operations officer. He was painting the walls of that little room a pale blue! Jack Newkirk and Bob Neale were helping. I asked: "And what do you think you're doing? Looks as if you were expecting the stork to deliver." Everyone laughed.

Harvey said: "Remember the trick the Dutch had in Java of painting their meat markets blue? Well, that's what I am doing. To keep the flies out."

We were all standing around watching the painter when Colonel Chennault appeared. As usual, he was smoking a Camel cigarette, hanging from his lower lip as if it had been glued there. His eyes narrowed to keep the smoke out. He said: "Harvey, what in holy Christ's name are you doing?" Harvey told him. "Well I'll be dogged!" continued the Colonel, "you're finally doing it. You wanted to do it in Toungoo, too, but I bet you then, as I bet you now, that the flies won't stay out. I am willing to pay for the paint, brushes and all, and pay you fifty cents an hour that that stuff won't keep them out!"

I didn't say anything. I knew the Javanese flies had kept out of the meat markets, but I didn't know about Chinese flies.

"Colonel," said Harvey, "I might have the wrong shade of blue. You have to keep that in mind."

The bets began. Two to one—even money. The funny thing was, the flies were staying out. Maybe they didn't like the smell of the fresh paint.

I asked the Colonel: "Will you please tell me who are the generals, and why?"

He said: "You'll meet them tonight at dinner."

"Dinner? Am I invited?"

"Sure," said the Old Man. "You're the A.V.G. hostess, aren't you?"

"It wouldn't be my birthday party, would it, Colonel?"

"Birthday?"

"Yes. Today, March 20th. Sweet sixteen, no more no less."

"Exactly why all the generals are here, to celebrate your birthday," said the Old Man. As he left he said: "Harvey, let me know when the flies start coming in." He took a few steps and turned around, "Olga, fix yourself up pretty tonight and don't forget that nice-smelling stuff you use. I like it."

At seven o'clock I was dressed in my green brocade robe, white flowers in my hair and jade jewelry on my fingers, arms and neck. A timid knock on my door was followed by a soft voice that said: "May I come in?" General Mao stood before me in full dress uniform. "Are you ready?" he asked. "They are waiting."

I wanted the boys to see me now, all dressed up, looking pretty, I thought, and arm in arm with the Chief of Staff of the Chinese Air Force. I felt so proud. We walked down the stairs, along the hall and into the private dining room. Immediately I noticed other women present—Mrs. Huang and Mrs. Chung accompanied by their husbands. Colonel Chennault and Harvey were standing in a corner of the room by a buffet table with three men in American Air Corps uniforms, stars on their shoulder straps. Generals! I knew Generals McGruder and Hearn, but I didn't know the other one. Colonel Chennault introduced him—General Naiden. I liked him. Not too tall, slender, trim. I thought: "He thinks he is a devil with women." There were two British officers and two Dutch naval officers, one in civilian clothes. I couldn't understand the name, but everyone called him "Doctor." I spent most of the evening with him arguing—Democracy, Communism, heritage, environment and patriotism! I don't remember just what point I was arguing.

It was a good dinner. Later I found out it was given by General Mao, not to celebrate my birthday, but to entertain the generals. However, I felt as if it had been my party.

When Harvey and I returned to our quarters we found Tom Jones there. He was holding a small package. "For you," he said, "happy birthday." I unwrapped it—it was a .25 Colt automatic! At last I had a gun! Harvey said: "Fine thing to give a man's wife. . ."

Chapter X

IN Yunnan the first day of Spring falls on March 21st, just the same as anywhere else, but to me it was just another cold, windy day. I had a vile cold and a rasping sore throat, was miles behind with my office work which defied all my efforts to catch up and was mean and disagreeable and mad at the world in general when the gentleman who is my husband came home accompanied by Colonel Chennault.

"Look at her, Colonel," said Harvey. "Did you ever see a witch as bad-tempered as this one?"

They finally diagnosed my trouble as inability to complete my work due to too many visitors. The Colonel thought he would put a stop to that by issuing an order. He dictated and I wrote:

MEMORANDUM: ALL CONCERNED.

1. During the hours of 0700 to 1600 this room is the office of the *War Diary* Statistician and the Editor of the *A.V.G. News.* Members of this command will not enter unless on official business.

C. L. Chennault,
Commanding

He took my fountain pen and signed it. "Now," he said, "I am going to tack this on your door. If anyone disobeys it, I'll slap 'em with a stiff fine."

He had no more than gone when people started drifting in, reading and snickering at the posted order. I knew then it wouldn't work—so decided my only salvation would be a week in the hospital where, I was silly enough to believe, I could lock my door and get a little rest and sleep.

Sam Prevo arranged for a room for me at the French Hospital and, the following morning, came to pick me up. I had already packed a bag with the usual nightgowns, slippers and my Elizabeth Arden make-up box, which was of pin seal. I noticed for the first time that the box, bottles and jars were "Made in Germany," although the cosmetics were made in Paris.

The hospital was in a large compound surrounded by a high wall—in the very heart of the city next to the Hotel du Commerce, where I had slept the first night I arrived from Toungoo, which seemed years ago. So much had happened since then.

Sam escorted me to a second floor room which looked even smaller than it really was because of the huge bed which covered most of the floor—a nine foot square somnambulistic delight with blue linnette canopy and blue cover. Not even in their hospital beds can the French escape that DuBarry influence! I peeked into the bathroom—a charming view for a lady who had daily been contesting bathroom privileges with a couple of dozen men. There was a bathtub in the abbreviated French style, wash basin, toilet and that inevitable Gallic plumbing feature, a *bidet*. The French, who, in Indo-China at least, are a funny race, are not addicted to the daily shower or tub. In lieu thereof they use the wash basin sparingly, the *bidet* perhaps a bit more generously—and then drench themselves with cologne—and finish the job off with talcum powder.

Sam went in search of Dr. Lanzalavi, the resident physician, and a nurse. While he was gone I unpacked—and was in bed when the doctors returned.

Dr. Lanzalavi was a tall, thin, handsome fellow in his late thirties. He asked what my trouble was. Nothing, I explained, except a bad head cold, sore throat and a complete inability to generate any motive power. In short, I needed a rest.

The head nurse entered. She was an Annamite, a good-looking woman fairly young with, I thought, a dash of French ancestry as she did not have the flat Annamite features.

Methodically she took my temperature, noted it on a chart—and left. All she ever said was *"Bonjour, Madame"* and *"Merci, Madame."*

Dr. Lanzalavi promised to send my *"de jeuneur"* from his own kitchen as the only food served from the hospital kitchen was Chinese. I looked forward to good French meals.

Later in the day the doctor came in again. I thought him a bit nonchalant. He was more interested in finding out things about the A.V.G. than about my health. He asked many questions about Indo-China—who I knew there, what they did at the time I knew them, but I did not commit myself in any way. He was Vichy-French. My friends in Indo-China were all Free-French.

During the afternoon I was very lonesome. No one but the nurse came in, she to paint my throat with something pink and nasty. She said I was not to smoke—doctor's orders.

At six-thirty Harvey arrived—and oh! was I glad to see him, for by that time I was feeling I had been forgotten by everyone. He sat on my bed and suddenly said:

"We've got bad news, babe. The Japs bombed hell out of Magwe yesterday afternoon. J. E. Fauth, one of the crew chiefs, was killed and Frank Swartz got hit by shrapnel. Poor Kids! They were caught on the ground—without a God-damn word of warning, as usual! Four or five of our planes were ruined."

Harvey said they had flown Frank Swartz to Calcutta, accompanied by Dr. Richards. He went on to say that Mc-Millan and three others had returned with new planes from Africa. Jack Newkirk, Bob Neale, McGarry and Boyington had left that morning for Magwe to operate under Olson's orders.

He bent over and kissed me on the forehead, "I've got to get back to the field." I hated to see him leave—and asked if he'd bring Lucy the next time he came over—to keep me company. He said he would, kissed me again and left.

I lay there thinking about poor Frank Swartz. Only a few days before he had been singing at our quarters while we made phonograph recordings. He was one of those kids who loved to harmonize—along with Newkirk, Ole Olson, Paxton, Pete Petach and some others. Well, wounded or not he could at least keep on doing that.

The door opened. It was Harvey. He stood there a moment. "Olga, I thought I'd better tell you. Frank Swartz lost one eye, one hand was terribly torn—and his whole jaw was blown off."

Mercifully, Frank died in Calcutta a few days later.

Later, Dr. Lanzalavi came in again. He only stayed a moment. I heard him walking up the other flight of stairs to the third floor where his quarters were—right above mine. He sat out on his veranda and began to sing in a low, soft voice. I was curious so I got out of bed and looked up from my window. There he was sitting on a rattan chair, smoking a cigarette, looking out over the city and singing—a song that I like very much, *J'Attendrai*, one of the few French songs I know. When General Ralph Royce, then a colonel in our Air Corps, was our guest at our Villa in Doson, he brought me this record. I learned it then. I stood by the window a long time listening to the doctor's voice.

The next afternoon Doreen Davis popped in bringing along her Number One Boy who had escaped with her from Hong Kong. "Just in case you don't like the service here, I've brought you Jowa. He is a very good boy."

Jowa bowed. I liked the way he was dressed, neat and clean. No boys like the Hong Kong boys, I thought.

"Missy have got bad cold," he beamed, "Me fix medicine. You well soon. Doctors, no goody. No savvy."

"Good," I said, "from now on you are my doctor. How much money you need for medicine."

"Not much, Missy—twenty, thirty dollars, mebbe. Me bring changee."

Doreen gave him the money and Jowa disappeared. "He's marvelous," Doreen said. "Without him I'd never have gotten here."

I asked her to tell me about her escape from Hong Kong, which, heretofore, she had seemed reluctant to talk about. She curled up on the bed. There really wasn't very much to it, she insisted. The Japs held her in a filthy old Chinese hotel with other British prisoners. She'd been there a week when she realized she had a Danish passport, having been married to a Dane. She spoke Japanese well, which eventually got her an audience with a Jap officer.

"I asked why he had me locked up—I was a Danish subject," Doreen explained.

I interrupted. "But you're British."

"Of course, but they didn't know I had divorced my husband four years ago, so they released me from the hotel and told me I was free. Later, I saw a Jap official and told him I wanted to leave Hong Kong and would they let me take my money out of the city. He said not only would they permit that, but a Jap boat would take me wherever I wanted to go!

"I crossed over to Kowloon and went to see a Chinese doctor I knew. He wasn't really my friend but I took a chance —told him I wanted to borrow 800 Hong Kong dollars. Without a word he gave it to me.

"I found Jowa and we sailed on a Jap boat for Kwanche-wang with a boatload of Jap soldiers going to Hainan and Haiphong. Jowa and I got off at Pahkoi, walked out of town that night and were in open country headed north. From there on it was easy—we rode trucks to Kweilin. The Chinese were wonderful about helping us—even offered money if I needed it—but I didn't."

There was a long silence.

"Hong Kong was terrible—terrible! From December 10th to the 24th there were continuous raids. I was with the

Lewises in their house on the top of the Peak. We were all in the basement when a bomb demolished the house. We moved to the house below—the one belonging to Texaco, remember? They bombed hell out of that—so we moved into a little apartment at the bottom of the Peak. We were running out of food, the water was bad. On Christmas Day the Japanese came in and rounded us up.

"They made us march through the streets, carrying our bundles. As we passed the soldiers, they spat on us. The Japs made our navy, army and high civilian officials carry the British flag, dragging it on the ground as they walked. . . ."

She suddenly burst into tears. "They can't beat us, Olga, they simply can't!"

I tried to comfort her. I had never seen her cry. She had always been a stout little fellow. I told her to forget all that.

"No," she said, "I can't forget it. I never will. The humiliation—if there is a God, some day we shall have revenge. Some day we will make them take it all back."

Jowa returned, carrying bundles. Without a word, he started to build a fire in the little iron stove that was in the corner of the room near the bathroom door. "Here, me cookim; me fixim your chow." Jowa's medicine was a Chinese pear filled with strong spices and Chinese rock sugar. He placed it in an empty coffee tin which he put in a pot half filled with water. He steamed it for two hours and served it to me very hot. "Missy, you chow. Plenty hot—plenty goody."

It *was* "plenty goody." The flavor was delicious, the effect on my throat quite soothing. Better than the Doctor's ikky concoctions.

Harvey came in at seven with Colonel Chennault and Lucy, who jumped on the bed and licked my face, then cuddled up beside me and went to sleep. The Colonel and Harvey sat on the bed across from Doreen.

"You aren't sick. You just think you are," said the Colonel. He put his hand into his coat and pulled out two packages of

Lucky Strikes. "Don't tell anybody I gave you these. The boys brought me a carton from Cairo." Harvey produced a pint bottle of Hennessy which he had found at Kwang Sueng Yang, hidden back of the counter. Jowa took the bottle and poured out four drinks. This was more like it, I thought—a party about to start. I loved having Harvey and the Colonel there with me and listening to their stories. But they didn't stay long. When they left Jowa took one of the chairs and sat outside my door. He had brought his folding bed and set it up in the hallway in case I wanted anything during the night.

To explain why would be impossible, but on the morning of March 24th I awakened with a strange fear that something was going to happen. I was restless all morning and felt, somehow as if I were imprisoned. I kept getting out of bed and looking out of the large bathroom window. What I expected to see out there in that compound, walled in, I don't know. But I kept scanning the sky. That day it was sunny and the sky was blue to infinity—but I had gotten so I no longer trusted the sky.

Jowa's voice: "Missy! *Ginbao!* Missy, wanchee go out?"

He stood there in the middle of the room, hands crossed in front of him, not moving an eyelash. What was one more *ginbao* to him after the hell he had been through in Hong Kong?

I said, "Jowa—you and I stay here in this room. Japanese no come. If Japanese come, no bomb here. This French Hospital. Big French flag painted topside on roof. Doctor topside too. He sing. He no worry—you make coffee."

"*Ho, ho.* Me savvy. Missy no scare. Missy *ding-how!*" "*Ho, ho*" meant all right and "*ding-how*" was equivalent to our "okay." Because I wasn't frightened, Jowa said I was "*ding-how*." It pleased me to see his broad smile and to know he approved of me.

The *ginbao* was a false alarm but my apprehension did not subside. About ten o'clock the two Sutter youngsters, a little girl and boy about ten and five, scurried into the room shout-

ing, "Auntie, auntie. We bring you flowers." Their father,
Harry Sutter was a Swiss who worked for the Commission on
Aeronautical Affairs. Mrs. Sutter, his wife, was a strange mixture of Chinese and Indian which turned out quite well—an
exotic-looking woman of perhaps thirty-five. She followed her
children into my room. She wore a print silk dress and a leopard skin coat, Chinese made, and was extremely attractive with
the coloring of the Chinese and the eyes of the Indian. I noticed
how small and well-kept her hands were. Her head was covered
with black curls which she must have been fixing for hours. I
offered her coffee, after which she became very intimate, as if
we had been old friends meeting for the first time in years.

She said, among other things, that the social whirl of Kunming was tiring her out—she hardly ever had time to herself.

"Social business?" I asked. I did not know there was such a
thing in Kunming.

She assured me there was—that at least forty French women
there were always giving parties which, unfortunately, weren't
what they used to be in the old days when there was plenty of
champagne and caviar.

It turned out she had come to see a girl who was very ill in
the hospital. I asked her about it. She said:

"Didn't you know? She is one of the Anglo-Indians whom
the boys brought up in a convoy. Pitiful! Why those girls ever
followed these American boys up here, I don't know. Everyone of them is coming to me asking for ways to perform abor-
tions. Fancy that! Me! The girl says that she has stomach
trouble, cholera or something. But I only looked at her once
and I knew what it was. She had a miscarriage, a forced one.
She hasn't any money, and she is worried to death. I think that
it is the greatest part of her illness—worry. The boy, who
brought her, won't help her. Beast!"

I said I would have Dr. Lanzalavi take care of her—and pay
for it myself—and if she could find out who the fellow was it
would help.

That apparently settled the subject, so she started again on

Cantonese pilot.

Chinese soldiers.

Shanghai skyline.

her social activities. She finally left, gathering up her two children, promising to come back tomorrow.

I dozed most of the afternoon, cleaned up a little about six o'clock and, with the day nearly gone, was about to conclude my earlier apprehensions were nothing more than frazzled nerves when Colonel Chennault and Harvey came in. The Colonel's arms were filled with flowers and Harvey carried a small potted dwarfed cheery tree in full bloom. They placed their gifts on the table and both sat on the bed. I suddenly sensed that whatever the trouble was, it was here—none of the usual cheerful greetings, faces serious, not a word. I finally said:

"Well? Out with it. What happened?"

Harvey said: "Jack Newkirk is dead."

The Colonel added: "And we lost Black McGarry."

That stopped me—completely. I couldn't say a word. I only swallowed my tears. I looked at the Old Man. His eyes were moist. I looked at Harvey. His eyes were dry, but the way his mouth was set, the grim half-smile which he always has when angry or hurt, told me how he felt. Jack had been one of his best friends—Jack and Arvid Olson.

I said, "Tell me about it."

The Colonel looked at Harvey. "Go on," he said, "you might as well tell her."

I was thinking of the last time I saw Jack—the night we all felt happy singing and making silly phonograph records. Jack was in his cups and unusually gay. He came close to me and whispered in my ear:

> Olga, in between drinking
> I do some serious thinking
> I get down to brass tacks
> Oil my guns, get my plane on the run
> And get ready to tackle the Japs

He stood straight and tall, looking down at me. "Didn't know I was a poet, did you? Want some more?" he grinned.

I said sure—more.

He continued, singing this time to a tune which might have
been *Gloomy Sunday* which was one of our favorites:

> I learned the beauty of precious stones,
>   Ho hum
> And to drink tea with buttered scones,
>   Ho hum
> I wear bush shirts and drink chota pegs
> 'Til I can't move my unsteady legs . . .
>
> But in between drinking
> I do some serious thinking . . .

"How's that?" he laughed. "Or would you rather I'd sing
On the Road to Mandalay?"

Harvey was speaking: "We don't know all the details yet.
This morning a flight of nine went to Chiengmai to strafe the
airdrome. Jack, Frank Lawlor and Gesselbrach were to meet
Neale's flight near Chiengmai, after strafing Lampang sixty
miles away—but something went wrong with the rendezvous.
Jack dove at a truck convoy but was hit by machine-gun fire—
we think. The others saw his plane burst into flames and crash.
Black Mac had to bail out before getting back to the Chinese
border."

"Will Black Mac get out of it, do you think?" I asked. I had
to ask something. The Colonel said sure—all the Chinese down
there were looking for him. But the Colonel's confidence didn't
calm my fears for McGarry. I knew that jungle along the
Salween. If the Japs didn't get him, the jungle and the ants
would.

Luckily I didn't have any time alone to grieve over Jack for
Sam Prevo entered as Harvey and the Old Man were leaving.
I told Sam about the Anglo-Indian girl. Sam said, "Yes, it's
unfortunate—but boys will be boys," he laughed. I told him
he ought to be ashamed to laugh at such a thing.

"Look, Pollyanna," he said, "Nobody urged those girls to
come up here. They're all of age. They know very well the

boys' intentions are strictly dishonorable—so what do you expect—and why should I feel sorry for them? If they want to be damn fools that's their business. Have you got any decent cigarettes? I'm sick of these *Cotabs*."

I offered him one of the Lucky Strikes the Colonel had given me and slapped his hand when he tried to take more. He lit it and inhaled deeply. "Oh! Nothing like an American weed. You know, I always say that it pays to be a woman. Look at you, you never lack anything, whether cigarettes or French perfume. You seem to pull things out of the air, where there aren't any." He sighed deeply. "I'm tired—would you mind moving over and letting me take a nap?"

I said, "I think it would be wonderful—but Jowa wouldn't approve and he's my guardian."

Sam turned his huge bulky figure toward the door, then stood for a moment leaning against it. "I came to talk to you about Jack," he said soberly. "He was a good friend of mine—we had a lot of swell times together. I'm going to miss him. Well, good night—see you tomorrow."

"Sam!" I called. "How about another cigarette before you go." He helped himself to two and left without saying a word. I knew I had been watching a pretty fair imitation of a guy with a breaking heart because Sam Prevo liked Jack Newkirk about as much as one man can like another.

I thought Sam was my last visitor but I was mistaken. C. E. Smith drifted in later, plopped himself down on the bed and tossed a special order in my direction.

I read that W. R. Wyke had been dishonorably discharged for submitting his resignation when the Group was in contact with the enemy and our country was at war. I handed the paper back to Smith without comment.

"Aren't you going to say anything?" he asked.

"Me? Nothing, except that you better watch out—somebody may stab you in the back some night. Why don't *you* resign?"

"Why should I? I'm getting wingman's pay for an office job. Six hundred smackers! What do you mean a stab in the back?"

I said: "Figure it out for yourself."

By three o'clock the next morning I still hadn't gotten to sleep. I arose, built a fire in the corner stove, made some coffee and smoked two of the Colonel's cigarettes—which I shouldn't have done as the doctor had made me promise I wouldn't smoke. I sat by the fire wondering what this was all about. I thought of Harvey—and felt very sorry for him. He looked so tired and haggard. He was always busy, always worried, didn't have time to eat, smoked too much and was as nervous as a cat. I didn't think he was well but of course he wouldn't admit it —on the contrary he snapped at me if I even mentioned it.

Then I began to feel sorry for myself. Things were, apparently, beginning to pile up. I had been in the hospital three days and gotten a shock a day—Swartz, Jack Newkirk and McGarry, Wyke's resignation, girl trouble, the outfit fighting against steadily increasing odds with steadily decreasing support. It was becoming more and more apparent to me that these kids were going right on winning fight after fight until they dropped from exhaustion. And what was I doing here? Why wasn't I just a normal housewife raising three or four kids, keeping house, cooking and doing the things every wife does? Why was I living out here with all these men—crying for them, laughing with them, listening to their stories, their troubles, their heartbreaks, watching them die, watching them beginning to crack under the strain of overwhelming odds. I'm no sissy—but that night I was afraid—as only a woman can be afraid.

At noon the next day, Greg Boyington, Red Probst and Bob Neale came in. I thought they were still at Magwe. All three sat on the bed—everybody sat on the bed!—and talked about the raid on Chiengmai, Jack's death and Black Mac. Bob Neale said:

"We certainly burned hell out of fourteen Jap planes—caught them just as they were about to take off—but God! did we pay through the nose! You know, we were all of us around a jar of water about four o'clock in the morning—about to brush our teeth with the damn muddy stuff when one of the R.A.F. fellows shouted 'Don't use that water—it's polluted!' But Jack said 'What the hell, a few bugs won't bother me any.' He was the only one to brush his teeth."

Boyington said, "Sure enough, the bugs didn't bother him any—they burned up with him. Poor Jack!"

If that remark was meant to be funny, I didn't like it.

Boyington continued, "Black Mac was funny as hell. Remember, Bob, when he hit the ground he untangled himself from that chute harness like a flash . . . just waited long enough to pick up the map Bond dropped him, the chocolate bar Gessel threw, and then started running hell bent for election into the jungle. I think he'll make it. He's strong and healthy—wouldn't be surprised to see him walking in here one of these days."

I prayed Boyington was right. They talked themselves out of most of their stories, and left. Red Probst had been very silent. For once he had nothing to say. I felt sorry for him. He was not being sent on any more missions down in Burma because no one wanted to fly with him. Everytime he had gone on a mission from Kunming, he had either gotten lost or had to crash-land his ship. Tough luck, I thought—but the trouble was that none of the rest of the Group thought the way I did.

The Colonel sent Harvey back to Burma the next day, to work with General Ling and General "Uncle Joe" Stilwell. The situation was becoming increasingly serious. Our planes had been forced to evacuate Magwe and move north to Loiwing. The R.A.F. had dissolved into thin air.

"If Burma folds it will be the end of the A.V.G.—unless we can get co-operation from the American Tenth Air Force in India," Harvey said.

I asked if I could follow him to Lashio. Kunming was getting too mild—nothing but false alarms. I wanted to be where things were happening. Harvey said I could come down later if there was anything there for me to do. He left that afternoon on a C.N.A.C. plane. I hated to see him go. It was the first time in years we had been separated for more than a few days. But this time I knew it was going to be for weeks.

Harvey's departure didn't slow down things at the hospital any. The day after, early in the morning, the head nurse came in. I noticed how attractive she was. She was wearing a gold bracelet made of small flat links. I had seen several of the French officers in Indo-China wearing them. They called them "Slave Bracelets," and only those who were married had them. The nurse saw me looking at it. Without a word, she took it off and handed it to me. I inspected it closely. In small letters "Paris" was engraved on one of the links.

"*Voulez-vous acheter, Madame?*" she asked.

"*Oui,*" I answered. "*Combien?*"

"*Cent Piastres.*"

I had my purse under the pillow. I opened it and counted out 900 National dollars. The exchange at the Black Market was nine to one, so Jowa told me. I had no rupees, but apparently she was satisfied with the Chinese money. She said: "*Merci, Madame,*" and walked out.

What a strange woman, I thought. She must be hard up for money. I wondered what she wanted it for. Nine hundred is a lot of money for these people, whether Annamite or Chinese. I was paying my amah 500 a month which I knew was too much, as professors at the university only received 350 dollars a month. This nurse only got 200 a month, if she was lucky. I began some sewing and forgot all about her, although I was now wearing her bracelet.

The Colonel dropped in to see how I was and brought me a precious package of Camels.

A whole mob, who seemed to have decided I must be finding

life in the hospital unbearably dull and lonesome, arrived bearing pots and pans, fruit and flowers, two bottles of brandy and chow from the Kwang Sueng Yuang. The brandy was a gift from Boyington who had gone down to Loiwing that same afternoon. Jowa took over. He loved parties as do all Chinese boys—as they think they make a lot of "face" with other servants. When my guests decided they wanted to dance I decided it was time they went home.

Sam Prevo slipped in during the party. He had been attending Bill Williams, whose appendix he had removed that morning. He said he didn't think Mr. Fogarty, who had been terribly burned in Scotty's crash, was going to live. He had not been given adequate care immediately after the crash. Colonel Chennault and Harvey had had him removed to the French Hospital for better treatment but his burns had become infected and gangrene had set in.

Early Sunday morning, Captain Carney, who was in charge of the Chinese training school at Yunnanyi, arrived with two quart bottles of real champagne. "Morning, Precious," he said, "I bring you a delayed birthday present. I heard you had two tins of caviar left, so when you get out of bed, you can give yourself a party."

How thoughtful of him, how nice to remember. I thanked him. I asked him to tell me about Rose. Where was she?

"As a matter of fact," said Carney, "I want to talk to you about Rose. She's down in Lashio trying to get through with her last convoy and would be in Yunnanyi now if it wasn't for Harvey."

"Harvey?" I was surprised. "What do you mean?"

"Harvey stopped Rose's convoy. Not only that, he insulted her."

I said I didn't believe it—that Harvey liked Rose very much but if she was trying to *smuggle* things across the border and cheat the Chinese customs, then he would stop her if he could. Governor Lung had talked to Colonel Chennault and Harvey about a lot of smuggling which was being carried out in trucks and station wagons marked A.V.G. When Harvey left for Lashio the Colonel told him to be on the lookout. Harvey was very conscientious about carrying out orders. If he saw any trucks marked A.V.G., he'd inspect them whether they were Rose's or Governor Lung's or anyone's else.

Carney said, "That's all right, but I am part of the A.V.G. and Rose is my wife. Anything she brings up is mine, therefore it's A.V.G's."

"That's where you are wrong," I insisted. "The flying school is directly under the Chinese Government and has nothing to do with the A.V.G. Besides, how do you account for Rose bringing in a truck load of Kotex?"

He flushed.

"How do you know about that?"

"You'd be surprised. No, I'm sure Harvey wasn't insulting Rose. He was only carrying out the Governor's orders."

"Poor Rose," Carney mused. "She lost a lot of face, you know."

I said I should think she'd lose more face by cheating her own government out of custom's revenue. No, Rose had it coming to her. It wasn't the first time she had tried her hand at smuggling.

Carney laughed. "You're so damn frank. A person can't get sore at you." He changed the subject abruptly. "Are you going to ask me to the party? I mean when you crack open those caviar tins?"

I said: "When I drink that champagne and eat the caviar, it will be a very special occasion. You won't be there."

"What party will that be?"

"It'll be something to celebrate a victory, or perhaps a farewell, or wishing the boys luck on a dangerous mission. I don't know but it will have to be very special. I've been saving that caviar for a long, long time."

Right after Carney left, I began to pack my things. No use

staying in the hospital. My cold wasn't any better, I was getting no rest, the gang came just the same. So, why spend A.V.G. money? I had better get back to my quarters and my work.

I was getting impatient, as no one came after me, and was so glad to see Tom Jones when he strolled in unexpectedly that I kissed him like a long-lost friend.

"Came over to see Williams and thought I'd drop in," he said. "How are you?"

"Fine," I answered, "and will you get me out of here?"

"Sure," said Tom, "glad to."

He rolled the carpets and strapped my suitcases. Just as we were leaving Dr. Lanzalavi entered, and two Annamite servants with him. I had forgotten about the servants, but leave it to them to show up just in time for their tip. Although I felt they hadn't earned it, I gave them a good one.

Dr. Lanzalavi said: "Madame, why did you give my head nurse so much money?"

I said: "I didn't give it to her. I paid it to her for this bracelet. Why?"

"It might interest you to know that she is dead!"

"Dead?" I was shocked.

"I have been keeping back her salary," he explained, "because she is an opium addict. Whenever she had money, she bought opium. It is very hard to get now but she, being a nurse, was able to buy it from some of the Chinese druggists. I found her dead last night from an overdose. She was a very capable nurse, but had had a violent and tragic love affair—with a French officer at Langsang. When the Japanese came in they killed him. She never got over it. Poor woman."

I was delighted to get back to my quarters. The office room looked more attractive than ever. The amah and Tugboat had everything clean and in order, even fresh flowers in all the vases. The bedroom, too, was sparkling and the beds freshly made. I had the feeling of returning home after a long trip.

Chapter XI

I T wasn't long before the gang knew I was back. They paraded in, pilots, men, clerks. The whole outfit. I said: "Can't you fellows read the commanding officer's order there on the door?"

One of them said: "Yeah, but we came in through the bedroom. The Colonel can't get us for that."

Tom Jones offered to stay and keep as many visitors out as he could. I noticed with pleasure that he was beginning to look like himself again, the way I had first seen him in Toungoo before his tiger-hunting trip. His skin wasn't yellow any more; his eyes were much brighter although the whites were still amber. His body was filling out and his muscles growing stronger. He seemed taller perhaps because he was walking straighter, with his shoulders thrown back. He had come back to life, and knew it. He laughed at the slightest provocation, a loud, happy laugh; and even when he was silent, his lips were smiling. He was eager, expectant, full of ambition.

He sat on Harvey's bed. Beside him was an old rose-colored chenille robe I had bought in Hong Kong three years before. It had seen a lot of wear. He kept looking at it. Finally, he picked it up and said, "My wife has one of these. Funny thing —you remind me so much of her, and you even have a bath-robe like hers."

I felt sorry for him, so lonesome for that wife of his—and the baby whom he had never seen. Still holding the robe in his hands, he came close to me, threw the robe over the bed and pulled it up to my chin. "Yes, and you look like her—maybe it's your coloring." He moved to my bed and began to caress the robe.

200

I said: "Stop it, Jones! After all, I'm under the bathrobe now."

That brought him to. He shook his head slightly and laughed.

"You can have it," I added, "if you want it. But, you'll have to find another one for me because this is all I have."

I heard heavy steps outside the door. Sam Prevo walked in. "You're a fine patient," he scolded, "leaving the hospital without consulting me. What's the big idea?"

"You didn't come after me. If it hadn't been for Jones I would still be there."

The Doc placed his hand on my forehead, felt my pulse, looked at my tongue and said, "I'll give you a good tonic and some vitamin tablets. With all the attention you are getting, you'll either get well or be dead in a week." He looked at Jones. "What are you doing here? You ought to be in bed."

Jones blushed and said, "You'll have a hard time getting me back to that hospital shack, Doc. It won't be long before I start flying one of those new babies, the P-40 E. Gosh! I can hardly wait 'til I get into one of them."

"You know what happened the last time," Sam said. "You went over my head and got permission to fly from Dr. Gentry, even though you knew I didn't approve of it. What happened? You went back to the hospital. Well, this time I won't let you fly until I'm sure you are okay."

It was late, and I was hungry. "How about a party for three?" I suggested.

"Sure," said the Doc, "we can start right in with this champagne."

I shook my head, "The bar is open now. Ring for Tugboat and I'll buy you both a drink."

"You can't have any," said Sam, "but I'll drink yours."

Following Tugboat was Doreen and then Daffy. We all had dinner on Harvey's bed.

On April 2nd, for the first time in many days, I went to the field. I was in my office alone, again feeling sorry for myself, when G. B. McMillan, Vice Leader of the Third Squadron, wandered in. Tall, very slender Mac. I hadn't seen him for some time.

"Remember before I left for Cairo," he said, "I promised to bring you my diary for the trip? Well, here it is. Not much of a diary, just about the flight, stops, refueling, repairs, and so forth."

"How come you are not down in Loiwing with the Third Squadron?" I asked.

"On my last fight, I made a power dive and hurt my spleen. The Doc grounded me. Now I sit in Harvey's office all day—doing nothing. I'm just waiting for the Doc to send me to Chengtu to the hospital there."

Mac drove me to Harvey's office. It didn't look the same. When Harvey was there, that room was bustling with activity. Now it was deserted and dusty. I noticed some of Harvey's pipes still on top of the desk, as he had left them. Ceder was there.

He said: "You better take Pappy's pipes with you. I've had a hell of a time keeping every guy who comes in from walking off with one." I picked one up—one I had given him for his birthday. I promised Ceder I'd collect them on the way back to the hostel.

Mac and I visited the new quarters and gathered wild flowers from the banks of the canal. I thought of that time when it was Sandy's day off, and he and I had taken this same ride and inspection tour of the new quarters. I would never forget Sandy—or Scotty, or Newkirk. But Sandy—I felt a great tenderness at the mere thought of him. Gentle, sweet, serious Sandy.

Mac said: "Have you gone into a trance? I've been trying to tell you something, but you didn't hear me. What's wrong?"

I laughed. "Nothing. What were you saying?"

"I said, are you going to the Governor's dinner tonight?"

"I don't know anything about it."

"All staff members are supposed to go—Colonel's orders."

"If that's the case," I said, "you'd better take me back to the hostel. I have to find something to wear."

Bob Little was standing in front of the First Squadron's alert shack. Mac stopped the car. Bob said: "Move over. I'll drive."

Mac got out, and Little took his place behind the wheel. Soon we were out of the gate on the main road. Bob said: "Got an escort for tonight?"

I answered: "No."

He said: "Make yourself beautiful, and I'll call for you at seven-thirty."

The invitation card which I found on my desk read:

> Governor Lung requests the pleasure of your company at a banquet in honor of the American Volunteer Group.

Doreen dropped in looking for something to wear. I took a black dress out of the wardrobe trunk. It wasn't bad; at least it had good lines, and the emerald studded jacket was in good condition. We made it shorter and tightened it here and there until it fitted Doreen perfectly. I decided on the same white dinner dress that it seemed to me I wore perpetually.

We were discussing types of hair-do when Paul Frillman peeked in. He said: "Which one of you wants to be escorted by the Minister himself?" We told him we had our escorts already, but wouldn't mind an extra one. "A third party is always a good idea," he said. "I'll be the protector of the two fair damsels."

He was an amusing person, and we all liked him very much. He arranged flowers and made two corsages. "You didn't know I was artistic, did you?" he said. He evidently was enjoying himself watching us making up, fussing with our hair and dabbing perfume behind our ears. Finally, he said:

"You girls got me sidetracked. It's almost seven o'clock and

I'm not even dressed. Oh, what shall I wear? My pink, blue or red?" He placed his chin on one hand and pulled his hair with the other one.

"Get going," I said, "We're leaving at seven-thirty."

Bob Little and C. E. Smith, who was taking Doreen, arrived together, both in wool gabardine, olive-drab uniforms, looking very handsome and I told them so.

The Governor's Palace was on top of a round hill almost in the center of the city. To get to it, we had to go by devious streets and alleys. We drove into a large courtyard, the entrance of which was heavily guarded by the Governor's own well-armed soldiers.

"Not taking any chances, is he?" said Bob.

"Maybe he remembers what happened to his predecessor," I replied.

"What was that?" asked Smith.

"The old Governor and this one, Lung Yin, were very good friends. The old Governor was always preparing for his funeral, although he was still fairly young and in good health. He spent a million National dollars building himself a monument and his friend, Lung Yin, promised him a grand funeral if he died before he, Lung Yin, did. One day the old Governor died. Everyone suspected it wasn't from natural causes but were afraid to say anything. Right away Lung Yin made himself Governor, and as he had promised his friend, saw to it that he had a spectacular funeral.

"For ages Yunnan Province was governed by a warlord, and only recently has the Generalissimo been able to control this Province. Governor Lung Yin has his own standing army, but the Generalissimo has his own troops here also, and some say that they outnumber those of the Governor.

"The old Governor was very keen on aviation and it is to him that the city owes the airdrome we are now using.

"The new Governor is pro-French and before hostilities broke out, he made frequent visits to Hanoi. He is very fond of French wines and French women. At present he is rather quiet—taking care of his soldiers and governing the Province under the Generalissimo's directions."

We parked the car and walked down a lovely garden path to circular steps leading to a wide door. Guards were lined up along the steps, by the door, and even inside the large corridor. Major Shun greeted us and escorted us into the drawing room where the Governor was standing with his retinue. I wondered which one of them would be he.

Much to my surprise, an insignificant little figure stepped forward. I extended my hand, not knowing whether to or not. He bent over and raised it to his lips in true French fashion. When he straightened up, I looked into his eyes. They were crossed! His head was like a shining billiard ball. I introduced Doreen and the boys. The man at the Governor's left, also wearing the uniform of a general, stepped forward and said:

"You remember me, Mrs. Greenlaw? Saigon?"

I didn't remember him at all, but I said, "Yes, of course." He laughed, displaying large brown teeth and spoke to the Governor in Chinese. The Governor said: "Madame he says you have a good memory. A compliment, I think, for women usually have very bad ones." He laughed loud and long, probably thinking it was very amusing.

The General said: "Do you remember General Gaston Wong?"

"Yes," I answered, "where is he?"

"I haven't seen him since I last saw you in Saigon when we played mah-jongg together."

Suddenly it dawned on me who this man was.

"Governor," said he, "you should play with Mrs. Greenlaw. She is the best mah-jongg player of all the foreigners in China. I'll go further than that and say that she can equal our best Chinese women players."

"I am afraid you will be a dangerous opponent," said the Governor. "Shall we play?"

I answered: "I fear I would be an uninteresting player at the same table with your Excellency."

He bowed again: "You are too modest."

Guests were piling up behind us so we moved on. The General from Saigon went along to show us where the "play room," better known as "the bar," was located. After going through several large rooms we found it. It was Louis XIV; precious rugs were scattered all over the marble floor, heavy drapes over the walls. What confusion! The A.V.G. had of course, taken over. They were sitting on tables, chairs, on the floor. One of them had even removed a lovely vase from a small table. Dozens of white silk gowned servants were bringing more and more liquor on silver trays.

Bob said: "I'll try and find you girls a seat and a drink." A servant passed carrying a large tray of bottles of Cinzano, Pernod, brandy, gin, Burgundy, and a silver bucket with ice. Bob stopped him. "Champagne!" he said. "That's for us."

We expected the liquor would run out at the speed the boys were drinking it and I was afraid they would begin to serve *Ouyappee*, *Chaoshing*, and Lord knows what other Chinese dynamite.

The General from Saigon said: "Dinner will be served shortly on the summer terrace. Come with me, and avoid the rush. It won't be cold; it has glass walls and a glass roof. The cement floor has been covered with pine needles."

Bob Little appropriated another bottle of champagne, and we all went to the summer terrace. By the entrance was a table covered with small booklets. We each took one. On the first page was the menu, on the second a list of addresses to be given by different people, including the *Address of Welcome by Governor Lung Yin*, and a *Response by Colonel C. L. Chennault*. Adair would substitute for the Old Man, who was absent.

The third page had a list of toasts,—the first in honor of the President of the National Government of the Republic

of China, H. E. Lin Sen; the second for the President of the
United States; the third was for the Generalissimo and the
fourth and last for Colonel Claire L. Chennault. On the next
page was the program of entertainment, beginning with a
Chinese drama.

I said: "Looks as if this party is going to last all night."

"We can always leave," said Bob.

Our table was next to the Governor's. The addresses and
toasts proceeded according to the program. During the dinner
the French wines gave out and, as I expected, Chinese wines
appeared. The mixture was, to say the least, extremely potent.

The dinner was excellent: chicken soup with bamboo
shoots, green peas with ham, sliced spiced beef, tiger palm
mushrooms with bean sprouts, chicken in Yunnan style, eight
precious pudding, fruit and tea. . . .

Bob said: "What in the name of Heaven is Precious Eight
pudding?"

I explained it was a combination of eight different kinds
of pastes made of fruits and nuts, each paste a different color.
When mixed up, it looked very pretty.

"But why eight?"

"It has something to do with the Eight Immortals," I answered, "better ask someone else about it."

George Paxton, our financial wizard, came to our table.
"How about us boys putting on a little show?" he asked Bob
Little.

"Swell," said Bob. He rose. "You stay here 'til I come
back."

Ten minutes later six of the boys appeared on the stage,
dressed in the beautiful silk, embroidered robes of the Chinese
actors, their faces painted and false, heavy beards stuck on
their chins. Bob was wearing a horrible red mask. They sang
and danced and did a comedy wrestling match. The Chinese
enjoyed it hugely as they applauded and laughed.

After the party I thought I would be able to go home and

straight to bed, but I was mistaken. Bob Little, George Paxton, E. C. Smith, Tom Jones, Adair, all escorted us home. One of the C.N.A.C. pilots, Kessler, was making himself at home already in my quarters when we arrived, reclining amid the leopard skins.

The "actors" asked for cold cream to remove the grease paint. I took a little of the cream out of the jar with one finger and placed a dab on each one's nose. I said: "That will have to do. I don't trust you with the jar. It's hard to get."

Captain Kessler said: "What the devil is going on here?"

We explained we had been to the Governor's dinner.

Adair suggested a crap game.

"No," I said, "I am going to bed. All of you get out!"

The next thing I knew, I was on the floor shooting craps with them.

When I had the dice, I told them to bet anything. Paxton bet me 500 rupees. I lost, but still had the dice. Paxton doubled the bet, and I lost again. I passed the dice to Little, who was next to me. I bet 500. Bob lost. When the dice came to Paxton I said: "Bet 500."

"Hell, no," he said, "I'll only bet you five."

I couldn't believe my ears. When the game broke up, I had still lost a thousand rupees to George Paxton.

Kessler and Bob Little remained after the others had gone. Kessler said: "Who is that guy?"

"That," I answered, "is our financial wizard."

Kessler made a wry face. "You ain't kidding!"

"Oh, well!" I said, "all kinds of men make our group what it is—a damn good fighting outfit."

As they were leaving, Bob turned and said: "Good night, Sucker!"

The group insignia long promised by Walt Disney finally arrived. I didn't like it at first. It was a pin in the shape of a "V" lying on its side, a tiger with small wings leaping out of it. The V, blue; the tiger, gold, blue and black. I was in the supply office when Adair unwrapped the pins. He and all the rest standing by were laughing.

One of the clerks said: "My God, do we have to wear those things? Looks like something we used to buy at the five and ten back home."

"Well," said Adair, "we'll have to wear them and like it."

"Where are we going to wear them?" I asked.

Adair said: "One on each shoulder, but since there aren't enough, I think we'll wear them over the right-hand side pocket. I'll ask the Old Man when he comes back."

All of us were given one each. I took two, one for Harvey, but like the rest, I had to sign for them.

"Whose idea was this, anyway?" somebody asked.

Adair said: "Walt Disney's."

At first we felt a bit conspicuous, but by night time, when everybody was wearing one, I began to get used to the funny pin and wound up eventually liking it.

A few mornings later, Ceder, now Provost Marshal, came in. He looked very official, with his uniform and heavy gun in leather holster, the lower end of which was strapped to his leg. I said: "Dressed to kill. What's going on?"

"Somebody has been stealing our telephone wire. Every night hundreds of yards of it disappear. We finally caught two of the thieves. I took them to the Chinese headquarters. This morning civilian and military authorities sent me an invitation to witness their execution, so I am going."

"Oh, Ceder," I pleaded, "please take me with you!"

"Are you crazy, Mrs. G.? Ever seen one?"

"Yes," I answered, "once in Hangchow. Four thieves were shot."

"That's not so bad," he said, "but these are not going to be shot. These will be tortured. I don't think you'd like it."

I said: "There's only one way to find out."

"Okay," he said doubtfully. "Get your coat on."

The execution took place at the beginning of the straight road that led to the airdrome—a courtyard surrounded by old crumbling walls, which afforded a good clear view. A mob was already there. Idle people of the streets—beggars with running sores; farmers; women carrying dirty children, with mud and mucous-matted faces. Peddlers carrying their wares, howling and clanging brass to attract attention; lepers with parts of their faces eaten away; toothless hags, grinning with expectancy. They were all laughing, all having a good time, just as we would at a picnic.

"My God," said Ceder, "look at them. They think they have come to celebrate. What is it? Why is it these people laugh at other's pain?"

I tried to explain: "A Chinese will laugh when he has great sorrow. He will laugh if you fall down and break your teeth, but he will be feeling sorry for you all the time. It isn't a bad idea, Ceder, to laugh at things when they go wrong—to laugh instead of cry. That's what they do. Otherwise, how could they survive all their hardships, all their poverty? Could you or I?"

Ceder was going to say something, but the appearance of the two culprits kept him silent. We both watched. Four guards were busy tying rope around the thieves' wrists. Both arms were pulled up, the two ropes tied together, and these in turn tied to another rope, which hung from a wooden contraption that looked like a gallows.

The thieves were raised from their feet and were floating in the air. Then we saw an awful thing—huge boulders were tied to their feet increasing the weight of their bodies. The poor devils began to scream for all they were worth, and to make matters worse, four more guards proceeded to lash the thin flesh off the fellows' legs and buttocks with leather and steel whips.

By this time the screaming was hideous. The howling and laughter of the mob, their obscene comments, was more than I could bear!

"Ceder, let's go home."

"No," he said, "you wanted to come, now you stay and see it through."

"Are they going to die, Ceder? Will their arms tear? Please, let's go. I thought it was going to be just an execution—with guns."

"They're almost gone now. They have been whipping them for over an hour. Hear that? They are only moaning now, not screaming as before."

I didn't answer. I had my eyes closed and was trying to keep the awful sound of tearing flesh and moans out of my ears. Ceder took me by the shoulder.

"Come," he said, "I'm sorry. I shouldn't have brought you. It's only a matter of minutes now before they die. The trouble is, this execution won't do any good. Others will keep on stealing telephone wire. They already shot four but that didn't teach the others a lesson. That's why they are doing it this way. Maybe it will put the fear of God into them."

We returned to my quarters. I felt weak. Ceder was very contrite. "We'd better keep this a secret. I don't think Mr. Greenlaw would like it."

I didn't think so, either.

At five o'clock, Easter Sunday, the Colonel, Madame and Generalissimo Chiang Kai Shek returned from Chungking. The Colonel remained, but the Generalissimo and Madame went on to Lashio. Word had been received that they would arrive at ten in the morning, so a covering flight was sent up and used four hours of precious gasoline for nothing. By the time the Army transport came in, all of our planes were on the ground.

The Colonel came into my quarters before dinner to say hello, and to see how things were going. I asked him if he had seen the insignia. "Yes," he said laughing, "I saw them before you did. I took a couple to Chungking but the Madame took them away from me. She liked them. Now I'll have to go and draw a couple more."

I said: "There aren't enough to go around. I already have mine and Harvey's."

"Why don't you wear it then?" he said.

"Not with what I have on, Colonel. I am having people over for dinner tonight. Will you join us?"

The Colonel was eyeing me with curiosity. "I like that white robe trimmed with black you have on. It's remarkable the way you produce clothes. Where did you get it?"

I explained to him that I had bought it in Hong Kong. "Colonel," I asked, "where is Harvey now?"

"Calcutta."

"Could I go, too?"

"No," he said. "You stay here. I want you to send a copy of the *Diary* tomorrow to Lin Wei Kui, the Chinese Secretariat. He will forward it to Chungking to the Commission on Aeronautical Affairs."

"Yes, Sir," I answered and added, "are you coming for dinner?"

"No," he said, "I have too much to do. Just got in, and maybe I'll have to leave tomorrow for Lashio."

"Can I go with you, please?"

"No. If I need you, I'll send for you."

"Is that a promise?"

"Yes. Good night, and don't stay up too late. I don't want you down with pneumonia."

Chapter XII

WITH the Old Man and Harvey absent it wasn't strange that discipline at Kunming began to deteriorate rapidly. Almost every member of the Group was beginning to show signs of war weariness. Pilots and ground crews had taken a terrific pounding and their nerves were starting to fray along the edges. Wear and tear on the planes was enormous and our general situation was growing steadily worse. We didn't have enough of anything—plane replacements, spare parts, anti-aircraft weapons. The odds the boys fought against were consistently so overwhelming as to be almost ridiculous. No matter how many Jap planes they shot down an equal number—or more—appeared on the next raid. And look as we might—and did—we could see no relief in sight.

Although everyone realized we were fighting a losing battle and would inevitably be chased out of Burma and perhaps even farther than that, nobody talked about it much. The pilots just kept on knocking down Japs and the ground crews laughed off repeated bombings, threw away the clock and worked heroically to "keep 'em flying." The only thing the A.V.G. had more than enough of was a collective sense of humor and an inexhaustible supply of guts. Under the circumstances our disciplinary difficulties were probably no worse than might have been expected.

Ceder dropped by one morning to say he had a little matter to attend to at Number Two Hostel. He suspected some of the First Squadron pilots and men had been smuggling contraband up from Burma in our convoys. Trucks left the border fully loaded and arrived practically empty—or even not at all. Machine guns and ammunition had disappeared into thin air.

Ceder said: "Colonel's orders to go along with McMillan and search the quarters. There'll be trouble."

I suggested he go fully armed.

"The hell of it is," said Ceder, "with the Old Man in Lashio and Pappy in Calcutta there's nobody here the guys have any respect for." He sighed dismally. "I'm afraid I'll get the short end of the deal."

He really was worried as he left to carry out his orders. I didn't envy him the job.

I was having lunch with the Chaplain, Adair, McMillan and Sam Prevo, when a mess boy told the Chaplain: "Man outside wanchee talk see."

The Padre went to the door, spoke to someone we couldn't see and returned quickly. He said to McMillan: "Two men out there say there's some kind of trouble at the field."

Mac no sooner reached the door than we heard a terrific scuffling. Then Mac staggered back into the room. Someone had slugged him. Adair rushed out. I started to follow, but the Padre grabbed me. Mac wanted to go after them but the Padre grabbed him, too. Mac said:

"Those bastards. They're sore because we searched their quarters."

Adair, six feet three and husky, made short work of the two attackers. He was gone some time and returned to say he had placed the men under arrest—confined to quarters. I wondered why they weren't behind bars.

"They beat the daylights out of Ceder," he said. "He's in the hospital. Sam Prevo just went over there."

When I got to the hospital Sam didn't want to let me in. I heard Ceder mumbling, "I want to see her." His eyes were closed and his head jerked from side to side like a robot.

"He may have a concussion," Sam said. "If he snaps out of it he'll be damn lucky. I gave him a shot—he's out like a light—wouldn't even know you."

While there I stopped in to see Boyington. I had received

a note from him saying: "Dear Mrs. G.: Why don't you bring a guy American cigarettes when he is in the hospital?" Luckily, I had one package of Camels left, which Red Probst had given me. I was saving them and had been smoking *Cotabs*. There were still American cigarettes at the Kwang Sueng Yang, at 200 National dollars for a tin of fifty, but four dollars for each was too much for me.

Boyington was flat on his back—head bandaged and his two knees covered with adhesive tape.

"Hello, handsome," I said.

"Gee! You did come. I didn't think you would, but I was hoping. Gets kind of lonesome here."

I opened the package of Camels, lit one and placed it between his lips. "What happened to you?" I asked.

"Well, starting from the beginning: when we were at Magwe, the Japs strafed hell out of the place. That's when Frank Swartz got it. We had so many planes shot to pieces we had to move up to Loiwing. A few days after we arrived, the Japs came over—ten of 'em. We were in the air—at 20,000 feet. Suddenly our radios said the little yellow-bellies were having a picnic over the field. We blasted down and crashed seven of them in flames. I made a lousy landing, overshot the field and banged my head."

He puffed on his cigarette. "Two days later, the Japs surprised us at dawn. It was still dark—I was in the club house frying some eggs, when I heard machine guns. I made a dash to the nearest ditch. Nobody told me it was thirty feet deep!"

"How unromantic," was my only comment.

"What do you mean?"

"Your injuries. Falling into a ditch."

As I was leaving, Boyington said: "Got any clean pajamas, Mrs. G.? I haven't been to my quarters yet, and I feel pretty dirty with what I have on."

I said, "Harvey may have left some. I'll look around."

Outside, near the tennis court, I found J. E. Terry, who,

several weeks before, had cracked up with an American instructor of the cadet school at Yunnanyi. The instructor had been killed and when poor Terry came to he discovered both his legs were broken in many places. He gave some coolies instructions on how to make a stretcher out of bamboo poles, and by signs made them understand he wanted to get to a village. Then he passed out.

Three days later he woke up in a hut, with a Chinese doctor by his side telling him he was going to live because he was very strong and had the will to live. Terry had been a prize fighter. He had been in the hospital over three months. His bones were finally healing, although one of his legs was slightly bent. I stopped to talk to him.

"You're a sight for sore eyes, Mrs. G.," he said. "A guy sure gets lonesome in this awful place." Sam Prevo came out of the little building and joined us. "When do I get permission to leave this compound, Doc?" Terry asked. "I'm fed up. If it wasn't for Jones and Mrs. G. I'd go nuts."

"Another two months ought to do it," said the Doctor. "You're lucky to be alive."

Terry said: "I'm no use to anyone here. I tried to resign, but they won't let me."

I bent low and whispered into Terry's ear. As we walked away, I looked back. Terry's face was beaming. Sam saw me smile, looked back, and then asked me: "Say—what do you do to these guys?"

"That," I said, "is a secret."

I worked hard all next day so as to be through by four o'clock. I had Tugboat and the amah clean my quarters and place fresh flowers in the vases, ordered a special tea for afternoon, opened the last tin of Kraft cheese I had and a jar of pickles and placed the remaining Camel cigarettes in a box on top of the chow bench.

At exactly four o'clock, there was a racket outside my door. I opened it. Poor Terry, all dressed up in his best pajamas, was lying on a stretcher, four hospital coolies trying to lower it gently to the floor.

I said, "Come on in, before anyone sees you."

Terry was grinning, a mischievous light in his eyes. "Gee, Mrs. G., this is swell of you."

We lifted him off the stretcher and settled him on the leopard-covered sofa with pillows behind his back to make him comfortable. He gazed about the room.

"Say—this is some place! Looks like home. I like it!"

I fussed over him like an old hen, trying to make him feel at ease.

"No one saw me leave, but Boyington," he said. "I had to tell him you had asked me to tea."

He had no more than spoken when the door opened and Boyington entered, his arms over the shoulders of two coolies. He wore a blue bathrobe over Harvey's white silk pajamas.

Tugboat brought the tea things, and the amah waited on us. After we finished, she passed the American cigarettes. The boys sat silently smoking, enjoying the good tobacco. It was getting late, and I wondered if they were thinking of staying for dinner. That I knew couldn't be done because they would be missed at the hospital. I began to get nervous, as I knew I had no business inviting them over for tea.

So who should barge in at this critical moment, but the Doc himself—Sam Prevo! "Well, well!" he said.

I said, "Now just be a regular guy, Sam. Terry hasn't been out for months and Greg's well enough to get around."

"It's okay by me," said Sam, "but if Dr. Gentry finds out——"

"Who's going to tell him?"

"Not me," said Sam. "Tell you what I'll do—I'll get the ambulance, drive it myself, pile you guys in and put you to bed. But for God's sake keep your mouths shut."

Pretty soon he returned with the four hospital coolies. He had parked the ambulance in the back. The coast was clear.

"Boyington," he said, "you use Terry's crutches, and we'll carry him down on the stretcher."

In the evening after dinner, Dr. Gentry came in. He was very businesslike. "What's this I hear of you getting two sick men out of the hospital and entertaining them for tea?"

"Who told you that?" I asked.

"Things get around."

"Did it do any harm?"

"No," said Gentry, "it didn't. But it might have. What if Terry had rolled down the stairs? How did he get here anyway?

I told him about the stretcher and the four coolies.

"And how did he get back?"

"The same way he came."

The doctor relented appreciably. "Well, don't do it again—but I guess it did do Terry a lot of good. Gets pretty tiresome, that hospital."

After dinner I talked to the Colonel. He had just returned from Lashio and was plainly worried. He said Harvey was still in Calcutta, but was expected back soon. "Things aren't so hot at Loiwing," he said. "I'm going back there tonight."

I asked if I could go with him.

"Not this time. You stay here and hold the fort." He laughed. "Tell you what—I'll send for you in two or three days."

I pleaded: "Take me now. The Group historian should be at the scene of combat—that's what regulations say."

"True, true, but I'll give you another job while I am gone."

"What's that?" I hoped it would be interesting.

"You can look after Joe."

Joe was his dachshund.

The unexpected arrival of a rather famous lady relieved the boredom of one of our Kunming nights. Eric Shilling, who had been to the Gold Coast to ferry back a new plane, brought me a box of perfume from Ahmed Soliman, Cairo's renowned perfumer. I was glad to get it as the French perfumes I had bought in Indo-China were nearly gone. Eric said Pilot Adkins, who had crashed on the Persian Desert on his way back from Cairo, had arrived by transport from India and could the two of them come over that night and play the phonograph?

They arrived with some new records, a soda siphon and a bottle of whisky which Eric displayed proudly. He had flown it all the way from Cairo. They said Tom Jones and Greg Boyington might drop in, too.

Jones showed up with a new record.

"Want to hear it?"

We said sure—so he played, *The Last Time I Saw Paris* which, out there, we had not heard before. We listened silently and almost tearfully.

Then Shilling cleared away the chairs and chow bench and I danced, by turns, with the three of them.

Boyington hobbled in on crutches and we all sat on the floor and listened to the music. In the midst of our concert, the lights flicked out and the music stopped abruptly. I had candles for such emergencies and placed two over the radio and two on the chest of drawers beneath the large mirror.

We were grousing about the Kunming Edison Company— or whatever they call it—when someone knocked on the door. Shilling opened it. In the dim candlelight I barely distinguished a woman in slacks, but thought I was mistaken.

Shilling said: "It's Whitehead, Mrs. Greenlaw."

That was strange, as Whitehead had never before come to my quarters. I went to the door. He said: "I was at the C.N.A.C. office when the plane came in. This lady arrived. I was told to bring her to you."

That was wrong. Our quarters were barred to everyone except the military. A woman. I wondered who she was, and what she was doing there. "Come in," I said.

She entered. The first thing she said was: "Madame, your name precedes you. I bring you a message from Cairo, from the Free French Headquarters."

Boyington inquired: "And who in the hell are you?"

Only then did I realize the woman had been speaking to me in French. She spoke again—in English this time: "I am Clara Boothe Luce, the playwright, and part owner of *Life* and *Time* magazines!"

This didn't make much impression. It had been some time since any of us had worried about theatres, or even magazines.

"Sit down please," I said, "and may I take your things?"

She gave me her coat, but remained standing. I introduced the boys and asked if she would like a drink.

Shilling poured her one. She evidently was quite thirsty because she drank it all.

I asked why she spoke to me in French.

"*Madame est Russe,*" she answered.

"No," I said, "Madame is not Russian, Madame is American. Speak to me in English. I understand it better.

"Maybe Mrs. Luce—Boothe?" I hesitated over the name. "Maybe she would like to look around."

Shilling and Adkins said they had met her in Cairo. They'd show her what there was to see.

While they were gone, Jones, Boyington and I wondered what had brought her there to that God-forsaken place. "Well, let's not worry about it," said Jones philosophically. "Maybe we'll find out tomorrow."

The lights came on again and Jones played *When It's Round-Up Time in Texas*. We listened to the lyric. Jones was wearing his saber silver chain. He took it off, put it around my right wrist and clasped it. "It looks like a bracelet," he said. "Will you wear it? I wish they were diamonds—diamonds suit you." He said it so wistfully that both Boyington and I looked at him.

"You know, Greg," he said, "to me Olga, the Colonel and

Mr. Greenlaw are the A.V.G. Without them, there is no such thing. Olga, you are the spirit of the A.V.G."

At first I thought he was kidding—or just talking to himself. I realized he was in earnest when he said:

"So far I've been unlucky with this malaria but as soon as I can I'll get into plenty of fights. If I shoot down three Japs, that ought to pay for my keep. So far, I have only been an—well, excess baggage."

As it was time to take Greg back to the hospital, I rang for Tugboat who popped in almost instantly. "Missy wanchee me?"

"Yes, Tugboat," I said. "Get some clean sheets and fix bed for new Missy. She sleep here tonight."

"Me catchum book. Missy sign."

"No, don't get the book, Tugboat. New Missy is my guest—no signing."

The hostel had a visitor's book. Everyone signed and was charged one dollar a day. But that was only for military visitors, and I didn't know just what rule to apply to Mrs. Luce. I thought it would simplify matters by having her as my guest, although no guests were allowed.

We took Boyington back to the hospital. When we returned, we found Adair, standing on the top step in front of the hostel. He was in his pajamas and had a robe over them.

"Did you two see anyone outside?" We said we hadn't and asked why.

"Someone broke into the bar, and one of the men told me it was Boyington."

I said "He couldn't have. He was with us all the time."

"The fellows swears it was he. Did you at any time notice Boyington's absence."

Jones said: "He went to the bathroom once, but when he came back he didn't have anything with him."

"That's the time he did it, then," said Adair. "We'll have to try him for that."

"Maybe the fellow who told you did it and is trying to put the blame on Boyington," I said.

"No," said Adair, "he isn't strong enough. The man who did it twisted the lock off the door with his bare hands. Only one guy in the Group can do that, and that's Boyington."

"Uhm," I said, "circumstantial evidence—and you are going to blame him on that?"

"We'll have a meeting tomorrow, and we will call both of you to testify that Boyington left the room."

"You won't get me to testify!" I said.

About ten-thirty, Mrs. Luce returned with Shilling and Adkins. I showed her the bed, and I went to bed myself, thinking about the message from Cairo, who had sent it and what it was. She never did tell me what it was.

Saturday morning, April 11th, Mrs. Luce and I were having breakfast in my office. She wore her brown slacks and jacket well, and the brown silk paisley scarf, placed far back on her head, made a pretty frame and was very becoming.

She asked me a lot of questions, but I evaded most of them, as we were not supposed to give out information to anyone. We were still eating when Shilling and Adkins came in.

"Play the A.V.G. records for Mrs. Luce, Olga," said Shilling.

I played all the records we had made one night when an American general was there. Mrs. Luce liked them and said: "May I take them with me?"

"No," I answered, "the Colonel and Harvey wouldn't like it."

"It would be good publicity for the A.V.G.," she said. "I could put them on the *March of Time* program. It would pay quite a bit of money...."

"Let her take them, Olga," Adkins urged.

Mrs. Luce wanted to go to the field. We went in Shilling's car. Outside we met George Paxton. I introduced him to Mrs. Luce. "This man," I told her, "will give you all the information you desire."

I knew very well Paxton would tell her only what he thought she ought to know and nothing more, and give her a lot of doubletalk.

I was right. In subsequent articles she described me as a white Russian, the wife of the paymaster. Paxton kidded her about the "furious-fighting-flying-tigers," who went up in the skies, bang-bagged-a-Jap, and hollered, "Eureka-certified check, —five hundred smackers!" "Certified-check,"—that's what she pounced upon and finally wrote about.

While at the field, we took her to the camouflaged repair shop, which was only a clearing under some trees covered with huge fishing nets, threaded with branches of trees, so that from the sky nothing could be seen but green trees and shrubbery. She took a lot of pictures there of me and Lucy standing by a plane, on top of one and up a ladder near the propeller. The boys were busy taking pictures of her. From there we went back to the airdrome proper, where she took more pictures of pilots and men in front of planes.

On the way back to the hostel, we stopped at the telegraph office. She wanted to send a message to New York, which took almost an hour.

We went back to the hostel for lunch. Shilling still insisted I give Mrs. Luce the records. I knew I would catch hell from the Colonel and Harvey. They were perfectly harmless— music and kidding and impromptu speeches but there was a danger of their being misunderstood by anyone who failed to consider the circumstances under which they had been recorded. However, I finally let her take one.

The C.N.A.C. plane was leaving at two o'clock. Mrs. Luce said good-by without bothering to thank me for the hospitality or for the record.

Her stay in Kunming had lasted exactly sixteen hours— scarcely enough for her to become an authority on the A.V.G.

The days went by and nothing of much importance happened in Kunming. Boyington's "trial" was dropped as he was certainly in the clear, but the real culprit was never found. Ceder was still in the hospital but recovering—the fellows that had attacked him were supposed to be confined to their quarters, but were not. Discipline was shot to pieces. I was planning a quiet evening when Jones came in.

"Aren't going to bed now, are you? It's only eight o'clock."

"I was," I said, "but now that you are here, I'll postpone it."

"I won't stay long," he said, smiling. 'I have good news, and knowing that you are interested, I came to tell you."

He placed both his hands on my shoulders. "I'm fit! Fit as a fiddle! And I'm off tomorrow to join our combat group at Loiwing!" His strong, long arms almost lifted me off the floor and swung me in a circle in the center of the room.

I had scarcely ever seen anyone so happy, so eager, so full of life and anticipation.

"Thank God," he said, "I'll be able to do my share. I am going down there, Olga, and fight like mad. I've got to make up for lost time." For a moment he was serious, then he smiled again. He handed me a letter, and pointed to a paragraph. "Read that."

I read it.

"Can you imagine," he said, "my wife has been spending all my money buying War Bonds. That's swell, but hell, I want my money put away so I can go back to the University. From now on everything I earn, including bonuses for shooting down a few Japs, I'm going to send directly to the University until I've paid up four years' tuition. I want to go to law school. You're going to laugh at this, but some day I'm going to be Governor of Washington State! What do you think of that?"

I said, "I think it's great—but it means a lot of work, a lot of study...."

He suddenly switched subjects, "I want to show you something I found in the Chinese storage house out at the field. I'll go and get it."

Before I could say "no," he was off. He returned shortly with a gadget that looked like a large camera with a handle on it.

"It's an instrument for star navigation. Come to the window and I'll show you."

I squeezed beside him in front of the small window. He showed me some of the stars and explained the use of the instrument for night navigation. The whole thing wasn't very clear to me, but I didn't want to disillusion him.

"All this leads to one thing," he said. "Just before the Colonel left, I presented a little plan. I talked to Harvey about it, too."

"What is it?" I was beginning to get impatient.

"A raid on Hanoi—Indo-China! A night raid! I've been on reconnaissance trips as far as Laokai, on the border. I know that country now like the palm of my hand. I could lead a flight down to Hanoi and back without the slightest hesitation—at night, I mean. We could sweep over them silently, make three passes over the field, drop all our bombs, and then ground strafe and get away before they knew what hit them!"

"Did the Colonel give you permission?"

"He did, and he didn't. First I have to go to Loiwing, get in a few fights, get the feel of it, and I'll be ready."

"Are you sure that you feel all right now? No dizzy spells? Perfectly all right?"

He looked at me sharply.

"Funny, you asking that. Swear you won't say a word?"

I promised I wouldn't.

"The other day I went on a flight by myself in one of the new P-40 E's I gave it the works for about an hour, then came in with a perfect landing. Here's the secret—when I got out of that cockpit I was so damn dizzy I had to lie on the ground beside the plane for about a half-hour. Lucky nobody saw me."

"What do you mean by 'the other day,' Jones?"

"Yesterday," he said, "but don't you tell anyone or they won't let me take off tomorrow."

"Jones," I said, "tell Sam Prevo. Just to see what he says. You are well, true, but maybe you are still weak. Tell him, Jones. Let me tell him."

"No, no, no!" he said, almost angry at me. "You swore you wouldn't say anything."

"You win," I said, "but if anything happens to you, I shall feel I was to blame—Tom."

"Tom," he repeated. "Sounds funny when you say it. You always call me 'Jones.' I got used to it, and I kind of like it. All the others call me 'Tom' but you are the only one who doesn't." He placed one arm around my shoulder. Seriously, he said: "You won't tell?"

"No," I said, "but if anything ever happens, if you get killed, it will be because of this. I shall never forgive myself. Dammit! I'm going to tell Sam!"

He held my face with both his hands and looked at me for a long time before he said: "You won't do it. You promised me. . . ." Quickly, gently, he kissed my lips and rushed out of the room.

I couldn't go to sleep thinking of him. My sense of duty told me to tell Sam. My pride in being able to keep a secret and a promise held me back. I prayed hard and long asking God to keep this boy safe, to spare him. Maybe he is all right, I thought. He certainly had no premonition of death, or any ill thing happening to him, as Sandy and Jack Newkirk had. After praying, I felt better and went to sleep.

I slept through the whole night and would have slept more if it hadn't been for the roaring noise of a plane diving right into the compound. I jumped out of bed and ran to the window—to see a plane zoom and circle. It turned back toward the compound, dove straight toward the building in front of my quarters. In that split second before the plane pulled up, I saw Jones' face and the wave of his hand!

I worked fast and hard all day. Late in the afternoon, I made a large pot of fresh coffee and took it to the hospital. I knew it would be a treat for Terry and Boyington.

"Thanks, old lady," said Boyington. He drank a cup of coffee all in one gulp and added: "Funny about Jones, the other night. Do you think he really meant what he said about you and the Colonel and Harvey being the A.V.G.? Do you really believe that he was in earnest when he said that shooting three Japs would pay for his keep?"

"Yes," I said, "I believe him. Jones is not much for saying things he doesn't mean. He left for Loiwing this morning."

"I know. I heard him buzzing you. For a moment I thought he was going to land in your bedroom!"

On the way back to my quarters, I met Adair. "Hello," I said, "how about writing out a special travel order for me? Official business to Loiwing!"

"Not without a confirmation from the Colonel. He didn't authorize me to do it."

I said: "He didn't have time before he left. But he told me he was going to send for me in two or three days."

"When he does I'll issue a travel order," said Adair drily.

Chapter XIII

I RECEIVED a letter from Harvey saying he had arrived at Loiwing from Calcutta, intended to continue to Kunming, but the Colonel had stopped him.

I was at breakfast when Adair came in, smiling and waving a paper.

"Read this, Mrs. G., special travel order for the *War Diary* Statistician—official business."

I was so happy I almost shouted. "Thanks, Skipper. Thanks a lot."

"The plane leaves at three o'clock. Come and see me before you push off. I have some messages and letters for you to take. And I want to see how you look."

"Yes, sir," I said, clicking my heels and saluting him, laughing all the time. He too, was laughing.

"You don't take things seriously, do you?"

"No use—life's too short."

"It'll be tough there. You still can back out."

"Nope—got my orders."

The news soon got around that I was going down to the front on official business. Red Petach came over with a letter for Pete.

"Gosh," she said, "I envy you—going down there where things are happening."

"What shall I tell Pete?"

"Tell him to hurry back—and give him a kiss for me."

After I had finished packing, I made out a will, of all things. But I thought it would be a good idea to be prepared, just in case. I didn't like the way they had been disposing of the dead pilot's belongings. I felt the same way Sandy had felt about it. So, to make sure they wouldn't trifle with mine, I made out the will to Doreen Davis.

"But," she said, "if anything happens to you, there's Harvey."

"Don't worry about him," I answered. "If nothing happens on my way to Lashio, you need not worry about Harvey, because from then on, we are traveling together. If I crash, he'll be on the same plane."

Ceder came in. "Are you really going Mrs. G.?" I told him I was.

"If you're wearing your uniform I have a very nice wool army shirt that's too small for me. I'll get it for you."

He returned with a beautifully tailored olive-drab shirt. The fit was perfect.

I wore Sandy's tunic, the one he had left with me, and a lighter-colored pair of gabardine slacks. Sandy's wings were still on just as he had left them. On the right side over the pocket, I had pinned the new A.V.G. insignia, the Flying Tiger, and the Chinese insignia, two white eagles on a red background, bordered by a blue circle.

Ceder gave me a letter for Harvey and drove me to Adair's office. "Pretty snappy," Adair said. "You're going down to Lashio where there are a lot of R.A.F. and American officers. You are one of us and you have to look right." He straightened the A.V.G. pin, fixed my overseas cap, looked at me again. "Okay," he said. He gave me a large package. "These papers on top are for the Colonel. Very important! The rest are letters for the fellows in Loiwing."

The plane was already in. The pilot, a good-looking, middle sized man about thirty came towards me. I knew him well— the only Australian pilot in China National Airways Company.

"Hello, D," I said. I always called him "D" as his name, DeCanzo, was hard for me to remember.

He smiled and said: "Well, Olga, I see you are my passenger. By Jove, they gave you priority, too. Big shot, eh?"

I was about to get into the plane, struggling with Lucy and the papers Adair gave me, when Boyington drove up. "Going, Mrs. G.? Not even saying good-by to a guy?"

He looked badly. The wound on his head hadn't completely healed. He kept brushing the flies off it. Lucy pulled impatiently at her leash.

"You aren't taking our mascot, are you?" he asked.

I said: "When I'm here she is your mascot—when I leave, she becomes my dog." I put out my hand and Boyington took it. "Good-by," I said. "Keep your chin up!"

"I'll miss you, sure as hell. I owe it to you that I have been able to check myself. . . . There are a lot of things a guy can't take, but I took them, on the chin. But now that you are going—I don't know. I have an idea you aren't coming back here." He was talking to himself, I thought.

As I was climbing the steps he said: "Wait! Bend down and let me whisper."

When he got through, I said: "No, Greg Boyington, you can't do that!"

I found a seat near the tail, remembering what Colonel Edwards told me: "Whenever you take a trip on a plane, ride in a seat near the tail." I thought of Scotty, my good friend— gloomy thoughts for one about to start on a trip.

I checked my baggage. The suitcase was up on the shelf, and my traveling kit. The portable typewriter I had drawn from supply was in the luggage compartment, I hoped. The plane was taxiing. I saw Ceder standing by his car and waved to him. We were off and flying over lovely Kunming lake. It was three o'clock. Lucy settled herself on my lap and began to shake and pant as she always does on a plane. This irritated me, but I didn't scold her as I knew she was extremely nervous. The plane was fully loaded with Chinese passengers, two war correspondents who had come from Chungking, and Doctor Evans.

The pilot told me there were no signs of enemy planes anywhere and the weather being fair, we would arrive at Lashio at six o'clock.

I wasn't feeling too well—the days in the hospital, the hard work in my office following that, the worry and the uncertainty of our group. I had a miserable headache, and was afraid of a nervous breakdown, although I had never had one before. Then, too, flying made me jittery. I hated to fly, but always seemed to find myself on a plane.

At five minutes of six we landed. The field was crowded—Americans, British, Indians, Burmese and Chinese. Most of them were waiting to get a seat on a transport to India—to safety.

The first person I recognized was Cox, a little fellow I knew in Batavia. I hadn't seen him since October, in Rangoon. Now he was in R.A.F. Intelligence. He said: "When you got off the plane, everybody said that you were one of those new American lady soldiers."

Cox drove me to the C.N.A.C. hostel. Captain Hensley was standing inside the small compound. He was one of the C.N.A.C. pilots, but became ill with some Oriental disease and was placed in charge of the Lashio hostel by the company while he was recuperating. He grinned: "A woman, by gosh! Long time no see. How are you?"

I told him I felt rotten. He said Harvey had reserved a room for me.

The room wasn't bad, rather small, but it had two beds covered with mosquito netting, dressing table and desk. It even boasted a bathroom!

"No running water," the Captain said, "but we still have plenty of servants."

I asked about a doctor. Cox said he would get the R.A.F. medico and returned presently with Doctor La Frenais. I told him I had pains in my lower abdomen and the small of my back.

He dissolved some tablets, put the liquor in a syringe and injected it into my arm. "I think you have kidney trouble," he said. "The water out here will do it. And you're badly run down. This will make you sleep. That's what you need, a good rest."

I began to get drowsy and could hardly hear what he was saying. He helped me undress, and put me to bed. I didn't see him leave the room, I was sound asleep.

It was almost noon when I woke up. The R.A.F. Doctor was standing by my bed. "How are you now?" he asked. I told him I felt slightly dizzy. He laughed. "Can you get up?"

For an answer I jumped out of bed. He rang for the boy. The Indian appeared immediately. When asked about coffee, he said he would see if he could get some. A little while later he returned, not with one cup but with a potful. The Doctor and I drank several cups of it. He then took some blood from one of my fingers, and left, promising me a report in about two hours.

The report was bad news. He thought I had sand in the bladder and advised me to go to Calcutta for at least two weeks in hospital and have a thorough examination. I thanked him and told him it would be impossible. I didn't have time to be ill. I asked for something to kill the pain, which he said I was sure to have often. He gave me some pink pills and instructions for taking them.

I lost both the pills and the instructions and didn't have any more pains which were, as I should have learned by then, merely the aftermath of the flight from Kunming. I always imagined all sorts of things were wrong with me after a flight in a plane.

It was hotter than blazes in Lashio, so I put on a thin cotton shirt and a pair of shorts. The hostel was a series of ten little rooms, in a row. The front doors led out to a narrow porch, and into the so-called garden, which was cluttered with Jeeps, trucks and all kinds of cars, from Fords to Packards. In the middle of the compound was an enormous old mango tree which bore no fruit.

A heavy-set, tall, handsome man about fifty, in khaki shorts and bush shirt, with the rank of a colonel, approached us. Captain Hensley introduced him—"Colonel St. John."

"I know Harvey very well," he said. "I'm at Maymyo with General Hearn."

It was getting late, but still light enough to see a Jeep come skidding into the compound—with Harvey at the wheel! With him were two American Air Corps officers—Lieutenant-Colonel Tex Sanders, and Major Hal Wright. Nice chaps and not bad to look at. They were stationed at Karachi with the 51st Pursuit Group.

They washed up a bit and we went in for dinner. Colonel St. John was already eating with Captain Hensley.

"Sardines, boys and girls," said Hensley. "Honey and biscuits and a dash of tea to fill you up."

That was our dinner.

Back in our room, Harvey said, "Catch!" A little blue box flew through the air and into my waiting hands. I opened it and saw a lovely white sparkling diamond in a plain platinum setting!

"Two and a half carats," he said, "for your birthday."

My birthday! Almost a month before, but he hadn't forgotten! Good old Harvey. "Got it in Calcutta," he said, "it came off a maharanee's ear, or nose. Supposed to be very good—like it?"

Did I like it! ! !

"What's new in Kunming?" he asked.

I told him about the "ganging up" on Ceder and Mac, and gave him Ceder's letter.

"Are you planning to stay very long?" I asked.

"I'll be here for some time."

"Why did you go to Calcutta?"

"To try and get replacements. These two boys who came

along with me would like to join us. The Army eventually will take over anyway, and it's a good idea to have some of the Army pilots going on missions with ours so that they can learn the ropes. Our men are very experienced and could be a lot of help to these new pilots coming into India. But the Big Shots over there in India think they know everything. They will probably bobble the details."

I didn't quite understand, so Harvey explained.

"I'll begin at the beginning. From Kunming I went to Lashio, talked to General Ling and went down to Maymyo to Stilwell's headquarters. He wasn't there, so I went down to the front at Pyawbwe. Talked to him. He advised that I go to India, contact General Brereton, of the Tenth Air Force, and ask him for some planes. I went back to Maymyo, stayed there a day waiting to see Stilwell again and General Wavell. They arrived almost at the same time. Wavell thought it was a good idea that I go to India. He gave me a letter to Air Vice Marshal Stevenson who was in Calcutta, and who, he said, would do anything he could to help us, the A.V.G. Here's the letter. When I got to Calcutta, Stevenson wasn't there, so I talked to Group Captain Manning, whom you know."

The letter read:

Government House

30.3.42

Dear Steve,

This is Greenlaw, Chennault's Chief of Staff, who is going to India to try and get re-equipment for A.V.G. and discuss air policy with Brereton.

He suggests our basing some light bombers in China to attack the Japanese air fields under protection of their fighters and warning system, which he says is quite adequate.

You might talk it over with him and when I pass through Calcutta on Thursday I might pick him up and have him at Delhi to see Brereton and Peirse.

Whether what he proposes is best way to use some of our small forces I am not sure, but I am all for attacking the enemy on their grounds, if we can.

The signature was a long, heavy, vertical line with curlicues which resembled hieroglyphics. I thought of the name, General Sir Archibald Wavell and tried to connect the scrawl with any of the capital letters, but couldn't.

Harvey continued: "Before I left Kunming, the Old Man gave me these notes."

He tossed them on the bed. In the Old Man's handwriting I read:

NOTES FOR H. K. GREENLAW

1. Improvement aircraft reporting service at Lashio and Mandalay.
   a—A.V.G. radio station, BP-3 (Station at Lashio), can be used as intelligence center for net if:
      1. Provided with additional receivers, operators and mechanics. (Quarters, messes, dugouts, telephones, transportation)
      2. Additional landing strips and dispersal areas: Lashio, Mandalay, Schwebo, Myitkyina, Kutkai.
         a—Command Post radio stations, quarters, mess, transportation, office huts, telephone communications, refuelers, fuel, ammunition, bombs, mechanics, laborers.
2. Reinforcements: Draw on Group at Karachi for:
   a—50 pursuit planes and pilots to be attached to A.V.G. and commanded by experienced A.V.G. pilots.
   b—30 light bombers, Lockheed Hudson preferred or Blenheim, to be drawn from R.A.F., India, and operated under China Command.
   c—50 pursuit pilots, 100 crew chiefs, 50 armorers, 20 radio operators, 30 radio mechanics, 50 clerical administrative, 12 staff officers (American)
   d—Complete crew for bombers, plus key men for technical and administrative work (British) Chinese bases will be used for bombers and part of pursuit units with advanced fields in Burma. Chinese personnel and facilities will be available.
3. United States Army Ferry Command to bring in personnel, food and vital equipment such as radio sets, telephone sets, ammunition, etc.

"What happened in Calcutta?"

"As I said, Stevenson wasn't there. On Thursday, General Wavell came through and I went with him in his own Lockheed Hudson to Delhi. Air Vice Marshal Peirse wasn't there. I stayed at the Imperial Hotel, in New Delhi, which is probably the finest hotel in Asia. The Tenth Air Force has taken it over as headquarters—and boy-oh-boy!, air-conditioning, wonderful service, millions of beautiful secretaries—that's the way to fight the war! On Sunday I received this note:

> Sunday
> 11:25 A.M.
>
> Mr. Greenlaw,
>
> General Wavell's A.D.C. has just telephoned to ask you to lunch with him today at 1:30.
>
> Will you please call him at 3120, or send me a note whether or not you can accept and I will call him.
>
> D. W. Jepson
> (Secretary to General Brereton)

"Did you go to lunch?" I asked.

"Yes," he said, "I went to the palace of the C. in C. It is right next to the Viceroy's Palace. I liked Lady Wavell very much, and their two lovely, charming daughters."

"And then?"

"I had a long talk with General Brereton that same afternoon, but he said he had no bombers at this time, that is, no medium bombers. I got the same story from the R.A.F., although they, at least, promised to send some Blenheims over."

"Then your trip wasn't very successful, was it?"

"I didn't expect it to be."

"And what is the program now?"

"I'm going back to report to General Stilwell."

"What did the Old Man say about it?"

"I forgot to tell you—the Old Man has been inducted! They made him a colonel!"

I said: "A colonel! After all he's done! That's damn generous of them!"

"The colonel isn't squawking so why should you?"

It still made me angry. The woods were full of colonels who hadn't smelled a whiff of gunpowder or done a single thing more than shuffle papers and sign their names to reports and yet a silver eagle was all they saw fit to give the man who stood out clearly as the most effective American aerial strategist and tactician the war had produced so far. I calmed down enough to ask:

"Do you think we are going to fold up here, then?"

"No doubt if we don't get replacements. We have no proper fields, no nets, no operating bases. I suggested we build up and hold Paoshan, Loiwing, Myitkyina, Wanting and Kunming. With these bases well supplied, under our operational control, we can hold on and keep the Japs back. But, we need a hell of a lot of help."

We went to bed. It was late. I was still mad about the colonel.

The next morning I went through Harvey's suitcases, as wives will do, and found six tins of Nest-cafe, the powdered coffee which is so easy to make; six tins of corned beef, a few tins of baked beans, two of milk, three little bottles of perfume, and a large jar of Elizabeth Arden's cleansing cream! What a husband! He never forgot anything.

We were at the R.A.F. headquarters about ten o'clock when suddenly, sweeping out from the clouds, came three P-40's. One of them seemed to be in trouble. He came low, circled the field, climbed again and circled several more times.

"His wheels are stuck," Harvey said. "Let's go to the field and see what happens."

We arrived just in time to see the plane hit the runway with a loud, rasping noise, make a complete circle on its belly, and finally pin one wing into the ground.

Several Gurkha and Indian guards were standing about,

mouths open, doing nothing. Harvey ran to the middle of the runway frantically signalling to the third P-40 which was coming in for a landing, not knowing the other one had crashed. It pulled up just in time to avoid a collison.

A tall, husky figure, dressed in a flying suit with the Chinese insignia crawled out of the crash. Tom Jones! He was swearing, the first time I ever heard him do it. His face was pale, and his lips set with a grim grin. "God damned ship! The wheels *would* lock. This was my first mission."

He smiled and came toward me. "Trouble seems to be my middle name."

By this time Harvey had gotten hold of a heavy International truck, some cables and a few Indians. Tex Sanders and Hal Wright helped pull the plane off the runway, gasoline spilling all over the place. The pilot of the first ship that landed came toward us—Frank Schiel, who was the Intelligence Officer at Loiwing. Just the man I wanted to see!

Harvey asked what had happened. Jones said: "Well, we were supposed to escort the Blenheims on the mission the Old Man planned. We got to Namsam at the appointed hour and waited and waited for the bombers to show up. We were to attack at dawn this morning. We three took off to find out what had happened to them. Guess the rest of the flight went on to Loiwing."

Harvey said to Schiel, "You'd better go on to Loiwing and report. I'll give Jones my Jeep to drive back there."

From there we all went to a Chinese restaurant Captain Hensley had spoken about. It was a filthy place, the lower part crowded with Burmese, Indian and Chinese. As usual, the best rooms were upstairs.

The rickety stairs led to a small room and there we found Colonel St. John and of all people, Tommy Thomson, Standard Oil man who used to live in Nanning and stole ducks and turkeys to send to me for Christmas.

"What in hell are you doing here?" he boomed.

I laughed. "Official business. And you—all dressed up in khaki. Are you in the Army?"

"Yes and no. I guess you could call me the unofficial supervisor of the Burma Road—what's left of it."

Colonel St. John said: "Your official title, my boy, is 'Scavenger.'"

"What's that?" I asked.

"Well," explained the Colonel, "if we want a radio, he gets it. If the Chinese want a generator, he gets it. If you want a bottle of beer, he gets it. I don't know how he manages, but that Jeep of his is always loaded with stuff either for us or for the Chinese."

Tommy beamed with delight. "I am a sort of a Burmese Trader Horn."

We all had lunch together—native bacon, frilled spare ribs, rice and mustard greens, and flies, of course.

When we got back to the hostel Harvey said: "Get yourself together. We're going to the front to see Stilwell. I've borrowed Colonel St. John's car. He'll follow us later."

I packed hurriedly and put on a khaki-colored uniform of cheap, thin cotton, faded from many washings. It was the coolest thing besides shorts. I didn't wear shorts, thinking that I might have to run into the bushes if we happened to meet Jap snipers. I did not say anything to Harvey, as he might have thought I was silly.

Outside, Hal Wright and Tex Sanders were waiting. Each had a Tommy gun. I said: "Hope we won't have to use them."

Hal said: "We might, and we might not. But they're handy to shoo cows and natives off the roads."

After we passed Hsipaw, a small town about forty miles south of Lashio, the road was quite clear of traffic. The going was slow, however, because of hundreds of sharp curves, and numerous hills. We went over the supension bridge at the Gohtek Gorge and, I thought, a single bomb on that bridge would put the road out of commission for good. What a dangerous road, and how beautiful the scenery was at that part.

We drove into Maymyo at six-thirty. It wasn't much of a city as far as I could see. The usual brick and wooden houses were in the center of compounds. We drove straight into a very pretentious compound, in the center of which was a large brick church. To the left of it was a large brick house with vine-covered portecochere. There were many beds of chrysanthemums, daisies and roses in front of the house. Back of this two-storey building was a small wooden bungalow, and scattered around in back of these were several comfortable guest cottages.

"The Baptist Mission Compound," said Harvey. "These missionaries certainly do themselves well!"

Several men in uniform came out to meet us. One of them was General Hearn, and a tall, slender figure was Dan de Luce, war correspondent. He too, was wearing khaki shorts and a bush shirt. A tall, thin man in his early fifties was Colonel Williams, the chief medical officer of General Stilwell's staff. The compound was Stilwell's main headquarters, although the General spent most of his time at the front with the Chinese soldiers.

I met more majors, colonels and generals. They all seemed to be twiddling their thumbs, nervous, nothing to do except write reports approved by one and signed by another and handed over to still another.

At dinner, I sat next to Colonel Williams who said he supervised all the meals. For dessert we had strawberries that had been parboiled.

"What for?" I asked the Doctor.

"My orders," he answered. "Everything is thoroughly disinfected. I don't let them eat anything raw."

"Are there any fresh berries in the kitchen?" I asked.

He told a mess boy to bring me a dish of fresh strawberries.

When the boy returned I poured milk and sugar over them and began to eat them.

"That's suicide," said the doctor. "You must be crazy, girl!"

"No," I said, "that's the only way to keep myself immune. I eat everything. Otherwise, how can one build up a resistance? What if all of you have to walk out of here and eat off the land as you go along? You'll all be sick." I didn't realize then what a prophet I was.

After dinner we all retired to the large drawing room. I began to fool with the radio and turned the dial to Tokyo. "Listen, everybody!" I said. "Listen to this—Tokyo says that American airmen bombed Tokyo, Yokohama and Kobe." They told me to keep quiet and they all gathered about the radio.

I was getting ready for bed when Col. St. John knocked on the door and asked if I needed anything. I went out to the porch to talk to him.

"Just what is your job, Colonel?" I asked.

He grinned. "Well, the last exciting job I had was when I was in Rangoon I got myself appointed a one-man demolition crew. But I did a stupid thing. I went into a warehouse that was full of drums of gasoline and oil and boxes of dynamite. I ignited the place, but instead of doing it from the outside, I did it from the inside. The next thing I knew, I was spinning through the door into Kingdom Come. How I escaped being killed, I don't know."

A faint wind began to waft the most unhappy odors our way. "Whew," I said. "What in the world is that?"

"Two or three days ago, a load of bombs fell on a stable full of horses. They were all killed. The natives dragged the bodies off to a small ravine about a quarter of a mile away. Everytime the winds blows this way, we get the smell. Delightful, isn't it?"

"Were any people killed?"

"All of them that were in the houses nearby. Some of the bodies are still there. The natives won't bury them because they say they are leaving anyway. There's hardly anyone left here. All the whites, all the Indians, have moved out. The Burmese population took to the hills."

"Any of the British Army left?" I asked.

"Oh, yes, a few—and by the way, one of them says he is a friend of yours."

"Who?"

"Stanley Robins. He is a Colonel now. Come to think of it, there's another friend of yours stationed over there across the Irrawaddy past Madaya. Jelf, I think his name is, a young fellow, tall, dark hair—said he knew you in Rangoon." I remembered him well, a charming British captain.

When Harvey came in I asked him what had happened to Edna Robins, Stanley's wife.

"Forgot to tell you—I put her on a transport at Lashio before I went to Calcutta? She and her two Siamese cats. She's in India now, perfectly safe."

He knew about Stanley—had seen him when he was there before.

Harvey said, "I am going down to Pyawbwe tomorrow morning to see General Stilwell."

"Am I going too?"

He shook his head. "Too close to the front line."

I knew it would do no good to argue, so I didn't.

The next morning about seven I was getting dressed when the sirens went off. Finished dressing and went outside where I met Harvey, Hal Wright and Tex Sanders. "Let's go to the Botanical Gardens," I said. "That's what Colonel St. John told me to do." I didn't see another soul besides ourselves. "What happened to the others?" I asked.

Harvey said: "They're way to hell-and-gone by now. It doesn't take them long. Guess we might as well go too, and get a grandstand seat."

We drove through the city past the Gymkana Club and into the beautiful, well-kept Botanical Gardens. We stayed on the top of a hill, watching and waiting for the bombers. Nothing happened—another false alarm. I asked myself, "am I ever going to see and experience another raid, or not?" I was getting tired of always running for cover.

"The next time we have an alarm," I said aloud, "I'll be darned if I run."

Stanley Robins came after us at five o'clock and took us to his bungalow near the Gymkana Club. I asked him when he had left Rangoon.

He said: "I was one of the last to leave. That is, the last British fellow. I got out through Prome. The last two nights in Rangoon I spent shooting native looters. I was surprised at what a good shot I was, thought I'd lost the knack of it."

The dinner was magnificent. No shortage there. All kinds of wines and even good champagne. We said good night to Stanley, thanked him, and I wished him all the luck in the world.

"Don't you get caught out here," I said.

"Don't worry," he answered, "I am a good tracker, and I know the country. My tiger hunting experience will come in handy, yet."

Little did Stanley know then of the hell that was to be his, of the trek through the jungle, his body emaciated by fever— of weeks and weeks in the hospital not knowing who he was or why he was there in a little village in Assam. But he started to find out less than two weeks later.

Next morning, Sunday, Harvey left early for the main front, near Pyawbwe, to see General Stilwell and report on his trip to India.

I passed the afternoon with Thomson at the Botanical Gardens. He said that Mandalay was razed to the ground and was only smoking ruins. The only place left standing was the ancient King's Palace of Mandalay, and the brewery.

Harvey returned late in the evening. We went to bed after

he had a long talk with General Hearn. He told me that General Bruce Scott, our friend in Toungoo, had been cut off with three thousand native troops at the Yennangyaung oil fields north of Magwe. The Japs were now scattered all over Burma. He also told me that there was danger of the Japs cutting the other narrow road that ran almost parallel to the road from Maymyo to Lashio. But, he said, they were still quite far away, and we could make it easily to Lashio without being attacked.

Hal Wright and Tex Sanders had already left for Calcutta. I wished they had stayed and gone back with us. Four were better than two, I thought, remembering the two Tommy guns they had.

We had breakfast early and left Maymyo at six o'clock. Harvey was very silent so I had lots of time to observe things as we went along. The road was dusty and glaring white. The bordering jungle was covered with dust but at a little distance it was a brilliant green. We stopped at various villages on the way, trying to buy eggs or chickens but there were none to be had. At one place we bought some bananas and were very fortunate to get them.

Along the roadside were hundreds of trucks parked under the trees. They were loaded with empty gasoline drums, going to the oil fields to load up before the storage tanks were demolished. Some were also going to the front, or near there, to move back four million pounds of rice and the thousands of soldiers who were steadily retreating. Harvey said the situation looked pretty bad.

Chapter XIV

WE arrived at Lashio at two-thirty in the afternoon. I was so tired I slept for three hours before dinner, went back to bed right after—and the next thing I knew Harvey was shaking me.

"Come on, get up," he insisted. "I finally borrowed a car from the R.A.F."

"What time is it? Where are we going?"

"Loiwing."

Reluctantly, I dragged myself out of bed. It was still dark, but we didn't get started till bright daylight. Our driver, a little Welsh chap, was so short he had to sit on a cushion in order to see the road and slide down on the small of his back to step on clutch or brake. Harvey slept most of the way. Several times we came to places where a truck had a flat tire, holding up a long string of trucks behind it. The only way we could get the Chinese and Burmese drivers to pull aside for us was for Harvey to shoot his .45 in the air. Some of them paid no attention at all.

The road was sharp, steep, winding and very narrow in parts. Hundreds of people were trudging wearily through the dust and heat but they scrambled off the road when they heard a car approaching. They had to, or the native drivers would simply drive over them or crowd them off into the deep ravines. Many were camping, ready for the night to come. During the daytime they could choose better spots, a little flat land near running water, disregarding the millions of mosquitoes. If they only realized this part of the world was famous for its virulent malaria!

We drove about a hundred miles up the Burma Road and then turned left on a dirt road which was so narrow it was difficult to keep the car steady. After two hours of bumping we came upon a large steel bridge crossing the wide Schweli creek, one of the tributaries of the Irrawaddy—and were in Chinese territory—Yunnan Province again! The guards on the far side stopped us, but on seeing the insignia on Harvey's cap and shoulder straps, they saluted and let us pass.

We made a wide turn, climbed a hill, rattled through two small villages, climbed a higher hill and there was Loiwing, where Bill Pawley had built his airplane factory. The buildings were whitewashed, with camouflaged corrugated iron roofs. An attractive place and a perfect target for the Japs.

"Where's the airdrome?" I asked.

"It's about eight miles from that large building on the hill. That's the club house. The little houses are the pilots' and crew chiefs' quarters."

"Who lives in the club house?"

"Some of Bill Pawley's men, our staff, the Colonel and some of the pilots. Visiting firemen. We all mess there."

We parked the car around the house in front of one of the entrances. It was seven-thirty in the evening. Five and a half hours of traveling, and Harvey said we had made good time.

My hair was white with dust, and my face felt broiled. I tried to sneak into the house without seeing anyone, but met Mrs. Davidson, the housekeeper. I had heard the boys speak of "Ma Davidson," never realizing she was the same woman who used to run the dining room of the American Club in Hong Kong. She led me into one of the bedrooms.

What a surprise! For a moment I thought I was back in the Peninsula Hotel in Kowloon. A fine, thick Chinese rug on the floor; soft beds covered with green taffeta spreads, and over them, eider-down quilts. The furniture was good, too. Off the room was a small bathroom with tub, shower, toilet and basin, all blue tile.

"This used to be Ed Pawley's room," said Mrs. Davidson.

"The Colonel is using Bill Pawley's quarters which are at the end of this hall." I asked her how long she had been there. She answered: "Since November. I was still with the American Club when Bill offered me this job. Glad I took it now, or I would have been caught in Hong Kong."

It was evident she enjoyed feeding the A.V.G. She hustled about trying to make me feel comfortable. She saw me scrutinizing her and said: "Didn't I get fat, though? That's because I eat at such irregular hours. Every time the boys come in to eat, I eat with them." She laughed.

I washed up, changed my clothes and gave my hair a good brushing. Harvey was locked up in conference with the Colonel. Mrs. Davidson took me into the large lounge, which was used also as dining, recreation and projection room.

It was a lovely room. One whole side was a plateglass window giving a magnificent view of the small valley below. The drapes were flowered chintz, the same material being used for covering sofas and large, comfortable chairs. On one side of the room was a huge fireplace. Everything was in good taste and very cheerful-looking. A fine place, I thought, for the boys to rest when they come "home" from missions. At the other end of the room, opposite the plate-glass window, were four rows of tables, already set for dinner.

The boys began to drift in. David Lee Hill—"Tex" to all of us—who had taken Jack Newkirk's place came forward when he saw me. A slim, towering figure, shoulders slightly bent, lips parted in a smile, exposing long, widely-spaced sharp teeth. He was wearing his flight uniform and Texas boots.

"Hello, Olga," he said. "Glad to see you. When did you leave Kunming?"

I told him.

"Then it was before Boyington resigned. . . ."

"What do you mean—resigned?" I asked.

"Didn't you know? He got into trouble with Bob Neale— reported drunk at night alert. Greg is easy going, but something happened to him that night. When Neale accused him of drinking on duty, Greg said: 'Have you got the keys to your car?' It took Neale unawares, as the question was so foreign to the subject. Neale gave him the keys. 'Good-by, fellows,' he said, 'I am going over to the Adjutant's office and turn in my resignation. . . . Guess that's what you all want .' "

"Did he?" I asked.

"Yes, he did," said Tex.

I thought of what he had whispered in my ear, and I had answered, "No, Greg Boyington, don't do it." I heard his words again: "They're ganging up on me, Olga. Next time I'll fool 'em,—I'll resign. To hell with it."

R. P. Hedman came in, then Frank Lawlor, Geselbracht, Keaton and Petach. I called Pete over and gave him a letter from his wife. "Bend over," I said, "I have a kiss to deliver— a poor substitute, but here it is." He bent down and I kissed the side of his cheek.

Moss was the next to appear—leading a little girl by the arm. Moss and his little gals—but this wasn't a Florida one, this was an Anglo-Indian. She was one of the prettiest I had seen. Her skin was fair, and she had dark brown hair, but the eyes had the unmistakable pull at the corners, and the bluish-yellow shadow under the lower eye-lids. He saw me, and blushed a deep red. I smiled and waved at him. He and the girl sat at the far corner of the room.

Another pilot came in, also with a girl. She couldn't have been more than sixteen, tall and thin, also an Anglo-Indian, darker than the other one and not so attractive. She tried her best to flirt with the rest of the boys behind her escort's back, but accomplished little.

"Are they allowed to bring girls in here?" I asked.

"No," said Tex. "Only tonight because there will be a movie."

Harvey and Colonel Chennault joined us for dinner, which was good, although Mrs. Davidson said she had difficulty in buying green vegetables—tinned supplies were still holding out, "but not for long."

Later, Tex Hill and I sat together to watch the show, *Border Town*. We didn't see much of the picture, however, because of what Tex was telling me.

"We had a little insurrection here, did you know?"

I told him I didn't know anything.

"The Old Man planned a mission escorting some R.A.F. Blenheims. The fellows refused to go, saying it was a suicide mission because the Blenheims are too slow and undependable. We have thirty-two pilots here, and only five of us volunteered to go. Twenty-seven submitted their resignations on one piece of paper."

"Come outside," I said. "I want to hear the whole story."

We sneaked out of the room and bumped into Tom Jones and R. T. Smith, the tall, thin, twenty-four-year-old Flight Leader of the Third Squadron, one of Olson's staunch supporters and friends. We exchanged greetings, talked about the picture and gradually drifted to the subject I was interested in.

Smith said: "Tex, you wouldn't refuse the mission because you are a new Squadron Leader, and you thought you might lose your squadron. Ed Rector naturally followed your lead. And Jones here wouldn't because he hasn't seen action and didn't want to miss out. Frank Schiel wouldn't because he feels he is important now, being Intelligence Officer."

I said: "You fellow are talking in riddles. Are you referring to the Blenheims I saw flying over Lashio last Friday, when you, Jones, landed on your belly?"

"That's it," said Jones.

Tex cut in: "Thursday afternoon we were supposed to go to Namsam and meet the Blenheims, take off early next morning and strafe and bomb Chiengmai."

"You know," said Smith, "that it wouldn't have materialized. We all got together and discussed every angle. We were to escort the Blenheims, they were to drop their bombs, and then we were to strafe! We wouldn't have had a dog's chance to get away. By the time the Blenheims got there, it would have been too late—there wouldn't have been any element of surprise. We had planned on hitting the Japs before dawn, giving them no chance to be ready for us. The Blenheims can't hit anything anyway, and they would have only delayed us. Well, we refused to escort them, knowing just what would have happened, from previous experiences with them.

"The Colonel came in, and three of us, Frank Lawlor, Keaton and myself wanted no part of the mission. Olson had already talked to the Old Man in private, and as he had had his say, he kept silent.

"The Colonel said: 'If you want to show the white feather, you can all quit!' "

"My God; white feather!" continued Smith, "after what guys like Tex Hill, Lawlor, Keaton, Older and even I have shown we can do in the air, with all the odds against us. I came right out and said he knew damn well we were no cowards. The Colonel said: 'By white feather I mean insubordination.' I insisted it meant 'cowardice.'

"The whole trouble in a nutshell was that we didn't want to escort the Blenheims—not at the time they would be ready. We wanted to get off long before dawn and surprise the Japs. The Blenheims wanted to start at seven! They're late risers."

Tex lit a cigarette and handed it to me.

Smith continued. "The Colonel was sore as hell at all of us and more so at those he thought were the ringleaders, five of us—Olson, Jack Croft, Frank Lawlor, Buster Keaton and myself. The Old Man's hands were tied because he knew if he tried to replace Olson the whole Third Squadron would have resigned. We all have great respect and regard for Ole and everyone of us would go to bat for him."

"Who did you say wouldn't sign the resignation slip?"

"Frank Schiel, Tex Hill, Rector, Pete Wright and myself,"

said Jones. "We went, but the mission fizzled—Blenheims never showed up. On the way back we strafed hell out of a Jap convoy that was moving up—"

"Yeah," Tex cut in. "You should have seen those Japs! We made a pass and dropped our bombs—right in the middle of the road. We knew that all of those that could would leave the trucks and run to the ditches so we made three more passes and strafed them on both sides. . . ."

"We went on another mission yesterday," said Jones. "We had word of enemy planes approaching so we went to intercept. We tangled with them near Lashio—shot down two." Jones' face expanded in a broad smile. "One of them was mine, Olga—shot down my first Jap!"

The movie was over and the crowd dispersing, so I said good night to the boys and went to my room. I thought of Jones and his first kill. It must have happened when we were travelling north of Maymyo towards Lashio. And I worried about the misunderstanding which had arisen between the boys and the Old Man, who had his own side of the case to consider. I'm sure he knew the missions were dangerous but he was fighting a losing campaign and it was his duty to support the Chinese who certainly were getting no support from anyone else.

One o'clock in the morning—I woke up. The lights were still on. Harvey wasn't in his bed. But, sitting on mine and holding a huge chocolate cake right under my nose, was a handsome young fellow. "What the—," I said. "What's going on here?" I opened my eyes wide and set up. I recognized Mickey Mickelson, Hennessy's co-pilot.

Mickey said: "Wake up, sleepy-head. It's my birthday! We're celebrating in the room across the hall. Ma Davidson and Hennessy are there. Mr. Greenlaw promised to come over and eat a piece of cake. Coming? Get up!"

"Get out," I said, "and I'll get up. Your birthday? Yesterday, or today?"

"Tonight," he answered.

"Well," I said, "it isn't tonight any longer—it's tomorrow morning, so it isn't your birthday any more."

"Anyway, we're celebrating. Hurry up!"

I dressed and crossed the hall to their room where some were sitting on the beds, and others squatting on the floor. The large chocolate cake with Happy Birthday written on it in white was also on the floor.

"We got in this afternoon," said Hennessy, "from Lashio. We picked up some of the mail they had there in the post office. No one gave it to us, we just went in and took it. We are leaving for Kunming very early. Anything you want to send up there, Olga?"

I went back to bed and didn't get up until eight o'clock. I was having breakfast when a girl came in. She was not over twenty, of medium height, and a little on the plump side. Her round face was framed by a glorious wealth of light brown hair neatly arranged in curls. Her eyes were large and pale brown, her mouth full and generous. She wore a sheer black dress and high-heeled black pumps.

Mrs. Davidson said: "This is Freddie Hodges' wife—Helen."

After breakfast Helen went with me to my room to see the lipsticks I had, as I had promised to give her one. We sat on the bed and talked. I asked her when she and Freddie had been married.

She said: "About a week ago. Right here. When Freddie left Kunming, I didn't want to stay by myself in the Taho Hotel with the Anglo-Indian girls, so I caught a ride in a truck that was coming to Loiwing. I was here three days when Freddie and I talked it over. He said that it wouldn't do for me to be here as people would start to talk. But having no place to go, and not knowing where my mother and father are, I didn't know what to do. Freddie suggested we get married. We had been engaged ever since you were stationed in Toungoo. I wanted a real wedding.

"The bombing of Rangoon started, and with Freddie always moving about with his squadron, we didn't have time to get married."

"Who married you here?" I asked.

"Freddie said that it was an American custom to elect a Mayor whenever a group of Americans lived together in one place. So, he and the boys got together and elected Mr. M. D. Walsh. Once elected Mayor of Loiwing, he had the authority to perform marriages, at least that's what everyone said. He married us. Later we found a British chaplain and he performed the religious ceremony. Do you think I am really married?"

"Yes, of course," I answered. "You are Mrs. Fred S. Hodges."

She smiled—a pathetic little figure sitting there on my bed. Suddenly she began to cry. "What's the matter?" I asked placing my arms around her shoulders.

"I miss my mother. I don't know anything about marriage. I don't know what to do. Mother never told me anything. . . . I was brought up by the Catholic sisters, and when I went home on vacations I only played with my three brothers. I never talked about things to anybody. . . ."

I spent the next two hours explaining to her the facts of life to the best of my ability.

Just before dinner General Peter Mao and Mrs. Mao arrived. They had flown from Kunming in their own plane, a Beechcraft. I was happy to see Mrs. Mao—had not seen her since the days of Hangchow, eight years before. She still hadn't learned English. The General told me she thought it was too much trouble. "Besides," he said, "she tells me to tell you she thinks that people who come to our country should learn our language. If she ever goes to America, then only will she learn English."

Mrs. Mao looked very pretty. It was hard to believe she was the mother of six boys and was expecting another one.

She was dressed in a pale blue Chinese gown, completely embroidered in silver and crystal beads. Her arms, from the wrists to the elbows, were covered with diamond and sapphire bracelets. She wore many rings, including a huge square-cut diamond. Carelessly thrown over her shoulders was a priceless sable coat that reached below her knees. We had dinner together and afterwards saw a movie, *China Clipper*.

The General sat next to her translating the words as they were spoken by the actors. Now and then she would become bored with the picture and ask me about my sister Alicia. When I told her she only had two little boys, she was very much disappointed. And, of course, she was amazed by the fact that I had no children at all. "Be patient," the General translated, "the good God will give you a large family."

Rumors were rife. There was talk that the Generalissimo had sent General Mao to take over from Colonel Chennault. Some said that it was the result of the little demonstration of insubordination, and that the Old Man could no longer handle the A.V.G. Rumors, rumors—I don't know if they bore any truth or not. But I did notice that the Colonel was very worried.

Before going to bed Harvey came in with the good news: "The Colonel was promoted to the rank of Brigadier General!"

I was still annoyed that they hadn't made him a B.G. in the first place.

I was up at six-thirty and had breakfast with the Colonel and Colonel Bob Scott, who was to become leader of the 23rd Pursuit Group, which later was to succeed the A.V.G. Scott was a trim looking young man and what Jack Newkirk would have described as an 'eager beaver'—full out for flying and fighting.

I drove to the field with them. The Colonel said the weather at Lashio was bad—planes couldn't get through. We drove to the alert shack. The Colonel talked to some of the pilots,

Jap sentry.

Harvey K. Greenlaw on bombed street.

Crossing river in flight from Hengyang.

On the road to Hanoi, Tonkin, Indo China.

then off we went to the radio shack. The Colonel dumped me there. He was in no mood to be bothered with women that morning. I didn't stay long in the radio room—got nervous listening to the reports from out Lashio station—"Enemy planes approaching from the southeast—enemy planes escorted by fighters—" On and on.

I saw Frank Schiel, now Intelligence Officer and the right man to give me the dope for the *War Diary*—and we drove back to the airdrome.

Three transports were warming up on the runway. Good thing I got there as Harvey said he was going back to Lashio and I was to go with him. What a life! We had just come from there—now we were going back again. On asking about the radio report I had just heard he said it was correct but that the Japs had turned back because of the bad weather—which is still the best of all defenses.

One of the transport pilots, an American captain, said: "Going my way, babe?"

I answered: "Which way?"

"Lashio—taking off right now."

In the same chummy manner I replied: "Okay, pal—Lashio is my way, too."

Just then Harvey left the Colonel and told me to get aboard the plane on the right of the runway. I climbed on—with my brief-case and dog.

"Good grief," I said. "Where am I going to sit?"

The ship was full of ammunition boxes—no safety belts, no seats, no parachutes. I made the best of it and settled myself on the boxes. Harvey found a place close by. We took off and the other two ships followed. Then I saw six P-40's taking off also. When we were about 3,000 feet up they took position—two above us and two on either side. They were to escort us to Lashio just in case we did meet the Japs. Sitting as I was on a load of live ammunition I naturally hoped we wouldn't.

As we landed at Lashio the siren went off—the one at

British headquarters. Planes approaching from Magwe. Damn it! The transports were still loaded with explosives. The runways were lined with refugees, white and Indian, from all over Burma—poor devils trying to get out. Harvey ordered some of the Gurkha guards to unload the planes. He pitched right in himself.

He told me to get into a car standing by, go down the runway and tell the white people to run to the planes and get aboard. I did so, shouting: "Move up near the planes and get ready to leave for India!" That started a mild panic. Women, breathless, milled around carrying children and bundles. I told them to drop the bundles and take themselves and kids only. Some hesitated, but most of them left their belongings behind and ran toward the planes.

In twenty minutes the boxes and bombs were stacked on the field, the transports taxiing into position for a take-off. We loaded about sixty people, white and Indian, in each transport and got most everyone out. There was only one truck on the field, and moving the ammunition out of the way was a slow process. Harvey was sore as hell at the British. They knew we were coming and had made no arrangements to move the stuff. Three P-40's took off, escorting the transports as far as Loiwing. The other three Sharks had continued their flight on a reconnaissance mission.

I was dog-tired as I had been up early, and there had been too much excitement. Harvey told me to get off the field. A Chinese Captain, Dan Wang, drove me to the C.N.A.C. hostel.

Number four room again—we were gettting to be permanent residents in that little room.

All afternoon reports from Chinese and British Intelligence stated that Jap columns were moving up the old road to the east of the Burma Road. Objective: to cut off the road at a point thirty miles south of Lashio, isolating the Chinese Army from General's Alexander's forces south of Mandalay in the

Irrawaddy Valley, and cutting off General Stilwell and his Chinese forces at Pyawbwe.

Four American officers were at the hostel: Colonel St. John, Lieutenant Colonel Boatner, Major Wilson, and another one. They were part of General Stilwell's staff. Boatner advised me to get out of Lashio.

After a very skimpy dinner I looked out the door at Swarms of natives carrying bundles from one place to another and then moving out of the town along the different paths leading to the main road, the Burma Road. I was witnessing the evacuation of Lashio, and didn't know it. Only a few hours before I was talking to a British officer who declared the town was in no danger and the order for evacuation had not yet been given. Still, a lot of army trucks were moving northward loaded with Indian and Burmese soldiers.

British were driving the trucks, and several of them were loaded with white soldiers. The number one bearer of the hostel insisted that everyone was leaving and that the bearer of the British C.O. had told him that he was to be ready to move out. Maybe the British didn't want panic in the town, or to clutter up the roads—so they could have a clear way for their own evacuation.

The bearer said: "*Mem sahib*, please do not eat the bananas I brought you. Save them. Tomorrow I think you will need them."

I looked down at the miserable little bananas, four of them, not more than three inches long. I put them away carefully in my purse.

Harvey said he hadn't eaten yet and told me to get ready to take off for Kunming on a C.N.A.C. plane that was expected at seven o'clock. We went to the airdrome where there were several Chinese officers and business men who wanted to get on that plane for Kunming.

The Chinese C.N.A.C. manager came over to our car and told Harvey: "The British colonel in charge of this area has destroyed our radio station. That is bad! It was a Chinese station put there by us for the use of the C.N.A.C. They didn't even warn the Chinese authorities before destroying it."

Harvey told him to notify the people to get out by other means as without the field radio C.N.A.C. would not be able to land after dark any more.

We went back to the hostel. Harvey received more reports from Chinese Intelligence: "Japs moving up the road and traveling fast. They are closing in from two directions."

By this time the evacuation had really begun in a big way. What a stampede! The road back of the hostel was jammed— like a crowd leaving a big football game. Some were on foot, others packed into cars and trucks—hundreds, thousands of them—Indians, Burmans, ox-carts, wheelbarrows, shoulder yokes. It was pouring rain and dark as pitch. About ten-thirty Harvey decided I had to get out, whether by Jeep, car or on horseback. "You're a God-damn nuisance and this is getting dangerous," he said. "I can't keep you here and I hate to send you up that road alone—but you've got to get out."

Harvey meant to stay behind as long as possible. The British had carried out no demolition whatsoever. Our radio station, which was in the middle of the jungle two miles north of town, was well camouflaged. He said we couldn't afford to lose the equipment and that he and two A.V.G. radio men would hold out till the last minute as it was the only remaining means of getting out information. "If we can't salvage it we'll blow it up," he declared.

Major Wilson passed by and told me he had to get through to Maymyo and deliver a message to General Hearn who was still there. He was driving a Jeep and carried a Tommy gun. I wished him luck and hoped he would make it.

Then I saw Elsum, an Englishman we had met in Rangoon two years before. He wanted me to take a package containing jewels to Kunming. I told him that I didn't know if I would get there and wouldn't accept the responsibility. He insisted and said I could have any piece I liked out of the lot. I refused.

I stood there, alone, thinking of the trip on the transport from Loiwing to Lashio, scared stiff because of the ammunition and no 'chute. All for nothing. Now I had to get out! In a hurry!

Midnight. There was absolutely no warning system now. We didn't know exactly where the Japs were or how fast they were approaching. I passed the time taking down curtains and folding them. I figured I could make good use of them in Kunming. Seemed silly, me worrying about curtains at that time. The rain was still falling in torrents. Nobody had found a truck, Jeep, or horse and buggy to get me out in. I finally said: "The hell with it!"—and went to bed.

Harvey woke me up a couple of hours later. He shouted: "I got hold of Little Ole. He salvaged an R.A.F. Ford truck from Magwe. He has been in Heho and just got in. The Japs were just two jumps behind him. He'll take you up to Loiwing."

"Who is 'Little Ole'?"

"One of our crew chiefs—nice little fellow. You'll be perfectly safe with him."

"I am not worrying about that," I said. "I just want to know is he a good driver."

"He got here from Heho, didn't he?"

"Okay," I said, "when do we start?"

"In a few hours."

"And you?"

"I am staying here to see that all our equipment is moved out. I'll have some notes for you to give the Old Man. See you later."

"Where are you going?"

"Look around the town. Maybe do some looting."

"Let me go with you."

"You've done your looting. You certainly left the rooms in this place bare and empty."

"I only took curtains."

Harvey laughed. "Might as well. I'm going to burn the place down before I leave. If the Japs are sleepy when they get here they can sleep out in the rain."

After he had gone I looked around the room—at the walls, the ceiling, the furniture. It gave me a curious feeling to know that before another night they would be a smouldering pile of ashes.

Chapter XV

PERHAPS someone got to sleep that last night in Lashio but I know I didn't. There was no use trying. The activity going on all over the dirty little town was frenzied and noisy. People shouting and running around in the rain, repairing tires and motors, loading trucks and all sorts of vehicles in frantic haste and confusion. This was the last chance to escape. In a few hours, or less, it would all be over.

Harvey came back, and with him Little Ole. They had a Jeep and the Ford truck with "R.A.F." still painted on it, loaded with all kinds of stuff—cases of whisky and gin, cigarettes, boxes of sugar, tins of hard candy and biscuits.

"Loot," said Harvey, "and food for the A.V.G. They're running short now over there."

"Where did you get all of that?"

"Some from the British quarters, some from the open shops. Nobody in them—they just walked out and left everything for anyone who wants to take it—or for the Japs."

"You better go to sleep, Mrs. Greenlaw," said Little Ole. "We'll have a tough trip. I will load our truck now."

"By the way," I said, "I also looted two good mattresses from this hostel. How about packing them, too, on the floor of the truck? We might need them—you never can tell."

"I'll pack 'em in," he said. "Don't worry about a thing."

The same old words hammering in my ears: "Wake up!" But it wasn't Harvey this time, it was Little Ole. "Seven o'clock," he said. "You overslept."

"Where's Harvey?" I asked.

"Over talking to some Chinese officers. Get up and take a look outside. If we make the trip in less than fifteen hours, we'll be lucky. You ought to see the people, soldiers and the R.A.F. moving out."

Harvey came in. "Take this message and deliver it to the Old Man," he said.

I jumped out of bed, dug my fountain pen out of the battered old purse.

Harvey dictated: "One: C.N.A.C. radio station destroyed by British at 1430 yesterday by order of Colonel Day without notifying Chinese authorities. Two: British moving out—much confusion. Three: Our radio station will hold on as long as possible. If possible, will move it out, if not, shall destroy it. Four: Americans also moving out as soon as possible. Five: C.N.A.C. hostel personnel moving up to Myikytina. Six: Gin, purchased at rupees eighteen, each bottle, two cases. One case butter. Seven: Cannot get through to Maymyo now. Japs now at Hsipaw, will begin moving northwards toward Lashio before morning. Only thing between enemy forces and Lashio is one battalion infantry on each road. Chinese not equipped with any anti-tank guns. Eight: Will try and be in touch with you in the morning if still here. Nine: Suggest you signal Dinjan about transport, preparatory to moving out of Loiwing when Japs get to Lashio."

"Is that all?" I asked.

"That's enough," said Harvey. "Get going, you two. Truck's loaded."

I picked up Lucy and my purse, strapped on the .25 Colt automatic that Jones gave me for my birthday, and climbed into the truck beside Little Ole.

We moved slowly the first two hours and only covered ten miles. There, in a terrible traffic jam, we saw Captain Hensley. His big truck loaded with supplies and his station wagon loaded with his baggage and his servants, were stuck in the middle of it. As we passed by, we waved to him. No use stopping to help.

When we got near Kutkai, there was another traffic snarl.

We had to stop, as it was impossible to to get through. A Chinese colonel was directing traffic. When he saw us trying to move up and noticed the R.A.F. markings on the truck, he came toward us, fury written all over his face. "You God-damned British—blocking the road. Can't you see that Chinese Army is trying to get through from the north, going toward Lashio to cover your retreat? Pull up there on the side of the road!"

Then I recognized him. "Colonel Wang!"

Now his face was one big smile. "Mrs. Greenlaw! What in the world are you doing in this R.A.F. truck?"

I introduced him to Little Ole and told him we had to get through.

He said, "I'll get you through."

In ten minutes we were out of that jam. Ole was certainly a wonderful driver, the way he wiggled in and out of traffic along the sharp edges of the steep road. When we crossed the bridge a few miles north of Kutkai. We noticed that the railing on both sides of the bridge on the far end had been completely knocked out. I looked back and saw something at the bottom—forty feet below.

"Stop, Ole," I said. "Some people down there need help."

We pulled to the side and scrambled down the hill to the river bed. Sure enough, there was a brand-new Red Cross ambulance turned over on its side. Inside, at the driver's seat, a figure slumped over the wheel, head smashed and covered with blood. "Chinese," we both said at the same time.

In the back of the ambulance Little Ole found two women nurses, also Chinese, and a child not more than four years old. All were dead and covered with blood. There were packages of bandages, medicine bottles, thermos jugs, books—all scattered. Evidently we were the first ones to arrive at the wreck as the bodies had not been looted.

Across the river on the other side, I saw two Chinese soldiers digging holes into the brick retaining walls of the bridge—

completely disregarding the wrecked car—going on about their own business. I knew what it was—those holes were to be loaded with dynamite to destroy the bridge when the signal was given.

"Ole," I said, "let's take some of these medicines with us. Someone else will come here and loot everything they can carry."

"You collect that stuff," he said, "while I empty the tanks. There's a lot of gas left. Wish I had some tools. I'd take off these tires. Look at them—brand-new."

I collected the stuff and Little Ole got the gasoline. A slow process, as he had to pierce the tank and let the liquid drip into an empty five-gallon tin. I found a brand-new pair of shoes, American-made, size four. I couldn't wear them, but maybe someone else could, so I cleaned the blood off and wrapped them in a piece of paper. By the doctor's body I found a good fountain pen. I picked it up and put it in my purse. An hour afterwards, we continued our journey.

When we climbed up to about 4,000 feet, the road was very winding and very narrow. Here again we found trucks piled on top of each other, and those trying to pass the wrecks were blocking the road. Little Ole spotted a small clearing. "We'll make it through here, if that other guy doesn't speed up. Hold on, here we go."

Just then, the other truck tried to speed up, too.

"Get your gun out," said Little Ole, "and shoot at his tires."

I had to shoot with my left hand as the wheel of the truck was on the right-hand side. Bang! Bang! went the little gun, and I was yelling at the same time: "Get over on the side!"

It was evident that these people, Indian, Burmese and Chinese civilians, were having a good time. Once on the road, they thought they were no longer menaced by the Japs. To them it was a regular outing. I had to fire several shots before they finally moved over, and Little Ole got through. Went on for another five miles when we had a flat tire.

"Damn!" said Little Ole, "one of your bullets ricocheted and hit one of our tires!" We both laughed. We weren't up against it, however, as Little Ole had stolen a Jeep tire in Lashio which fitted our truck. He said, "If we have no more flats, we'll make it."

We got to a small village and reported the accident. About eight miles further, the road straightened out a bit. Many natives were walking toward the village we had passed. Evidently it was bazaar day. I wished we could have stopped there to buy the lovely Shan bags. The natives were colorfully dressed in the costume of the northern Shan States and didn't seem the least bit disturbed about the war.

"Perfect line here," said Ole, "all these hundreds of trucks on the road, loaded with people and bundles. What a wonderful target for the Japs to strafe!"

Just then we heard motors—many motors—many planes.

I said: "Here they come!"

"Don't worry," he said. "Those are ours."

Six of them roared overhead—flying low. But the natives in the other trucks didn't know who they were. They left their trucks and dashed for the ditches. Several trucks ran into each other. The one in front of us was carrying wounded Chinese soldiers and two women with young children in their arms. I got off, took the tin of hard candy with me and gave the two mothers handsful of it for the children. They were very grateful, but it was hard for their poor frightened faces to smile.

We went on. When we got to the 102 4/10 mile mark, we left the Burma Road and turned left, thank God!—out of that terrible traffic and into a clear road—the dusty one that led to Loiwing.

Later on, we had another flat tire near an R.A.F. camp. The camp consisted of two large new tents. Two British officers were lying on the ground. We stopped the truck near them, and Ole and I got off.

"Hello, there!" I shouted. "How about a tire?"

One of them rolled over on his side and opened his eyes. "Sorry," he said, "no tires."

Over in the distance we saw a Jeep. Little Ole said: "How about one of those Jeep tires? They will fit our truck."

"No," said the officer, "can't spare it. By the way, have you any cigarettes? We're clean out."

"Sure," I said, "plenty. Got whisky and gin, too. We'll trade you a carton of cigarettes and a bottle of whisky for one of those Jeep tires."

At the mention of whisky, the other officer woke up. "What's this? What's this?" he said.

I was glad I had spoken because Little Ole was going to give them the cigarettes for nothing. He looked at me and smiled— stretched out his hand and pointed one thumb up. We both laughed.

"All right," said the first officer, "go and get it and it's yours."

"You are certainly taking it easy, aren't you?" I said to the first officer.

"Oh, well," he answered, "we can't do anything about it. No planes to fly, might as well get out of the way and move north." He laughed.

I said, "Why don't you get hold of a gun and do a little fighting."

"What for?" he asked. "Something went wrong here. Maybe it is because we are not in the spirit of the thing. Now, back there in Dunkirk—that was different. There we were fighting for something. But here, who the hell cares for these Burmans?"

I thought to myself—so that's the attitude of these British soldiers toward the country they conquered. They take from it but give nothing in return.

He interrupted my thoughts. "Who are you anyway, and what are you doing here? It strikes me as amusing, seeing a woman on this God-forsaken road."

"Just an American," I answered, "looking for trouble."

By this time Little Ole returned with the precious tire. We gave the officers a bottle of rye and a carton of cigarettes and were on our way again.

We got into Loiwing at six-fifteen. Ten and a half hours of driving—and only dry bread and bananas to eat!

Several of the boys in the club house came out to meet us. "Unload, boys unload!" I shouted, "We bring you liquor, cigarettes and candy!"

Shilling, Tom Jones, Tex Hill and Mrs. Davidson helped to unload.

"C.N.A.C. plane come in yet?" I asked. "I want to go to Kunming."

"Just left," said Shilling, "ten minutes ago."

"Where's the Colonel?"

"Out at the field," said Jones.

"Got a message for him," I said. "Any transportation going that way?"

"Nope," said Tex. "Why don't you wait till he gets here? You are all tired out. Take it easy."

They took the stuff into the room Freddie Hodges and Helen had occupied. "What happened to them?" I asked. They informed me that they had just left on the C.N.A.C. plane.

We sat on the beds, talked about the Japs and the British, about the looting in Lashio, the traffic on the road. Later, the Colonel returned and I delivered the message that Harvey sent. I also gave him a bottle of Bourbon, which was indeed a treat for him, as it was his favorite drink. After taking three baths to get the filth of the road off me, I went to bed. Mrs. Davidson brought in my dinner on a tray.

I slept soundly that night and was up bright and early the next morning. I was packing again so as to be ready to take the first available transportation to Kunming, when Jones came in.

"Shot my second Jap yesterday morning, Olga," he said, smiling and happy as could be.

"Congratulations," I said. "Tell me about it. But, first, tell me how are you feeling. Any more dizzy spells?"

"No," he answered, "fit as anything. Never felt better in my life."

"Fine," I said, "but if you do, will you tell Dr. Richards?"

"Yes, yes," he said impatiently. "I want to tell you what happened yesterday. We went on a mission in the morning—eleven of us. For the first time the P-40's were loaded with bombs. We dropped them on a line of trucks. The way we did it was this: first, we spotted the Jap convoy moving up the road north of Hsipaw. We got into position for bombing. Of course, the Japs had already seen us and had enough time to get out of the trucks and run for it. This made it just right for us because one flight bombed the trucks, and the other two strafed both sides of the road. We got them and got the trucks. The bombs hit the first trucks and set them on fire, blocking the road for any more to come. We left twelve of them blazing! On the way back, we met a bunch of Jap planes. We let them have it, and ran like hell. We couldn't stay and fight it out because we didn't have much gas left. We shot down four of them at least."

"Do you think they'll come back today, Jones?"

"Not in this weather. Got to go now. See you later."

Had breakfast with Colonel Chennault and went to the field with him. It was almost eleven o'clock when he stopped by the radio shack, about one mile from the runways. The weather had cleared, and the Colonel said he wouldn't be surprised if the Japs did come. I followed him into the radio room. The operator was saying: "Twenty-eight enemy planes approaching. Nine of them bombers, the rest escort fighters."

The Old Man quickly took the man's place at the radio. Seventeen of our own planes were already up. Seventeen was all we had that could fly. All the others were out of commission, the engines were so worn out.

"Find yourself a ditch!" the Old Man snapped.

I ran outside. Back to the same old ditch where I had been two or three days ago. I waited ten minutes in perfect agony, thinking that after all, only a direct hit would bother me. Next thing I knew there was a hell of a racket! The clatter of our too few anti-aircraft guns, the scream and whistle of falling bombs, and then the boom-bang when they hit the ground. I had heard the planes overhead coming in our direction, but since our own planes were up, I couldn't tell which were which until the bombs began to fall. When I heard the "salvo" I left the hole and went back to the radio shack. The Colonel was still at the radio.

"All bombs fell on the field," he said. "Damn accurate bombing. One fell close to here on the dry paddy field."

No wonder the earth shook. That was a close one—about 200 yards or less from where I had been in my hole.

"The boys intercepted the escort but couldn't get to the bombers. They sneaked through and dropped their eggs," said the Colonel.

Thirty minutes after the announcement of "enemy planes approaching," the boys reported: "Japs on the run; between six and ten shot down. All our ships okay."

When we got back to the club house, we found that the servants had not returned from the *Ginbao*, and that there was no food. It was almost one o'clock, and we were all hungry. I went into the kitchen to see what I could find. There was some uncooked chicken in the Frigidaire, but no bread. I suddenly thought of biscuits. I'd make some. Found some flour and lard, salt and baking powder and went to work. Some of the boys were watching me. "Bet you we can't eat them," they said. "They'll be hard as nails."

Frank Schiel came in: "If you want to go to Kunming, get ready," he said. "Beechcraft leaving."

"Where's the Old Man?" I asked.

"Outside," said Schiel. "He told me to tell you to take that ship."

With my hands covered with flour, I went outside, looking for the Colonel.

"Colonel," I said, "I don't want to leave yet, not until I know what happened to Harvey. I am worried."

"Don't worry about him—he knows how to take care of himself."

"Yes, sir," I answered, "but one of the truck drivers said that when he last saw Harvey yesterday afternoon about five o'clock, he was already half way up the road and had turned back to Lashio. "What do you suppose he did that for?"

"Maybe he forgot his hat," said the Colonel.

"I don't want to go in the Beechcraft unless it is an order."

The Old Man pulled a paper out of his pocket and gave it to me. "Deliver this to Adair, and good luck to you."

"Yes, sir"—What else could I say?

It was an order. I went back to my room, strapped my suitcase, picked up Lucy and got into the Jeep with Frank Schiel.

"Airdrome, James," I said, "and don't spare the horses."

I was standing by the Beechcraft waiting for the pilot when I saw a Jeep coming in a cloud of dust. It was muddy and dirty, no windshield, no top, and Harvey driving it. How glad I was to see him!

"What in the hell are you doing here?" That was his greeting.

"On my way to Kunming," I yelled back.

"In this broken-down old crate—are you nuts?"

"I've got my orders," I said.

"Who gave you orders?"

"The Old Man."

"Well, you are not going in that lousy crate."

"Oh, yes I am."

"You are like hell. Get in here!"

He threw my baggage in the back of the Jeep then we began a wrestling match for Lucy, who was barking and wiggling, happy to see Harvey.

No use arguing, I thought and meekly did as I was told. We went back to the club—back to the Hodges' room. Nothing else to do, I went to bed thinking that I might as well rest up while I could. No more *Ginbaos* for the rest of the day as it was raining hard. I went to sleep and didn't wake up until seven-thirty. I couldn't figure out whether it was morning or night. Tom Jones came in.

"Harvey said for me to wake you, but I am too late, I see," he said. "He's with the Colonel in a conference."

"By themselves?"

"No," said Jones, "some fellows of the Tenth Air Force are with them. Two transports came in from India when you were asleep."

"Who are the men?" I asked.

"I don't know. Big shots, maybe."

He was smiling and I asked him why. He said: "This morning when we had the fight, I didn't come in with the rest of the flight. I drifted off towards Lashio, having plenty of gas because my plane was fully loaded before I took off. I was flying high, and down below I saw some planes. At first I thought they were ours, they were flying our same formation style—by twos, and scattered at that, just like we fly. Suddenly, I saw the red dots on the wings! They were too many to attack. All Zeros. I turned back and beat it for home."

He was shaking with laughter. I noticed how gray his hair was turning—his temples were almost white.

"I don't think that's a bit funny, Jones," I said. "You ought to be spanked. Come, let's go to dinner."

In the large room we found Colonel Chennault sitting with a stranger whom he introduced as "Colonel Cooper." Later I was to find out this was the same Meriam C. Cooper who had, some years before, made those memorable motion pictures, *Grass* and *Chang* and who had subsequently been production head of one of the large Hollywood studios.

"Going to Kunming?" I asked.

"I think so," said Colonel Cooper. "Want to come along?"

I said I did—if he had room.

Harvey said if they were too crowded I could go on the C.N.A.C. plane which had just arrived a short time before. Moon Shen was flying it.

I saw Moon Shen, the Chinese pilot, across the room so I went over to talk to him. "Sure," he said, "We'll have plenty of room, I may have to fly up to Myitkyina first to pick up a message there from General Ling—but maybe I won't have to."

I said good night to Moon Shen, had dinner and went back to my room. Mrs. Davidson came in. "Olga," she said, "I think I'll go with you to Kunming. They are getting ready to evacuate here and if I don't get out now maybe I'll be stranded. What do you think?"

I thought she'd be a dunce not to leave while there was a chance—and said so.

"How about my dog, Pooch?" she asked.

I told her to bring him along, too. At this stage of the proceedings I couldn't see where one dog more or less would make any difference.

Chapter XVI

PEOPLE walking by the room and speaking loudly woke me up. It was two o'clock in the morning. It was no use trying to sleep any more since we were leaving at dawn; that is, if Moon Shen had received the message he was expecting.

I dressed and went across the hall to Mrs. Davidson's room and found her packing. By the time we got through packing and feeding the dogs, it was four o'clock. Harvey was still asleep and I didn't wish to wake him. We found Dave Harris who volunteered to drive us to the field in his car, as there was no other transportation. We stopped directly in front of the alert shack. Hanging on the front of the shack was a long, narrow board with "OLSON & COMPANY, EXTERMINATORS—24 HOUR SERVICE," painted with black ink.

We waited there for Moon Shen. When he finally showed up he said the message from General Ling had not yet arrived. That meant more waiting and it was getting too light—for comfort.

"How about having your co-pilot load our baggage?" I asked Shen. He, his co-pilot and I walked over to the plane and loaded it.

Another car drove in and stopped by the C.N.A.C. plane. The driver was a Chinese doctor employed by C.A.M.C.O. With him were three women and eight children. He asked me if that plane was about to leave and if there would be room for the women and children. I told him I didn't know, but that the women could wait in the hut next to the alert shack.

The Doctor introduced me to his wife, Mrs. Kwang. She was pregnant—about five months, I figured. By her side was her little boy about five years old. The Doctor introduced me to the other women. One was eight months pregnant, he said, and the mother of five of the children. The other woman had two small babies.

"I have to leave," he said. "I have several patients in the hospital whom I wish to evacuate by car. Too bad I can't put them on this plane. Will you be so kind, dear Mrs. Greenlaw, as to take care of my wife and the others? They haven't flown much and are very frightened."

"I would be delighted to be of any help," I said, thinking as I said it, that I too, was frightened and didn't like flying. But I put up a brave front and took over the care of the three women and eight children.

I went into the alert shack and chiselled some doughnuts and coffee from the boys. I drank the coffee and took the doughnuts to the children, who like myself, had no breakfast. The children liked the doughnuts but wanted tea.

There we were, sitting around still waiting, and no signs of any plane getting ready to take off. Mrs. Davidson and the Chinese were getting impatient, not to mention myself. I was really getting nervous. The sky was clear. A fine day for bombing! As if in answer to my thoughts, off went the siren! The children and the three women shouted, *"Ginbao!,"* the women turned green, gathered their babies about them and began to dash around in circles.

"No use running," I said to them. "There are no holes near here."

At this moment another car drove up and Colonel Chennault and Harvey jumped out. Without even looking in our direction, they went inside the shack to talk to the pilots. I didn't dare follow them in, but I stood by the door and listened to the voice of the radio. It was giving positions of enemy planes coming in our direction. The various stations of the "Net" reported eighty-seven enemy planes! This, I thought, is the finish of all of us—caught like rats on this airdrome.

Harvey came out of the shack. "Get yourself and your kindergarten in one of those cars and get the hell out of here."

The women were hysterical when I told them. The children screamed when they saw how frightened their mothers were. Finally, we all got into one car, including the two dogs. How we ever managed it, I don't know. We were on the main path going towards the control shack when I saw the C.N.A.C. plane taking off!

"There goes our baggage, Mrs. Davidson. We'll have a fine time finding it again."

"Where is the plane going?" she asked.

"Myitkyina," I replied.

We got to the control shack. I hustled the whole outfit into the dugout and told them to stay there. I was too nervous to join them, so I went into the room to listen to the reports. It was all very exciting but tough on the nerves until finally, I had a feeling of not giving a damn. All of our planes had already taken off and were flying in the direction of Lashio. There were only fifteen up this time—two of the total seventeen we had yesterday had developed engine trouble. The Japs did not show up—but the alarm lasted until eleven o'clock.

We all went back to the runway. Three Americans in khaki were fussing about and loading boxes into an Army transport, a Douglas DC-3. I walked over to find out if they were going to take off.

"Good morning, how did you like the excitement, Mrs. Greenlaw?" It was Colonel Cooper.

"Not too well," I answered. "Ready to take off?"

"In a few minutes. Have you met Colonel Powell and Captain Carleton?"

I recognized the tall-young-and-handsome fellow as the one who had flown us out of Loiwing in the loaded ammunition plane. He was Captain Carleton.

"Are you flying this crate, Captain?" I asked.

"You bet," he smiled. "I haven't flown this course to Kunming yet, but I think we'll manage to get there."

I didn't like that at all. The flight was a difficult one over treacherous mountains and I felt that only the experienced pilots of C.N.A.C. could handle it.

"Beside myself," I said, "how about carrying a load of women, children and dogs?"

"Bring them in," said Colonel Cooper. "The plane is practically empty—maybe we won't bump around so much if we put a little weight in it."

I was walking back to the shack to get the women when I met R. C. Moss.

"Olga," he said, "could you do something for me?"

"Sure," I answered, "what?"

"Those two Anglo-Indian girls—you know the ones—they ought to get out of here. Could you take care of them?"

"Why not?" I said. "Better get them over here quickly. We're about to take off."

"Will you give this letter to Hastey? He'll take care of the girls when you get there."

The situation struck me as very amusing, and I began to laugh. Moss laughed too, probably knowing why I was laughing.

"Any more contraband?" I asked.

Moss grinned. "Isn't that enough?"

Colonel Cooper signalled they were ready.

Off went the sirens!

I didn't think twice. I gathered the women and the kids and Moss's two Anglo-Indian girls and loaded them into the army transport. I forgot Lucy and ran back for her. When I got into the ship Mrs. Davidson was already there with her dog. The Chinese women were busy strapping themselves to the aluminum seats. There were four other passengers—two Chinese pilots, who had bandaged heads and looked very ill, and two Army mechanics.

Since we were flying in the opposite direction of that from which the Japs would approach, I didn't feel so apprehensive. Soon we climbed to 10,000 feet and turned northeast.

If all went well, we would get to Kunming in about three hours and a half.

Twenty minutes after the take-off, the Chinese women began to vomit all over the ship. I was worried about the one who was eight months' pregnant and feared she would give birth to the child at any moment—she was that large. She turned a sickly color, closed her eyes, and her body slumped. She was holding her youngest child who was about a year old. I unstrapped my belt and rushed toward her, picked up the infant and placed in on the lap I spotted first—Colonel Cooper's.

"Here," I said, "you take care of this while I look after the mother."

Why the Colonel blushed, I don't know, but even his bald head had turned crimson. I couldn't expect any help from the other two Chinese women because they, too, were deathly ill, and so were the Anglo-Indians. Mrs. Davidson wasn't, but she looked quite frightened and made no move to help me. I kept crossing the aisle from one side to the other, cleaning the mess off the women's dresses and off the heads of the little ones they were holding on their laps. What a mess—a good thing I have a strong stomach.

An hour and twenty-five minutes later, we were flying over Yunnanyi, the aviation training center where Captain Carney was stationed. Our plane began to lose altitude and was soon circling the field to land.

"Why?" I asked Colonel Cooper.

"It's overcast, and I don't think we can make it to Kunming. We'll get the weather report from here, and if it is okay, we'll take off again. If not, we will stay here for the night."

The Chinese women hoped we would stay, so they could rest. I hoped we wouldn't because it meant going through the same thing again. I wanted to get it over with. I had forgotten all about the baby the Colonel was still holding, when he said:

"Colonel Meriam C. Cooper reporting, Mrs. Greenlaw. The situation is critical."

I looked at him and at the baby and began to laugh. The Colonel's trousers were wet, and on the floor near his feet was a little puddle.

"You are now relieved, Colonel," I said, taking over the baby. By this time, the plane had come to a stop. It was good to feel the solid earth under my feet. I looked around the small airdrome and was surprised to find such little activity. Only two antiquated Curtiss Hawks were flying around.

Carney had gone north somewhere to another school, Van Shephard, one of the flying instructors, told me. He also said all the American instructors were resigning. He was the only one left. The other three had already gone to Kunming to start training as combat pilots with the A.V.G.

"Any of our men here?" I asked.

"Yes," he answered, "here they come now."

I looked up at the sky and saw three P-40's coming in.

"Three guard the field at a time," said Shephard. "They stay three days, and then are replaced by another three. They are all from the First Squadron. These three are the new replacements. Red Probst was in charge of the flight that left this morning."

Good for Red, I thought. Gives him another chance to do something.

The three sharks landed. Van Shephard and I walked toward the pilots. I recognized tall, blond, almost bald-headed J. T. Donovan even at a distance. He had been in Loiwing only a week before. The other two were Benny Foshee and Kuykendall.

"Hello," they all greeted.

"Hello," I answered and added, "any transportation around here?"

Donovan said: "We've got one car. How many are you?"

I counted them off on my fingers. "Two Anglo-Indian girls belonging to R. C. Moss; two Chinese mothers, pregnant; one Chinese mother, unpregnant; eight Chinese children, assorted sizes; one Mrs. Davidson; one Olga Greenlaw; and two dogs."

Donovan said: "Holy Moses! What are you running, a nursery?"

Benny Foshee said: "Or a maternity home?"

Donovan said the best place for us to stay was the hostel. He would drive us over there.

I asked about Rose Carney and Donovan suggested I stay with her. "Yes," I answered, "but not until I get the women fixed up."

That turned out to be some job, but after I had assumed the responsibility of the bill, the Chinese hostel manager gave me one six-room bungalow. The Chinese women and children took one side of the bungalow; Mrs. Davidson and I took one room on the other side next to the one I assigned to the Anglo-Indian girls. Then I went in search of Rose Carney's house.

The Carney's little house was within a very small compound. When I got there, four large vicious-looking dogs began to bark frantically. An amah appeared and let me into the house. Rose came out of the little room in back which she explained was the bedroom. She took me in there, asked a lot of questions and offered me a hot bath. Just what I wanted! While I was bathing, Rose stood by in the miniature bathroom, talking all the time, telling me stories about the pilots who were coming there to guard the field; about Carney, who had gone north, and about herself.

Having lost my luggage I had no underclothing, so when Rose offered me a pair of her own under-pants, I gladly accepted them. They were pink rayon trimmed with lace.

"Lace—nice?" she said.

"Yes," I answered, "beautiful. I hate to wear them."

"No, no," she said. "You keep. Me give you present." She laughed and her eyes closed. "Come, we have drink. Plenty liquor here. Look, I show you."

I followed her into the largest room which served as an office, dining room and sitting room. "Plenty liquor" was right! All the shelves built around the room were full of bottles and tins and tins of American cigarettes. Under the shelves on the floor were many more tins of foods, all kinds of food.

"Rose," I said, "you'll never go hungry."

"What-you-like? Chinese chow? American chow? I tell cook."

"Chinese chow," I said, "and tell them to hurry. I'm starving."

We were settling ourselves as comfortably as we could, smoking fresh Camels, when Mrs. Davidson made her appearance.

"My," she said, "I had trouble finding this house. How are you, Rose? I have heard Olga speak so much of you that I wanted to see you, too. My, my—you haven't changed a bit, and I haven't seen you for—let me see—almost five years. Or is it six? Remember, when you were working as a clerk in the Caravan shop at the Gloucester Hotel in Hong Kong?"

"Long time no see," said Rose. "I remember."

"What happened to your little boy?" asked Mrs. Davidson.

"Oh," said Rose in a small voice, "me worried. He Hong Kong with my father."

This was a new angle of Rose's past history of which I knew nothing. I wished Mrs. Davidson would stop talking. How catty women could be!

"Drink, Mrs. Davidson?" said Rose.

"Don't mind if I do," she said. She was silent for a moment, thinking, no doubt, what next to bring up.

"What happened to your first husband, Rose? The Chinese one?"

"Oh," said Rose, "we divorced—long, long time ago. He give me plenty money—thirty thousand dollars. I go Macao. I gamble all, play fan-tan. Play, play, play. Soon, all money gone—finishee! No money, I go to work Caravan shop. I meet you there. You work there, too. You broke, too?"

I had to laugh—I couldn't help it. Good for Rose, I thought.

The amah came in to say that chow was ready. We sat around the small, round table already loaded with food. It was Cantonese food—nothing fancy about it but awfully good.

"Olga," said Rose, "I have good stones. Wanchee look see? They no mine, they Mr. Law's. You know? Standard Oil man? He go away to America. He give me stones. He say can sell for anything, but first get his money back. I fix price—good profit. You can raise price, you profit, too. Yes?"

"No," I said, "no profit for me. Let me see the stones first, Rose, and I'll tell you what they are worth."

She left the table and came back with a little package wrapped in black silk. She untied the rag and opened the little box. What a collection of junk! Inferior, pale-looking cut sapphires; white, faded star sapphires with no stars, and a collection of very poor rubies and low-grade jade. On a piece of paper she had written down the prices. I read it and told Rose that she was asking 200 per cent too much for them.

"Never mind," she said, "you take to Kunming and sell to the boys." I told her I wouldn't sell anything, and certainly not stuff like that, that I would probably give them to the boys for souvenirs.

"You take," she insisted, "never mind no good. You sell."

I took the stones, wrapped them up in the same piece of rag and placed them in my purse, but not until I had counted and itemized the whole lot on a piece of paper. Then I had Rose and Mrs. Davidson sign it.

"What for?" asked Rose.

"You know why," I said. "You are too good a business woman, Rose." We both smiled.

Dinner over, Mrs. Davidson and I thanked Rose and left. Going to bed early didn't do us any good, there was too much talking going on in the next room. Someone knocked on our door. Mrs. Davidson opened it. It was Captain Carleton telling us that there was an air raid alarm, and that the Japs had bombed the airdrome at Loiwing just after we had left. No casualties, and our pilots shot down thirteen Zeros. The Flying Tigers were still in there slugging.

The boy woke us at six. I hated to get up, so tired and still very sleepy. The weather was bad, a heavy overcast.

The manager of the place presented me with the bill for all of us, 260 National. Since no one had any money, I signed for it.

Mrs. Davidson decided not to continue the journey with us, but instead got in a truck with Sasser, one of our radio men, and went south to Paoshan with him. She left instructions with me on how to take care of her dog, which was a Tibetan Spaniel.

We took off from Yunnanyi at ten o'clock. After circling over the field several times the ship gradually climbed to 13,000 feet so as to clear the tops of the mountains. The plane was travelling through a solid bank of clouds. An hour after we left, the pilot found a hole and got through it to find our bearings. We were lost. The ship was rocking from side to side and would suddenly pitch and drop a thousand feet. It was difficult for the passengers to stay in their seats, although they were strapped to them with safety belts.

The Chinese women and all the children, including the two Anglo-Indians and the two Chinese pilots who had head injuries, were terribly sick and repeated the previous day's performance.

One of the Chinese pilots who was sitting next to me signalled me to get his brief-case which was lying on a bag. I brought it to him. He opened it and took out some maps. We were still circling about in that clear hole and could clearly see the country below. The pilot pointed at a little spot on the map. "Here we are," he said.

I called Colonel Cooper. "Look, Colonel," I said, "this pilot knows where we are. Come and look at the map."

The pilot pointed out our location to the Colonel.

"I had better take this in to the pilot," said the Colonel.

He went into the pilot's compartment with the map. Five minutes later he came out again. "Leave it to us old-timers," he said. "We fly by the seat of our pants. I got him on the right course again."

"What do you mean, *you* did?" I asked.

He grinned, and I did, too.

The Chinese pilot said: "Ten minutes more, we fly over the tall mountain. Cross mountain, we are over big Kunming Lake." He was very pleased with himself. He sat back on his seat quite relaxed and no longer ill. "Chinese pilot not so bad," he said.

Soon we saw the range of the high mountains, then the Lake, then the city. We found the field and made a very fine approach after banking steeply, which made me sort of faint. The Chinese women were feeling worse, if possible.

It seemed as if all the A.V.G. came to meet the plane. Daffy Davis and Ceder were there. After exchanging greetings, I asked them if Moon Shen had arrived. They said he had but had not unloaded and had gone to Chungking. Well, I thought, I will never see my suitcases and stuff again. I saw Hastey in the crowd and gave him the letter R. C. Moss had sent him.

"Take over," I said. "The 'goods' are still in the plane."

Ceder drove me to the hostel. There we found Doreen, who was very glad to see me. She made some coffee, and the three of us sat down to talk. Doreen told me about Boyington and gave me a letter he had written to me. I read it aloud for the others to hear:

Dear Olga,

By the time you get here, I shall be gone. I have re-signed because I think it was the best thing to do. "For the good of the service" shall I say? I want you to know that I am not a coward, but I don't have to tell you that. Best of luck to you, and here's hoping we meet again.

Greg Boyington

Another friend gone! I felt sad and sorry for this boy who had bobbled his chances.

Harris, one of the clerks in the Adjutant's office, came up with a decoded message, it said:

FIFTY ENEMY PLANES RAIDED LOIWING THIS MORNING TEN O'CLOCK AVG SHOT DOWN TWENTY TWO WITHOUT LOSSES STOP FIFTEEN BOMBERS AND THE REST MODEL ZEROS.

"Ceder," I said, "Harvey wants you to get the next ship to Loiwing and take some Tommy guns and one Bren gun. Tell the Adjutant and have him write you out an order."

"Swell," said he. "I'll go right now."

Four of the pilots came in to see me and asked a lot of questions about Loiwing and Lashio, and also about the Tenth Air Force officers who were continuously arriving from India. They sat around, drank coffee and talked about resignation; getting back to the United States; joining the Ferry Command.

It was fun being back there, listening to the talk. It was fun and yet it wasn't. Something had gone wrong. The place was not the same. The Army was moving in.

Karl Esklund, the newspaper fellow, came to see me the next morning, "How about an interview?" he asked.

"Fine," I said, "what about?"

"The situation down there in Lashio."

"Don't you know anything yet?"

"No. No one is putting out any information, I don't think they know anything."

"Well, by this time, the Japanese are already in Lashio. When I left there, they were moving up north of Hsipaw. The main battle will take place in Kutkai, I think, as the Chinese Army is digging trenches there, and from what I heard, it is going to resist at that point. There was no one left in Lashio when I left, with the exception of Harvey, three

A.V.G. men and two American Officers. They all got out that night, except Harvey."

"Gee," he said, "what a story. I'll send it right away through Chungking to New York. Do you mind if I use your name and say you were the last woman to leave Lashio?"

"No," I answered, "I don't mind. It's the truth."

He left me after thanking me. After lunch he returned.

"Mrs. Greenlaw," he said, "I showed my article to Adair who is in charge of A.V.G. here now. He said that information was unconfirmed, that as far as he knew, the Chinese were at Lashio, and the Japs hadn't moved in."

"Suit yourself," I said. "But the Japs should be in Lashio now and getting in contact with the Chinese Army in Kutkai. Today is April 29th, Wednesday—I am sure of what I am telling you."

"I haven't been able to get through to Chungking. I'll have to wait, even if it takes me all night. I'll send the story through anyway."

Just before dinner, Adair came in. Doreen and Daffy were already with me. "Where did you get that information you gave Eskelund?" he asked.

"My own," I answered. "I happened to know what's going on down there."

"Well, it's incorrect."

He hadn't finished speaking when Major Lin Wei Kui of the Chinese Intelligence came in. He clicked his heels and saluted me as he always did, because, as I said before, Harvey had been his flying instructor in Hangchow years ago. He handed me a paper.

"Isn't that too bad?" he said.

I read aloud: "Japanese have taken Lashio and are moving northward. The next battle scene will be Kutkai."

It wasn't necessary for me to say anything. But I felt like the cat that ate the canary.

Two days later, Friday, twenty P-40's returned from Loiwing at 1530. Our mechanics had been able to repair four of the damaged ships well enough to fly to Kunming. One United States Army transport also arrived with General Chennault and other A.V.G. personnel. The A.V.G. completely evacuated Loiwing. All buildings were burned, including the lovely club house. Harvey was the last man to leave. General Chennault told me Harvey wanted to stay behind and destroy everything, and that he would come up later. Our convoys were already on the road.

Several Army officers were there in Kunming by that time —some on their way to Chungking and some on their way back to Dinjan, India. Captain Baumler, a United States Army pilot, had joined us. He told me he had spent a year of war in Spain.

General Stilwell was cut off and had started his historical trip through the jungles en route to India. Major Wilson, the chap who was going to Maymyo, was killed by a bomb in Mandalay. Reports said that Tommy Thomson, my old friend, was with him, but there were no reports of his having been killed. He was only missing.

Evacuation of Loiwing, May 4th, 1942. A. V. G. formation with Arvid Olson, Jr. leading flight (P-40 Mo. 68.)

(Photo by Major R. T. Smith, former Flight Leader, Third Pursuit Squadron, A. V. G.)

David Lee Hill ("Tex") who replaced Jack Newkirk Squadron Leader, Second Pursuit. Taken at Loiwing, May 1942, by Dan DeLuce, war correspondent.

"Fearless" Freddie Hedges and bride, Helen Anderson of Rangoon, with "Tex" Hill in Delhi.

Chapter XVII

IN the evening I played a few games of checkers with Tex Hill. General Chennault joined us, and I found myself playing against the two of them. I won three games and tied one out of the four we played. I was happy to know that I, at least, could beat the Old Man at some game. No one could beat him at cribbage or poker. Checkers—that was the General's Waterloo!

I hadn't seen Tom Jones since Loiwing, but in the afternoon of the next day, he came into my office. "Will you teach me some French?" he asked.

"What kind of French?"

He laughed. "French words. How to ask for water, bread, directions."

"You are going, then?"

Jones' face was serious as he asked me:

"Do you know Mr. X?"

"No. Who is he?"

"Mr. X is a Free-Frenchman. He was all morning with us—the fellows who are going on the raid to Indo-China. He gave each of us 1,000 piastres which he said would buy the silence of the natives and also food. He gave us the name of another Free-Frenchman in Hanoi who will do anything to help us. It's a good thing to be prepared, you know, Olga, in case something happens. Mr. X gave us a password to be used only when we come to that certain place outside Hanoi. On hearing the word, the Free-Frenchman will try to sneak us out of that area and direct us toward the China border."

"When are you going?"

"Tomorrow or the next night. Five of us. Donovan, myself, Frank Schiel, maybe Ed Conant, and another."

I remembered the champagne Carney had given me. Here was the occasion to open it. I invited Jones and the fellows who were going with him.

After Jones left, I received a message. "At 1400, 27 Jap bombers, escorted by 22 fighters, bombed, strafed and bombed again the field at Paoshan. They also bombed the town. There was no warning system at all. Eight of our planes were caught on the ground. The boys had just returned from a patrol when the Japs arrived. Bob Little's plane was still warm as he had just landed. Neale ordered his men to get out if they could to save the planes. Bob Little took off under fire and got away. Pilot Bond also took off but couldn't escape the Jap guns and had to bail out."

A short while later Red Probst came in, just back from Paoshan.

"Never saw so many Japs together at once—not since Rangoon. It was a shambles—a bloody slaughter house! At least five thousand were killed—and how stupid they were! They all came in from Burma, fleeing from the Japs, and parked their cars and carts together like sardines—just like sardines, Olga! People camped right by the cars. Jee-*zus!* what a mess! Talk about mass murder!" Red shook his head worriedly. "I think we lost Benny Foshee. He was running from one of the huts to a trench when a bomb got him."

"Killed?"

"When I left, Doc Richards didn't think he had a chance—"

"It was sickening," he continued. "I was lying low in one of the trenches when a little dog came along. I didn't want to see the little rascal blown to pieces so I called 'Here, doggie, nice doggie.' He understood English all right because he came into my trench. Then I saw what he was carrying in his mouth —a human hand—all bloody!"

There were seven of us for supper—Tex Hill, Schiel, Conant, Probst, Donovan, Jones and myself. We were rather silent as we ate, thinking of poor Benny Foshee and that massacre at Paoshan. Finally I proposed a toast in champagne to the success of the Indo-China mission. They started talking about it—how they intended to attack, what they'd do if forced to land—and Benny Foshee and 5,000 mangled Chinese were forgotten. A quick-lapsing memory is a handy thing for a flier to cultivate.

Ed Conant removed something from around his neck—a dirty string that had once been white. Attached to it was a scapular of the Sacred Heart of Jesus. He held it in his hand and looked at it for a long time. "My mother gave me this," he said. That reminded me that I was wearing a thin gold chain with a little cross. Harvey had bought it for me in Hanoi in 1939. I took it off and put it around Jones' neck.

"What is it?" asked Jones.

"A cross," I answered, "it always brought me luck. Will you wear it? And when you return from the mission, give it back to me."

"The General said I couldn't go on your mission, Tom," said Conant. "He says that I am not used to these fast pursuit ships. I flew the big fellows when I was in the Navy. Well, my tough luck. Since I am not going, will you wear this scapular? It certainly brought me luck."

"My God, Jones," said Donovan, "you'll be so festooned with charms and what-nots that Jap bullets won't be able to touch you."

"How about you wearing Conant's scapular, then?" said Jones.

"Yes," said Conant, "you take it. Olga's cross ought to be enough for Tom."

"Thanks a lot," said Donovan, "but, if my number is up— nothing is going to help."

We finished the champagne and about nine o'clock the boys left. I sat in my office alone, pondering the situation—that day, May 5th, the Japanese columns were advancing northward along the Burma Road and had entered Yunnan Province. A vanguard crossed the Salween River. Our planes had bombed the bridge on the Salween, checking the Japanese advance and giving the Chinese soldiers a chance to strengthen their positions.

Most of the men of the Second and Third Squadrons were at Kunming, resting after their strenuous fighting in Burma and Loiwing. The First Squadron had taken over the fighting, although some of the pilots of the Second Squadron and the Third, whose planes were still fit to fly, had gone down to Paoshan and Yunnanyi to support the Chinese Army.

The next morning Harvey returned on a transport with Bond, who was badly burned, Bob Neale, and the body of Ben Foshee. Harvey looked completely worn-out.

"Too bad about Benny. Caught on the ground and hit by shrapnel. He died yesterday. Doc Richards did everything he could to save him. Lucky thing I had a bottle of whisky with me when we got on that transport with Benny. We were dog-tired, no sleep for two nights and what with one thing and another, including the heat, it was about as unpleasant a flight as I've ever made."

Jones came in to say hello to Harvey. The mission to Hanoi had been postponed as all planes were being used to check the Jap advance. Jones said: "We had an accident this morning. Blackburn was practicing gunnery over the lake. He spun in. We haven't found him or his plane yet."

All I said was: "Too bad." My emotions, which had been so sensitive back in Toungoo when little Armstrong was killed, had become as dull as an old butter knife. I don't think my feelings had become hardened—just anesthetized by too much death and tragedy and disaster.

After dinner General Chennault—I still kept calling him "Colonel"—dropped by to tell Harvey he'd have to go back to India.

Harvey said: "Hell's bells!"

"You and I are the only ones that can handle the situation over there and I must stay here."

"If I go, I'll take Olga with me."

The Old Man said: "She'd better stay here."

"Colonel, I mean, General," I said. "If—"

"I heard you the first time," he smiled.

"If I go to India with Harvey, and our outfit gets inducted will you include me in it?"

"Sure, I will," he said. "But I don't want you to go. We need you here."

"If she doesn't go," said Harvey stubbornly, "I am not going either."

"Goddamit!" said the General. "All right, she goes. Tell the Adjutant to write out an order. Who else you want with you?"

"Ceder," said Harvey.

I noticed that the General was wearing a pair of sparkling silver stars. He saw me looking at them.

"Got them off Jimmie Doolittle as he went through here yesterday from his Tokyo raid on the way back to the States. He can get others in India."

"When do we leave?" asked Harvey.

"As soon as possible," said the Old Man.

Ceder and the convoy arrived with the curtains and mattresses I had looted from the C.N.A.C. hostel in Lashio.

"What happened to my car?" asked Harvey.

"I left it in Yunnanyi," said Ceder. "Captain Carney said he'd take care of it."

"Yea?" said Harvey. "And all the stuff I had in it, I bet I never see that again."

"What car?" I asked.

"Well, the last day in Lashio, I gave two English fellows a ride on one of our transports, the last plane, too. They were very grateful and they gave me their two Fords. I could only get one out of Lashio. They also gave me a bag full of silver rupees, close to a thousand, I guess, and some pieces of jewelry. I gave the jewelry to the fellows but kept an opal pendant for you. It's in there in one of the bags."

I decided to sell all the stuff I had brought from Toungoo—enough to furnish a house. Several Chinese ladies and their husbands came in and were more than glad to buy everything I had. They thought my prices were cheap, but I knew I was selling everything at a tremendous profit. For instance: I sold a radio for 1,000 rupees, and I only paid 400 for it; the dishes for 500 rupees for which I paid 150. The whole sale netted two thousand dollars United States currency. Not bad. But, if I had wished to buy the things back, I couldn't have for love or money.

Doreen wanted to know what I was going to do with the phonograph and records.

"Pilot Adkins bought them," I said. I began to separate the records. "If I don't see Bob Little," I told Doreen, "give him these two—with Olga's compliments."

I handed her Judy Garland's *Our Love Affair* and Dinah Shore's *The Nearness of You.* They were his favorites. The last time I had seen him, he said: "Olga, if I get killed, I'll will them to you."

I hated to see the phonograph and records go because we had had much fun playing them over and over. Suddenly I remembered that Jones' record, *The Last Time I Saw Paris* was amongst the ones Adkins took. But it was too late.

I asked Doreen to give the stones to Captain Carney when she saw him and to tell him to tell Rose they were no good and I couldn't sell them.

I went to bed. A little later I heard Harvey come into my office. I was almost asleep when I heard a familiar voice. It said: "Pappy, have you got a razor you could give me—or that you want to sell. Mine's busted. . . ."

It was Bob Little. I hadn't seen him in quite some time. I had been in Burma and at Loiwing and when I returned he was down at Paoshan. I wanted to see him, but being so tired I decided I'd wait until morning. I wondered, drowsily, if he were still carrying my black gloves.

We left Kunming on the morning of May 8th. It wasn't

until we were well on our way that I suddenly had a very positive feeling I had said my last farewell to Kunming and, as far as active service was concerned, to the A.V.G. It didn't bother me particularly then. I was tired, and was sure Calcutta would be a pleasant change. The flight across Northern Burma was rough and breezy and I was particularly worried about the possibility of bumping into a flock of Japs. We flew a hundred miles north to Myitkyina, the last British stronghold which the Japs had been bombing repeatedly and it was clear enough so we could see the broad Salween River meandering through the jungle. Now and then we caught a glimpse of the twisting, turning Burma Road, the now useless highway over which we had fought so hard and lost so many good friends—to no avail.

The plane, an Army C-47 transport, taken over by C.N.A.C. and flown by Frank Higgs, had the built-in aluminum benches and was thoroughly uncomfortable. There were nineteen passengers—mostly Chinese who, as usual, were inclined to be slightly unwell. The center of the cabin was covered with luggage, mostly mine—boxes, suitcases, a bundle of rugs and by Karenni drum which I refused to leave behind although everyone kidded me about it. In order to stretch my legs, and escape from the unsavory aromas of the indisposed Chinese, I spent part of the time in the pilot's cockpit with Frank Higgs.

Before we reached India the weather closed in solid and we found ourselves flying through a snowstorm so thick I couldn't see the wing-tips of the plane. Abruptly, we began to descend. I was afraid we might hit a mountain top—or had motor trouble. It never dawned on me that we were going down for a landing. I didn't see how we could—absolutely nothing was visible. But I was underestimating our pilot. I couldn't even see the tops of the trees, or the runway and yet Frank set us down as lightly as a feather. When I asked him how he did, he said:

"Instruments—how else? Or did you think it was yoga?"

We were at Dinjan, across the Burma border. India at last!

Big, bluff Colonel Caleb Haynes, who later was to command the bomber units of the American China Task Force, met us and asked Harvey if he could have, say, six or eight A.V.G. pilots and planes to defend this airdrome. Intelligence had reported that the Japapese intended to attack and bomb it at the earliest opportunity. We couldn't help but laugh. Here we were, on our way to Calcutta, Delhi and Karachi to try to beg, borrow or steal planes from the Tenth Air Force for the A.V.G., and Colonel Haynes of the Tenth Air Force was asking us for help! That was the limit, I thought.

Sawyer and Pete Wright were at Dinjan with brand-new ships flown in from Karachi and were on their way to Kunming, but were waiting for the weather to clear. It was raining cats and dogs and I found shelter under the huge wing of the plane. Sawyer saw me and splashed over.

"You sure get around," he said. I brought him up to date on the situation at Kunming. Frank Higgs, standing at the top of the boarding ladder and acting like a train conductor yelled: "A-a-a-ll aboard!" We got back into the plane. I hated it!

Taking off in the downpour and climbing up through the overcast wasn't as bad as landing. We got a glimpse of Dinjan—a few mud-and-straw huts, a few brick houses and a little church with a steeple. After an hour we came into clear weather. Higgs went down to the carpet, not over 500 feet, and chased along the beautiful Brahmaputra River, a wide, wandering stream with many tributaries. The whole countryside was a lucious green. At times we flew so low I could catch a glimpse of crocodiles basking in the sun along the riverbank.

We arrived at Dum Dum, the Calcutta airdrome, at seventhirty—eight hours of flying from Kunming, which was exactly eight hours too much for Olga Greenlaw. We took a bus to the city. There were no taxis. We went to the Great Eastern Hotel, Calcutta's finest. We had to go through the rigmarole of luggage inspection although it was made easy for us being of the A.V.G. They took the numbers of our guns and cameras and asked how much money we had. I was carrying 20,000 rupees that Harvey had drawn for expenses. He had turned the money over to me, saying I was to be the Finance Officer of the A.V.G. in India. My new job! I had to declare the amount of money.

It was hotter than blazes. I liked it, though, after Kunming weather. I felt my nose and throat clearing and was glad to realize that at last I was going to get rid of my sniffles.

I was too tired to sleep. I tossed about on my bed—wide awake and thinking of all the things that had happened in the last month. Everything seemed to move so fast. What, I wondered, was coming next?

Chapter XVIII

PERHAPS it was because I was unable, immediately, to unwind—or it might have been because of the uncertainty of our future plans—but Calcutta very quickly began to get on my nerves. We met a number of old acquaintances, many from Rangoon, but all of them seemed to be flitting around in circles and going nowhere in particular.

Everybody had the wind up. All buildings, small and large, were sandbagged. Air raid alarms were almost continuous—as bad as the early days at Kunming, but no enemy planes appeared. Shopping was a waste of time. Prices had soared out of sight because of shipping difficulties.

I felt uncomfortable and out of place and wished I were back in China, in the thick of things. The Battle of Burma was all but over and, to quote General Stilwell, "we took a hell of a beating" but the boys were still flying and fighting and I felt I should be with them—although what actual help I could have been I really don't know. But beyond that I had a strange and uneasy feeling that I was waiting for something to happen—something definite and conclusive which would write *finis* to the whole adventure.

The Calcutta newspapers annoyed me. I noticed how they were building up the R.A.F. and the new American Tenth Air Force and giving the A.V.G. slight credit—or none at all. I found one story—about the Jap Advance toward Yunnan Province—particularly irksome.

DRIVE TOWARD PAOSHAN

In north-east Burma another border battle is taking place, and the Japanese vanguards thrusting up the Burma Road are 60 miles to the west of Paoshan, 200 miles inside the Yunnan border. The Chinese have destroyed the bridges across the Salween River and are holding the east bank. Small parties of Chinese appear to be operating in many directions up the Burma Road, and the guerilla warfare stage appears to have been reached.

When the Japanese reached Lashio, they found that it was devoid of supplies, while buildings which might have been of use to them had been destroyed.

On and on it went. The whole thing so familiar to me. No mention of the A.V.G., who were the ones who had destroyed the large bridge across the Salween by dropping bombs. No mention of our whole First Squadron there at Paoshan, the new headquarters, the starting place for those raids over the advancing enemy. How well I recalled the destruction of Lashio—the day and night of waiting for Harvey to return from there—because he had stayed behind to carry out the destruction of the town!

Harvey soon found out that all our supplies were being shipped to Karachi and hence to Allahabad, or Delhi, from which they were sent by transport to China—so there wasn't much sense in our remaining in Calcutta as all business was being handled from Delhi, where the Tenth Air Force had its headquarters. We would proceed to Delhi as soon as Harvey could clean up loose ends at the A.V.G. Calcutta office, which was in charge of Commander R. DeWolfe, of the United States Navy.

A day or two after our arrival, Harvey received a coded message from General Chennault. We worked on decoding about a half hour and finally got it clear.

A flight of five, led by Jones, raided Hanoi. They bombed and strafed the main airdrome. Fifteen Japanese planes, including bombers, a large two-seater and single-seater fighters were burned on the ground. Two bombs hit the Administration building, and at least twenty-five more planes were damaged. All returned except Donovan.

Donovan!—who wouldn't wear any of our charms because if a bullet had his number on it, nothing would stop it!

I was sad about Donovan, and happy for Tom Jones. I could clearly see that smiling face of his. Fifteen planes and twenty-five probables! That was good. That meant that each one would be credited with three Japs because only fifteen were confirmed. Jones would have enough for his tuition expenses at law school.

The following afternoon several A.V.G. pilots came in; they were on their way to Karachi to ferry ships back to Kunming. How glad I was to see them—just as if the large family was getting together again. Tex Hill, who was heading the mission, Rossi, Cross, Hodges, Burgard. They left Kunming about eleven o'clock, they said.

All the boys, except Tex Hill, were going north to Delhi on a British transport. Tex decided to stay with us and go up by train. I didn't want to go by plane, as I wanted to see some of the country. Ceder would accompany the pilots to Delhi and from there try to get an Army transport to Karachi.

I asked Tex about the Hanoi raid. He said Jones was already planning another mission. "Too bad about Donovan," he said. I asked him if any of the other four had bullet holes in their planes. He answered:

"No, they didn't. They were damn lucky. Jones told me that they really caught the Japs with their trousers at half mast, as planned. You know, it's funny about Jones. We were playing football at the field the other day. Jones had nothing on but his slacks. He was still wearing your gold chain and cross, and all the fellows kidded him about it. He wears it all the time and says it's his good-luck charm."

"Tom isn't superstitious," I said, "he is only wearing it to please me. Hope the boys are not kidding him too much."

"Have you got another one?" asked Tex. "I'd like to have it."

"You're too mean," I said, "you don't need one."

We went to Delhi on May 16th by train and were lucky

to get an air conditioned compartment which made the twenty-eight-hour trip bearable.

We found Delhi 20° hotter than Calcutta, although it was the cool of the evening. We drove in an antiquated taxi to the Imperial Hotel in New Delhi, where Harvey had asked Ceder to make reservations. We found the place full up—completely taken over by the Tenth Air Force. So, we drove to Old Delhi to the Cecil Hotel. This too, was full up, but the clerk, an Austrian by the name of Karlini, said to me:

"Mrs. Greenlaw, we do have one suite, our best one. I might let you have it for a week, but no more."

"Why not more?" I asked.

"Well," he said, "we have it always reserved for Mr. Bill Pawley."

Funny how we were always coming across Bill Pawley. "He won't mind," I said. "If he comes, we'll let you put a cot in there for him."

The clerk laughed but let us into the suite just the same. He had to put another bed in the sitting room for Tex Hill. We sat up the rest of the night drinking beer and eating ham sandwiches and talking to Karlini.

It wasn't long before we three were settled and quite at home in the Cecil. Harvey made arrangements for purchasing a car, but not until General Naiden promised to buy it back from us at the same price. Taxi service there was difficult and very expensive, and Harvey thought he would save A.V.G. funds by purchasing the car. He bought a brand-new Buick for 9,500 rupees, and the Tenth Air Force supplied the gasoline.

The only cars used by the officers of the Tenth Air Force were Buicks and Packards. They had bought all of those cars in Delhi, and were much surprised when Harvey found one which was being reserved for the Governor of Burma, Dorman-Smith, who was able to get out of Burma a long time ago and was somewhere in India on his way to Delhi.

The hotel was cluttered up with war correspondents—so many of them it was difficult for me to remember their names —Bill Chaplin, International News Service; Bill Fisher, of Time; Dan de Luce, A. P.; Edgar Snow, free-lancing; Wiliam Mundy, Australian war correspondent; "Newsreel" Wong, famous Chinese cameraman; Ted White of Time and Life; Rogers, another photographer for Time; Maurice Ford, a cameraman for one of the British companies and the Peter Muirs of C.B.S. They all seemed to be stranded there as they couldn't get permits for the war zones. Having nothing else to do, they took turns visiting Gandhi.

Peter Muir showed me a paper on which he had written his broadcast, and I was quite amused reading about myself. It started out with: "Two men and one woman arrived in Delhi from China."

"Why," I asked Mr. Muir, "do you want to send stuff like that?"

"Because the Flying Tigers have been a sensation in the American newspapers—a glamorous and enormously popular fighting unit. Or didn't you know that?"

Frankly, I didn't. Of course there had been several newspaper men in Kunming and others in Rangoon but, with the exception of Karl Eskalund, I only regarded them as "snoopers" who were continually trying to find out things they weren't supposed to know. We didn't see many American newspapers or magazines in China or Burma, and those were always months old. So I was surprised to learn what a big play the A.V.G. had been given by the American press— and more surprised at some of the details. Jack Newkirk, I discovered, had been widely featured as "Scarsdale Jack." If he came from Scarsdale, nobody in the Group was aware of it—or even where Scarsdale was for that matter. And we never referred to ourselves as the Flying Tigers. We called ourselves the A.V.G.—or on infrequent special occasions, the American Volunteer Group.

Incidentally, if you think any airmen or soldiers who are in action on any front are the least bit concerned about their publicity in American papers you may disillusion yourself forthwith. Stories of hardship and heroism are for the home folks, not for the troops.

I saw a lot of Tex Hill. When we were not shopping or looking around the town, we were in the swimming pool, always surrounded by war correspondents, talking about the war or playing bridge.

Tall Tex, six feet two, and very slim—serious Tex who seldom smiled. I had seen him once when he was very angry, his whole expression changed—lips turned into a thin line, and his eyes narrow, blazing slits. But that day in the swimming pool he was smiling and his eyes were open wide and very blue. He talked to me about life in Texas, the country where he came from. He spoke a quasi-Spanish, learned there in the border towns. I noticed how his hair was thinning on top of his head, but he still had quite a bit left, and the wavy, blond strands covered the bald spot. He saw me looking at him, and his smile grew wider.

"I wish I had known you better in Kunming," he said.

"Your fault," I answered. "Why didn't you come around? All the others did."

"I was waiting for an invitation—you never asked me."

"No," I answered, "never asked you, nor did I ever ask the others. But then, didn't you once tell R. C. Moss way back there in Toungoo that I must be a cold-blooded woman. . . ?"

He laughed. "Yes," I did. "But I didn't know you then."

I said: "If and when we fold up, will you join the Tenth Air Force here, or will you go back to the States?"

He frowned and was silent for a while. "There's no reason why I shouldn't. Our country is at war, and I have to fight, whether it is here, Australia or Africa. It doesn't make any difference. As long as I'm fighting, I'll be doing my duty."

"But don't you want to go home first and rest up a bit?"

"Hell, no. I'm in stride now—why stop? Might lose my tech-ni-q."

"Will you ask for a commission?"

Tex nodded. "I'd like to get a majority."

I thought there was no reason why he shouldn't. India was crawling with majors and lieutenants colonels with no battle experience whatever and Tex, besides being a Squadron Leader, had nineteen Japs to his credit. When he later joined the American Air Forces these victories were, by some fantastic bit of reasoning, officially cancelled as far as compiling his total score was concerned, as were the victories of all the A.V.G. boys. As far as the Tenth Air Force was concerned, Japs shot down with the A.V.G. just didn't count, which must have been small consolation to the dead Japs.

I urged Tex to take care of himself when he got back to China. "Don't get too reckless, Tex. Remember what happened to the others."

"You'll see me again," he said confidently. "Ain't any goggle-eyed little monkey going to catch me asleep. I made up my mind a long time ago that I'll be ridin' those cayuses on my father's ranch back in Texas some day."

That vague feeling that I was waiting for something definite to happen which would clarify our situation continued to disturb me. The A.V.G., obviously, was going to be disbanded. Harvey had been offered an American commission but hadn't made up his mind whether or not to accept it at that time as it would mean staying on in India. We had been in the Orient for nearly five years and certain personal affairs at home demanded his attention. I wanted to go home—and yet I didn't. I was waiting for something—I didn't know what—something that was unfinished.

One morning, I went with Harvey and Tex to Willingdon Airdrome in the beautiful new Buick, a silver gray color. The Union Jack, and the R.A.F. flag were flying high upon their masts all over the airdrome and its entrances. But I saw only one R.A.F. officer there. All the rest were Americans. Hundreds of mechanics and dozens of pilots, all wearing United States Air Corps insignia. The Tenth Air Force certainly had taken over.

We drove back through the new city, passed through the Delhi Gate, and into Old Delhi proper. We drove along the broad avenue, Elgin Road, lawns on both sides, and past the famous old fort. The fort is known as "Lal Kila," or "Red Fort," because the massive walls of it are built of red sandstone. There are two fine gates to the fort, the Delhi Gate on the south side and the Lahore Gate on the west side, facing the end of one of the oldest streets of the world, Chandi Chauk, or "Silver Street."

We crossed Chandi Chauk and got into the Lothian Road, a continuation of Elgin Road. We drove along another few minutes and entered the ancient Kashmir Gate, the bloody scene of the Indian Mutiny of 1857. Not far from there, after a few twists and turns, we entered the Cecil Hotel.

The furniture of our suite was covered with the fine dust which was constantly blowing in from the desert. The rooms were hot, although we kept the ceiling fans going full-blast. Harvey decided to keep large tanks filled with ice directly under the fans so that the cool air would blow in all directions. We had three deliveries of ice during the afternoon so the coolness would last through, at least, midnight. We kept the windows tightly closed to keep the hot air out.

It wasn't long before Tex Hill left for Karachi. Tex hated to go, saying that since he had left the States the swimming pool at the Cecil was the pleasantest place he had found. He promised to return as soon as possible.

I was coming back from the swimming pool, my bathing suit dripping wet, when I heard voices in our sitting room through the open door, and I wondered who was there with Harvey. Suddenly I heard: "She wanted my hat to wear to the funeral. . . ."

I went in. There was Freddie Hodges and his wife, Helen.

"Hello," I said, happy to see them. "Whose funeral are you talking about, Helen?"

She said: "Tom Jones'."

I froze where I stood. "No, no! It can't be! Not Jones! It isn't true!" I kept saying to myself. "It isn't true!—it isn't true!—it isn't—"

Helen's voice was saying:

"It was Saturday, the 16th. I was waiting to get into the plane for India to join Freddie. One of the Anglo-Indian girls came by in a car and asked me to lend, sell or give her my hat, the only one I had. I asked her why she wanted a hat and she said she had to have one for Jones' funeral. That's all I know."

Harvey sighed deeply. "Strange we haven't heard anything about it. I'll send a message right away and ask for confirmation."

I was ill. My stomach had an empty feeling as if there wasn't anything in it—anything in my body at all. My head swam. I felt dizzy. I couldn't sit down. I was paralyzed on my feet. Only my brain seemed to function and it was going round and around. I could see pictures flashing by of Jones. Sometimes he was smiling, sometimes serious—his clear eyes fixed on the far horizons, seeing visions of his future, a future as he wanted it to be—with the wife who was waiting for him and the baby he had never seen. He was a lawyer. He was the Governor of Washington! I heard the music of his favorite piece, *The Last Time I Saw Paris*. I saw again the crazy instrument for star navigation he was so proud of. I saw the pure brilliance of the gold cross resting on his chest and I heard him saying: "I shall wear it always, Olga."

True, that. He had worn it always—until death.

The anxiously-awaited message from the Old Man in answer to Harvey's inquiry arrived a few hours later. And what a staggering blow it was! It was a long message and took some time to decode. And then, clear and sharp, the words burning through the thin paper—

JONES PRACTICING DIVE BOMBING NEAR FIELD SPUN
IN AND KILLED FRIDAY FIFTEENTH MAY STOP BOB
LITTLE KILLED SATURDAY TWENTY-THIRD BY EN-
EMY ANTI-AIRCRAFT FIRE OVER SALWEEN. . . .

There was a lot more to the message but I read nothing
else. My eyes were riveted on these few lines—JONES
KILLED—BOB LITTLE KILLED—

"Dear God! Dear God!" I kept saying to myself: "Not
Jones *and* Little!—Not you, too, Bob!" I began to cry. Harvey left his seat near the desk and placed his arms around me.

"Don't cry," he said. "You can't bring them back. I know
how you feel. I loved them, too—Jones and Little, Sandy and
Jack Newkirk. Remember when we were in Toungoo, at
the very beginning—remember what I told you? I told you
not to let yourself get too attached to these boys, not to love
them too much because, later, they'd tear your heart out. I
told you many of those boys would die, that many would go
and never return. I tried to warn you, dear, to keep you from
feeling the pain I felt when I was in the Army—when a lot
of my best friends went away and never came back. There,
now, don't cry any more. Harden yourself and forget about
it. You'll meet other boys you will love just as much." He
patted my shoulder. "Come on, Olga. you've got to be a
good soldier."

But I couldn't do it. I didn't want to be a good soldier. I
couldn't harden myself and forget. I kept on remembering
and thinking—wishing, hoping, praying that by some miracle
they would come back. I spent the rest of the day in bed, trying to read. Harvey had to go to New Delhi and I stayed
alone.

It was growing dark and I was still alone thinking—thinking about those boys—and what a lousy, rotten business this
all was—this war—this great adventure I'd gotten myself
into. Suddenly I wasn't alone any more. They were there
with me. I felt their presence so strongly I could almost see
them—clearly at times. Jones and Bob Little. They were both

laughing, as if at some huge joke. Little's eyes were luminous, like that night in Toungoo when we lit the kerosene lamps, and the pupils were larger than ever.

Jones was saying: "I was practicing dive-bombing near the field at Kunming. I got into a power dive, everything turned hazy—and I blacked out. I never came out of it. I spun right into the ground. Remember, Olga, when I told you I had to lie by the plane for a half hour after testing out that P-40-E? I made you promise not to tell Sam Prevo because he would have grounded me? I thought about that when I was diving—just before everything went blank."

"I remember it too well," I said. "It was all my fault that you spun in, Jones. I should have told Sam Prevo. It's all my fault."

"No it isn't," said Bob Little. "It isn't anybody's fault. Look at me. My ship and I exploded in mid-air—boom! and we disappear! Nothing left of me—ha,ha!—and nothing left of your black gloves, either. You told me black was bad luck. You must have a jinx—all your best friends get killed. You pick the wrong boy friends, Sucker."

"But it was fun," said Jones.

"It wasn't dull," said Little. "I took nineteen of them before they got me—from the ground. The fellows will tell you all about it, Olga. . . ."

The door in the next room opened. The room was so dark. It was late, and all the curtains were drawn. A light went on. Harvey came into the room.

"Get up, lazy woman. It is almost time for dinner."

"What's new, Harvey, over at headquarters?"

"Good news," he said, "Uncle Joe got in all right."

"Uncle Joe?"

"General Stilwell, stupid. After tramping through 150 miles of Burma jungle, they made it. It took him and his men eighteen days before they got to a town on the border of Assam from Wuntho, his last headquarters after he left Schwebo."

Tex and Duke Headman returned a few days later with news of Jones and Little.

Duke said: "He didn't have a dog's chance. I mean Jones. Neither did Bob, for that matter, but at least he went down fighting. Shot down by 37 mm. anti-aircraft. The other pilots with him saw his ship explode in the air—absolutely disintegrated!

"Bob Neale was leading that strafing mission over the Salween. The objective was to blast the Jap machine-gun nests and some anti-aircraft that was known to be in that location. Flying high, the fellows couldn't see anything, so Bob Little dove and flew at an altitude of 500 feet looking for the guns. That's when they got him. The rest of the flight dropped the heavy bombs they were carrying and strafed afterwards; then they returned to Paoshan.

"Bob Neale and Little were the closest of friends, almost like brothers. Maybe because they both hailed from the same place, Spokane, Washington. The pilots at Kunming were having a staff meeting, Olson presiding, when Bob Neale came in and told them about Little. He broke down completely, crying like a baby."

"Later the General ordered Neale on another mission, but he refused, saying it was suicide sending men out on a mission in those antiquated, worn-out planes that we have. The Old Man was really angry, but Neale said no more offensive work for him or the men of his squadron—only defensive. What can a guy do anyway, without the proper equipment? We have been losing men right and left in the last couple of weeks."

"And Bishop," said Tex Hill, "was lost in a raid over Indo-China. He had to bail out and probably was taken prisoner by the Japs."

"Like Black Mac," said Duke. "I wonder what happend to him—probably a prisoner, too. But the Chinese scouts found a body in the same location or thereabouts where Black Mac bailed out when Jack Newkirk got killed—in March.

The body was unrecognizable, as there was nothing left, the ants had eaten the flesh, but the uniform the bones were covered with was an A.V.G. flying suit with the insignia still on it."*

"It could have been any of the others," I said, "we lost several in that same location."

"Yes," said Tex, "never can tell who it was. But it gives us all hopes of some day seeing one of them walking back— Maybe Black Mac, Bishop, Mott, or Leibolt."

"But not Sandy, or Jones, or Little, or Old Newquack," I said.

Duke laughed: "I haven't heard Jack called Newquack for a hell of a long time. Sort of made me feel as if he were still alive."

Soon, too soon I thought, the boys' planes were ready and Harvey took them to the airdrome. At two o'clock in the afternoon I was in the swimming pool. It felt strange being alone without the boys, and only news correspondents about me. I heard the sound of motors and looked up at the sky. Two P-40's circled and dove straight down over the hotel. They buzzed the place twice, gained some altitude and leveled off in the direction of Allahabad.

"Good-bye," I said silently, hating to see them go, not knowing whether any of them would ever return. And as they faded into the dusty haze it dawned upon me that the vague something I had been waiting for to happen had happened. Unconsciously and without understanding why, I had been waiting for the last great misfortune—for Tom Jones and Bob Little to be killed. That was the finish as far as I was concerned. After that I didn't care what happened. I told Harvey I'd had enough. We decided to go home.

On June 23rd I found I was really ill—for the first time in years. Dengue fever!—which is something like malaria, but

---

*Since this was written, it has been officially announced that W. D. McGarry is a prisoner of the Japanese.

not so bad—it doesn't recur as malaria does. I felt miserable and had to go to bed, where I remained for several days. I was not lonesome—most of the war correspondents came to see me and Mr. Bond of Pan American Airways and C.N.A.C., who had just arrived from the States via Cairo, had many amusing stories to tell. He said that in the States the war was beginning to be felt—that it was difficult to obtain woolen clothing, that to buy toothpaste, one had to turn in the old tube. "Not the same place you left," he added. I said I imagined I'd be able to stand it.

When Edgar Snow came in one noontime, Newsreel Wong had just left. How sweet of Newsreel—he brought me flowers. When I asked him, "Where in the world did you get them?" he said:

"Oh, I just went around looking into peoples' gardens. I saw the flowers and I took them. As a matter of fact, they are all stolen."

I believed him because I knew it was impossible to buy flowers in Delhi.

One of the correspondents told me they had a Press conference at the Imperial Hotel that morning and that Colonel Scott, the chap I had met in Loiwing, so long ago, it seemed, had been there also. The mention of Scott reminded me of the article I had read that morning in *The Statesman*, one of the many Delhi papers. It said:

NEW LEADER OF THE A.V.G.

The 23rd Pursuit Group, which will take over the duties and equipment of the A.V.G., when that famous combat unit is formally disbanded on July 4th, is to be commanded by Colonel Robert L. Scott, according to an order issued today by General Brereton, commanding American Air Forces in India, China and Burma. Many pilots of the A.V.G. have been waiting to learn who their new C.O. would be before requesting transfer to the 23rd Pursuit Group. With a fine record of achievements, Colonel Scott is perhaps the best recruiting officer the Army could provide to entice the hard-hitting pilots of the A.V.G. to serve in the uniforms of the Army Air Forces.

With all due respect to Bob Scott, who has certainly proved himself to be a first-class fighting man and leader, it didn't turn out that way. None of the A.V.G. pilots were curious about who the commanding officer of the 23rd Pursuit Group would be, as all but five of them had already decided not to remain. The facts were, if I may speak freely:

The recruiting authorities did not handle the situation as tactfully as they might have. They brusquely presented our kids with applications for induction and said: "Sign here," not taking into consideration the fact that these boys felt their year's experience with the A.V.G. and their splendid fighting record entitled them to more rank than was generally offered.

A considerable proportion of both pilots and men were from the Navy and Marine Corps and preferred to return to their original services where they could take advantage of previous service.

The psychological fact was overlooked that these boys were war-weary and the super-sensitive from as long, strenuous and punishing a campaign as any single air unit has fought in this war. Our mail service had been atrocious, they were out of contact with their loved ones and the thought uppermost in most of their minds was to complete their contracts and go home. Had proper leave and transportation facilities been offered, I feel quite sure many more or them would have joined the American Air Forces.

Unfortunately, many of the old-line American officers regarded our boys as plain mercenaries, which did not make for the most cordial relationship. On the other hand, a lot of the A.V.G. didn't think the A.A.F. was so hot, either. As a single instance of this rivalry: while a guest of the A.V.G. at Kunming, a colonel commanding one of the 10th Air Force Pursuit groups suggested that our pilots were not so super and that he himself could take on our best pilot and beat him in a dog-fight. His face was plenty red when at least five thousand American dollars instantly appeared to say in a loud voice "You can't beat our *worst* pilot— and when do you want to start?" The colonel managed to laughingly wriggle his way out. Incidentally, this officer was on the board to induct our men into the A.A.F.

Last but not least, most of our boys had saved their money and wanted to go home and splurge a bit before returning to active service.

In any event, our boys had done a hell of a job. They were hardened, experienced veterans—invaluable, you would think, to the still untested American forces. They knew the terrain and the weather and they knew how to kill Japs. They also had learned how to get along with Orientals. It seemed to me a pity that a more understanding effort could not have been made to keep these men in the service of their country. They could have helped so much.

In the evening, Peter Muir and his wife came to see me. They said that they were going to Simla, one of the cool spots not far from Delhi, and suggested I go along with them as it might do me some good. But I felt too weak to travel—all my bones ached, even the tips of my nails. I was completely covered with the rash, something like prickly heat. The doctor told me it was "dengue rash" and that I was lucky to get it. He said that people who had it after the dengue fever never would get it again. That was some consolation!

Wayne Ricks, propeller man of the A.V.G., who had been stationed at Allahabad to push on supplies to Kunming, arrived and with him an Anglo-Indian girl, tall, dark and pretty, a night club singer from Bombay. Wayne introduced her as his fianceé and said they were going to be married shortly. Ceder also arrived that same day. He made his appearance all dolled up in one of the new uniforms the boys had been having made.

Harvey showed them both a message that had just come from the Old Man saying that he wanted Ceder and Ricks back in Kunming. Ceder didn't like it very much. He didn't like flying. Besides, he wanted to go back to Karachi to see

an American nurse there. She was one of ninety that had just
arrived on a transport. Harvey told both of them to get on
"their horses" and catch the next plane or if possible, a
bomber going to Kunming.

By the end of June, many of the boys began to drift in
from Kunming—their year's contracts were up. Of the first
to arrive were Wylie and Jordan, both of the finance office.
They said they were going to the New York C.A.M.C.O.
office to straighten out the finances and expected it would
take them about three months to do so. All the A.V.G. members were to receive $500 United States for passage home
and were to be paid one extra month's salary.

The boys asked me for news, so I told them what I had
heard: "A few days ago, General Brereton was sent to Egypt.
The 'grapevine' has it that he will remain there and that
Chennault is going to be sent to Washington to be fussed
over—but, then, other rumors state that he is in the dog-
house."

There was certainly a lot of gossip going on there at the
Imperial Hotel.

More of the A.V.G. arrived. Little Olson, my driving
partner on the memorable trip from Lashio to Loiwing;
Chuck Older; Bob Brouk, who was caught on the ground
at Namsam on April 22nd. He told me that he was by his
ship ready to take off when twenty model Zeros came and
strafed the field. Brouk got a lot of shrapnel and spent the
rest of the time in the hospital. Jernstedt, the pilot who said,
"No more pursuit for me—I like the big fellows better,"
and several others. It was like the old days seeing so many
of them together, although it was perhaps for the last time.

Brouk also told me that he had seen Tex Hill before leaving, and that he was very certain Tex and Frank Schiel would
stay, since they had been offered majorities, and that Daffy
Davis had joined the Americans and had been given a commission, First Lieutenant. That was good news. Doreen and
Daffy would be settled for the duration.

Nothing unusual happened in the next few days. The stream of A.V.G. was still coming in. Most of the time they were with us, either shopping for jewelry to take home to their girls, or swimming in the pool.

"Did you read the little piece about the A.V.G. in *The Statesman?*" Bob Brouk asked me, handing me the paper.

Little piece was right—it was down at the bottom of a column. The glamour of the A.V.G. was gone. It was only a dot and dash in the pages of history. I felt sad as I read:

CHINESE AWARDS FOR 36 A.V.G. MEN

The famous American Volunteer Group, which is operating with the Chinese Air Force, is to be disbanded as a volunteer unit tomorrow and formally inducted into the United States Army and Air Force in China. Brigadier General Chennault and most of the pilots and ground crews are remaining. Brigadier General Chennault has announced that he will not return to the States until he has seen the Japanese defeated.

The Chinese Government has conferred awards for outstanding bravery and achievement in combat on 33 pilots of the American Volunteer Group. Three ground crew chiefs have also received awards for "outstanding bravery and conduct while under fire."

"What do you think about it?" Brouk asked me.

"Nothing," I said, "except that the stuff about the pilots staying is not true. How many of the ground men are staying, Bob?"

"Not more than fifteen. Pilots, about five. Well, I guess that's the end of the A.V.G.—the Sharks—The Flying Tigers." He laughed.

The British were celebrating our Independence Day!

On the morning of July 4th, we received the following invitation:

The Viceroy and Marchioness of Linlithgow
request the pleasure of
Colonel and Mrs. Greenlaw's
company at a reception
on Saturday, the 4th of July, 1942, at 8 o'clock.

DRESS:

MILY.   Bush shirts and trousers.
CIVIL. Summer suits or Dinner
jackets or Indian dress.
No Decorations

I went to the Imperial Hotel and was talking to several of the many colonels and majors. They were all quite enthused over the coming event and amused at the idea of the British celebrating our Independence Day.

One of them said: "We might as well go. They tell me that the palace is air-conditioned. We'll have a breathing spell for a while and—free beer!"

I had planned to go, too, but in the evening before dressing, I had another spell of the dengue fever.

On the fifteenth of July we began packing and getting ready to go to Bombay. We were all supposed to return to the States by Ferry Command, but an order arrived from Washington that air transports were not to be used, not even by high-ranking officers, without a special permission. The returning transports were to carry war materials from the Oriental countries to the States.

That was that—but I felt a lot better about it because I had been wondering how in the world I was going to be allowed to carry my eight Persian carpets, Karenni drum and Lucy, when passengers were only allowed thirty pounds of luggage. That settled the matter, and it was one worry less for me.

Arvid Olson, Parker Dupouy, C. T. Smith, Tom Haywood and Bill Reed, A.V.G. pilots, had already left for Bombay. They were to wait there for the first available ship to America. I gave them four pieces of luggage because I had too many, and that way could avoid paying excess baggage.

Fearless Freddie Hodges returned with them from Kunming, but he and Helen left for Calcutta instead, where Freddie would join the C.N.A.C. This made Helen happy because she had no desire to go to America, a strange land, not knowing what had happened to her mother, who was still in Burma. One of her younger brothers was stationed in Calcutta with an Indian regiment, and she was pleased to be able to live near him. Her other two brothers were somewhere in England. She had not heard from them for many months.

We turned in the car to the Tenth Air Force, settled the account in the bank and paid off the driver. We decided to take the bearer to Bombay with us. Harvey gave all our phonograph records to Sergeant Grove, a chap of the Tenth Air Force, on condition he was to let all the soldiers of his barracks share them with him.

We had dinner, our last dinner there, with Bill Chaplin, Dr. Sargeson, and Colonels Frank Merrell and Bill Wyman who had taken the long walk out of Burma behind General Stilwell. After dinner, we sat by the swimming pool and talked about the things that might have been.

Bill Wyman said: "Your outfit put up a hell of a good show and you ought to be proud of it."

I was—but Harvey said: "With very little additional help it could have been so much better it makes me sick to think about it."

Bill wanted to know what he meant. Harvey said:

"Listen, Bill—our original plan was to operate as a group, taking advantage of numerical strength. The most airplanes we ever had in the air against the Japs at one time was eighteen—usually it was from eight to a dozen against many times that number. Imagine what we'd have done to the Japs at Rangoon if we could have fought them at our full group strength and had had a proper warning net. They wouldn't have gotten within fifty miles of the place. We proved that, as you know, at Kunming. Also, our original plan included a group of medium bombers which we were never able to get from anybody. If we'd had them to attack Jap airfields you wouldn't have had to walk out of Burma. You know yourself, Bill we didn't get any co-operation from the 10th Air Force and my time spent here has been utterly wasted. From the day we started it was a constant fight for existence. We never had enough planes, spare parts, anti-aircraft protection or replacements—and no possibility of getting them."

"How about the R.A.F.?" somebody asked.

Harvey said: "They did the best they could under the circumstances and their pilots and men had plenty of guts, but they didn't have nearly enough airplanes or experienced pilots to fly them. And incidentally, China has a great number of trained pilots ready and eager to take a crack at the Japs—but damn clever as the Chinese are, they can't fly without airplanes."

"Well," said Bill Wyman, "I guess there's nothing else to do but roll up our sleeves and chase the little bastards out."

It was agreed that unless Burma was retaken and the road to China reopened, it was going to be an awfully tough job to beat the Japs.

As we got up to leave, a group of British officers came out of the dining room. I immediately recognized the tall, slender figure and dark head of Captain Jelf, whom I had known in Rangoon—years ago, it seemed. He saw me and came over. I introduced him as "Captain" Jelf, not noticing his uniform.

"You mean 'Colonel,' " said Bill Chaplain.

"I was promoted," said Jelf, laughing. "Lieutenant Colonel. Do I look older?"

"No," I answered, "just the same. The chase through Burma didn't do you any harm. What happened to Stanley?"

"He got to Assam all right," he answered. "The last I heard of him he was in a small village very ill with malaria, poor chap. Edna is in Kashmir, waiting for him. They are both safe, and that's saying a lot."

I said good-by to all of them, and Jelf walked with me. We talked about other people we knew in Rangoon, and what had happened to them. He said that General Bruce Scott was still in Burma, but that it was believed he would get out all right. Mrs. Scott was in Simla helping out with the Red Cross. And that our friend, Mr. Fulton from Toungoo, was in one of the hill station hospitals recuperating from shock. We shook hands for the second time and stood there, silent for a while.

"I envy you," he said. "California!" Some day I wish to go there. After the war, maybe, if I am still alive."

"Look me up," I said, "if you do go."

Walking alone on my way up to our quarters I met an old friend, Mr. Espee, of the mines at Namtu, not far from Lashio. He was glad to see me. "Is it true about Tom Jones?" was the first thing he said. They had been good friends and Jones visited Namtu whenever he had the chance.

"We liked him very much," he added. "So young, so full of life. Poor boy. It's unbelievable—and I heard yesterday that Pete Petach was killed—plane exploded in mid-air."

I took that one standing up. It neither surprised nor shocked me. Nothing could surprise or shock me any more.

I said good night, wishing I hadn't seen him—that he hadn't told me about Petach or reminded me of Jones. The wound in my heart was still fresh. The memory of all of them was still vivid—Sandy, Bob Little, Jack Newkirk, Scotty, Cokey Hoffman, Pete Atkinson, little Armstrong and all the others. And to me who was privileged to be one of "the gang" it will always remain so.

On the morning of July 17th, exactly twelve months to the day since, in the Peninsula Hotel, I yelled at Harvey, "Little Mac's on the phone," we pulled out of Delhi on our way to Bombay and home—eighty of us who had been Flying Tigers—the American Volunteer Group.

It had been, I must confess, quite a busy year.

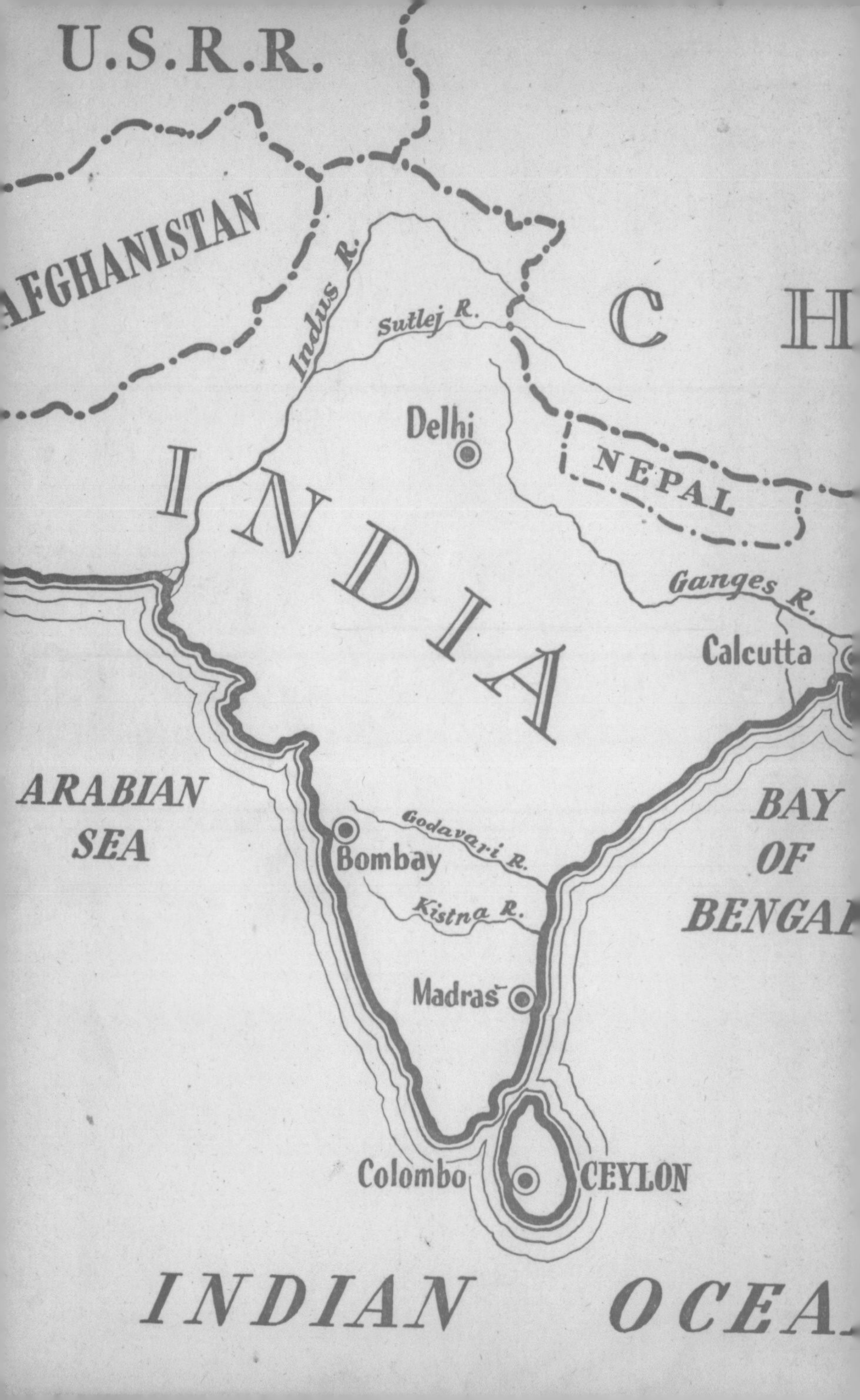
U.S.R.R.
AFGHANISTAN
Indus R.
Sutlej R.
C H
Delhi
NEPAL
INDIA
Ganges R.
Calcutta
ARABIAN
SEA
Godavari R.
Bombay
Kistna R.
BAY
OF
BENGA
Madras
Colombo
CEYLON
INDIAN OCEA